Endorsements

"We often look in the mirror and only see traits and shapes that draw our worst criticisms and assessments. Why do we do that? Who decided your value, your beauty, your purpose, your uniqueness? As you read through the pages of *The Red Geranium Sisterhood*, you will be guided into a personal, intimate and supernatural transformation. You will discover a new YOU! As you begin to see your inestimable beauty and worth, you will be amazed at the change that will surround you. You are not alone. We are with you. We are sisters. More than that, God — your Creator — has a plan for your life. Now let's journey together into the incomparable discovery of who you really are!"

—**Dr. LaDonna C. Osborn**, president of
the Women's International Network,
and author of *God's Big Picture*

"This book addresses untouchables in a way that gets into the personal world of any reader and enables them to see for themselves where they are and consider that there *is* a better way! The reader has no need to put up a guard to protect their coping mechanism of survival. Instead, they will desire to leave that behind and become transformed with truth! Very well done and keenly insightful."

—**Dr. Velma White**, author of *The Birth That Counts*

"Throughout our childhood and teenage years, we may have heard and experienced words and actions that have wrongly made us feel undeserving, unworthy, or unloved. Shelley compassionately and truthfully shows us that we are indeed the opposite of these abuses, based on the TRUE LOVE of the One who created us! I so wish this book had been available to me as a young woman. It is a 'letter of love' that will change the way you see yourself and change the way you love!"

—**Janet M. Little**, author of *My Tears Were for Her*

Dedication

This book is called *The Red Geranium Sisterhood*,
because together as females we can create an atmosphere
of esteem and kindness for women everywhere.

I dedicate this book to Emily and Claire,
and to my Sisterhood around the world.

May each of you who takes this book into your hands,
discover and embrace your extraordinary worth.

Forward

Shelley writes with compassion inspired by the Holy Spirit. She addresses the greatest longing of our hearts - the search for hope, identity, love and acceptance. Within these chapters are the answers to life's most pressing questions. May you find the treasure within, and experience this Person of love for yourself. It's my honor to recommend this book for you.

—**James W. Christian**

Table of Contents

Introduction 1

Discovering 5
Chapter 1: You're a Work of Art (Not a Piece of Work) 7
Chapter 2: Significant Beginnings 13
Chapter 3: The Grinch Factor 21
Chapter 4: From Chaos to Completeness 29

Loving...35
Chapter 5: Love + Truth = A Person..................................37
Chapter 6: Loving Your Own Self 43
Chapter 7: Keeping Your Colors 53
Chapter 8: Forgiving the Unforgivable 61
Chapter 9: Brokenness is Not Your Address......................69

Embracing..75
Chapter 10: The Camouflage of Comparison 77
Chapter 11: A New Family Album 87
Chapter 12: The Sisterhood of the Red Geranium.............95

Conclusion 101
Growing a Culture of Kindness..103
The Red Geranium Manifesto 107
Acknowledgements 111
About the Author...113

Introduction

When pressures in life close in, I like to slip outside and gaze at the stars, or go for quiet walks where nature nourishes my soul.

When scanning the starry network in the night sky, I see a divine order to the universe. The exact position of Earth in our solar system makes it unique in being the only planet that supports life. We know other planets have moons, atmospheres and even oceans, but only Earth has the right combination to sustain us humans. Even more stunning, is that the ancient book of Psalms tells us that every star and constellation has been given a name by the Creator.[1]

You and I are of *much more* value than the stars! We have priceless worth. The Designer of the universe created us unique, gifted, and with clear purpose. He knows our name.

Our Creator uses the simplest things in nature to bring hope into our beings. Several years ago, I was living in Northern Canada with our young family. My husband, an air ambulance pilot, flew day and night to remote locations. When we arrived in the North, the children and I sometimes

---

1. Ps. 147:4 (English Standard Version)

felt isolated because we didn't know a soul in the community. To make our home more welcoming, I brought several pots of red geraniums and placed them in our front window which faced the main street in town.

As seasons passed, my geraniums thrived. Those stunning, ruby blooms were the only color in the barren, winter whiteness. Gradually, the snow melted and patches of green began creeping over the landscape. I made friends in the community and found moss-carpeted trails to explore. Local indigenous women taught me how to make potato pancakes and discover the best spots to pick wild, mouth-watering blueberries.

All too soon, our time in the North was over and we began packing for the move home. A few days before we left, a young woman from the community stopped by. In a quiet voice she said, "Shelley, I want you to know something. This last winter was very hard for me. I didn't know if I could go on. But one very cold afternoon, I walked by your house and stopped short. My eyes drank in those bright geraniums in your window. Hope began to stir in me again. In fact, I came by almost every day to take in the beauty of those flowers. I...I just want to say thank you."

That was a profound moment. I brought the geraniums with me for my own happiness, but they did much more. These simple flowers helped a young woman through a difficult time in her life. They gave her hope and the will to rise above her sorrow. How wonderful is that?

I decided I needed to know what these particular geraniums signified. There is a language in flowers and each type of

flower has a significant meaning. When I checked red geraniums, I discovered one of the meanings was *esteem*.

The word *esteem* means to have a high regard, admira-
tion, and honor for someone — to value someone or something. When this young woman looked at the blooms in my
window, she felt a sense of esteem slowly make its way into
her hurting soul. May I ask you something? Do you believe
you are of high value? Do you have a high regard or esteem
for yourself and others? Many teenagers and women aren't
able to answer that question with a *yes*. As we take this
journey together, I believe you and I can rediscover our worth
and thrive on planet Earth.

DISCOVERING

artwork by Jan Louis

*"And God saw that His new
creation was beautiful and good."*

Gen. 1:12b (Voice)

Chapter 1

You're a Work of Art (Not a Piece of Work)

*"... you are altogether beautiful
and there is no blemish in you."*

Song of Songs 4:7 (ISV)

Each of us is born on purpose. Regardless of what anyone may have told you, you are not an accident. You and I are unique, irreplaceable, and one of a kind.

Did you know the DNA in every one of our cells that makes us who we are, can stretch to the sun and back sixty-one times? Think about it. The heredity material in you and I is twice the diameter of the solar system! No wonder we're described in Psalms as "mysteriously complex"[2] and crafted with delicate precision.

Every one of our bloodlines needs to be celebrated. Those who are our parents, grandparents, and great-grandparents,

---

2. Ps. 139:14 (The Passion Translation)

are unique individuals from every tribe, nation, and tongue. We may not have perfect people in our ancestry, but we have extraordinary ones. However, there is something far more important than our physical ancestry that we need to be aware of. And that is the spiritual DNA that is within *you*!

Our inner being was intentionally formed to be like the One who created us. Everything in creation spells out there is a designer behind it all. This loving, heavenly Being wanted, planned for, and *still* wants you! None of us came to earth as an afterthought. In your blueprint is dignity, worth, and purpose. We humans are phenomenal beings.

You and I may not share the same ancestry or similar background, but we do share something just as valuable; and that is our *womanhood*. As females, it's crucial this unique bond is strengthened so we can stand by and for each other. I don't have to be of the same culture or skin color to be your friend. You are female and I am female — that makes us a sisterhood.

When I started school at the age of six, it was a scary experience. I knew no one in my class. The first day on the playground, I fell from the monkey bars and bloodied up my knee. Another little girl came running over, dusted the gravel off my leg, and helped me to my feet. In her own way, she offered a red geranium to me. That simple act of kindness solidified a lifelong friendship that has lasted for decades. In fact, this girl was my only friend throughout a year of severe bullying in school. I believe her kindness and my parents' love kept me from thoughts of suicide. That's how important a sisterhood is.

Perhaps you have your own story of a friend who stood by you in difficult times. More of these relationships are necessary for our emotional health. We need these lifelines and connections on a daily basis.

I'm here to assure you, that from now on, you don't have to be alone in this earth journey. As my sister, I believe in your dignity and esteem. The fact you made it from the womb to the day you were born is a miracle in itself! The inception of your conception is of great significance, *never* forget that.

So why is it that many of us females don't have a high regard or esteem for ourselves?

Why is it so many of us females don't have high esteem for ourselves?

The findings in available data suggest that "in some countries, nearly one in four women may experience sexual violence by an intimate partner, and up to one-third of adolescent girls report their first sexual experience as being forced."[3] Sadly, some girls have been abused by their own relatives and caregivers. This only magnifies the pain.

Because this injustice happens every day, shouldn't we discover how this craziness started? And shouldn't we find out if there's a way we can be healed and restored? I don't know about you, but I want to know if the One who created us has a master plan to rescue us from this suffering.

---

3. excerpt from Chapter 6, pg. 149 on "Sexual Violence" (www.who.int)

Walk with me as we discover the personality and character of God through the extraordinary love story He gave to all people. It's vital to understand that the Bible is not white man's fiction of how life began. The pages were breathed by God Himself as He instructed brown-skinned people from the Middle East to record these living words. This written record explores in detail what our Creator had in mind when the human family was brought into being.

artwork by Jan Louis

Chapter 2

Significant Beginnings

"We see our baggage and bruises, but
God sees our belonging and beauty."

Shelley M. Christian

Have you hiked into a fragrant forest or climbed a mountain so awe-inspiring it took your breath away? Eden, the first home for humans, was pure and unspoiled before evil entered it. Earth's initial atmosphere was designed to be a place of peace, blessing and beauty. How do we know this? Because Genesis, the book of beginnings, describes the good life humans had before making choices which caused generational suffering.

Prior to the first couple's fateful decisions, the book of Genesis records there was *no* sickness, *no* inequality, *no* poverty, and *no* abuse polluting our planet. Adam and Eve weren't afraid of God or each other. In fact, they enjoyed a happy relationship with their Creator. Both of them were given a purposeful life in an atmosphere filled with everything good. If you were a parent, isn't that what you would want for your kids?

Our Creator isn't just a powerful force. God is a parent who *loves* His family. Understanding our original identity is crucial, because without this knowledge we will live far below what God intended. As a friend of mine once reminded me, "When we don't know who we are, we will act like someone we're not!"

**When we don't know who we are,
we will act like someone we're not.**

Chaos and evil took over when human beings said *No* to God's plan and headed in the opposite direction. This led to mass confusion and unbelievable pain. The word *sin* literally means to *miss the mark*. In the beginning of human life, there was a perfect bull's-eye God intended for us. He wanted us to feel the zing of accomplishing the high purpose we were given. When the first man and woman chose the direction of selfishness and pride, our human arrow ended up in tragedy. We fell far short of the happiness plan God designed for you and I.

This nature of sin infected every person on earth, just as a genetic disease passes down through generations. Every human alive today is born with this fallen nature; we can't help it. But I have excellent news! There is a cure for this sin disease. The medicine and healing are not found in a religious system, but in a Person.

A deep thinker by the name of Blaise Pascal, expressed our problem perfectly when he wrote, "What else does this craving and this helplessness proclaim, but that there was once in man a true happiness, of which all that now remains is the empty print and trace?"[4] He went on to say that all of us try to fill this empty space with everything around us, but find *nothing* can help, since the human spirit can only be filled by God Himself.

If I told you the solution to our desperation is actually found in the beginning pages of the Bible, wouldn't you want to search it out for your own good?

In the first few verses of Genesis, we find the whole earth was "...a bottomless emptiness, an inky blackness."[5] In other words it was a disorganized mess, kind of like some teenagers' bedrooms! This chaos was just waiting for the Master's touch to reveal the colors and creativity He paints everything with.

God's Spirit hovered over the darkness like a mother hen broods over her chicks. When God spoke "Let there be light" a brilliant radiance flooded the earth, kicking out the darkness! "God is light and in Him there is no darkness at all."[6]

Are things in your life out of control and robbing you of hope? Do you feel you can't climb out of a black hole, because you've made too many mistakes or been crushed too many times? I want to shout out some good news. The Designer of the universe has no problem taking our messes and making them into a *masterpiece*.

4. Blaise Pascal, *Pensées*, (New York: Penguin Books, 1966), pg. 75.

5. Gen. 1:2 (The Message)

6. 1 John 1:5 (English Standard Version)

If our loving Creator carefully shaped our solar system, lands, lakes, plants, and animals so we could thrive on this planet, don't you think He just might have a phenomenal plan for you? I believe when all the preparation for human beings was complete, that God laughed with sheer joy!

Then came the moment when creation stood on tiptoe to see what would happen next. This was God's pièce de résistance! In other words, it was *why* He designed it all in the first place. Everything God created was for the preparation of His new family. The formation of male and female was done with detailed, loving care. Adam, the first human, was formed from earth as a potter takes clay and skillfully shapes it on the wheel. Our Creator breathed into man's nostrils the breath of life, God's very own DNA!

Next, God put Adam to sleep in the first recorded surgery and carefully formed the woman from one of Adam's sides, not just his rib. She was bone of his bone, flesh of his flesh.[7] She wasn't taken from Adam's feet to be trampled on, or from his head to dominate him. God brought Eve into being as someone to be cherished and valued by her husband, even as she loved and esteemed him. Together they completed the picture of God's image bearers on earth. It was only at this point that our Creator looked over everything He had made and approved it as *very good*.

It's important we ask ourselves some critical questions. Do we believe being female is somehow less than? Do we accept injustice as what we deserve in life? If you answered *yes* to

---

7. Gen. 2:21–23 (English Standard Version)

any of those questions, it could be you have suffered at the hands of those who did not value your worth. But not for one minute is this the dignity design you were made for! And it's certainly *not* the future God has in store for you. That's why it is so important for us to understand the original plan God had for both women and men.

Eve wasn't designed superior or inferior to Adam. She was a perfect counterpart and partner with him. When God created male and female in His image,[8] He created us uniquely different, but totally equal. Neither one was given domination over the other. Instead, they were both given authority and care over creation. Men were not physically designed to subdue, violate, or harm a woman. A man's outward strength should always be used to *protect* someone who is physically weaker, not the opposite!

A husband is to lay down his life for his wife and cherish her. In the same way, a wife is to encourage and love her husband deeply. The form of help she gives is not demeaning in any way. Actually, the word *helper* used to describe Eve in Genesis, portrays powerful acts of rescue and support.[9] This same word is used to describe how God helps us in Psalm 121:2. Marriage was designed to be a "community of oneness, held together by love and to function by serving one another."[10] How amazing is this plan! Our relationships were meant to be a kind of heaven on earth.

---

8. Gen.1:27 (English Standard Version)

9. Gen. 2:18 (English Standard Version)

10. Dr. LaDonna Osborn (Principles of Biblical Relationships Study Course)

When our Designer created male and female in His like-ness, He blessed them and gave them *both* this instruction: "...Be fruitful and multiply. Populate the earth. I make you trustees of My estate, so care for My creation and rule over the fish of the sea, the birds of the sky, and every creature that roams across the earth."[11]

There is something unique to human nature which animals don't possess. In Genesis 1:27, we find that only humans are created in the image of God. Our Creator is a spiritual Being and as a result, so are we! Only humans can love God and worship Him out of our inner being.

The Creator has invited us to be adopted back into His family — a family of kindness, forgiveness and belonging.

Animals have a mind and will and are capable of great loyalty and affection. We are supposed to enjoy them and care for them with kindness. But animals are *not* designed in the same class as God. They are not spiritual beings. Only people made in God's likeness have the ability to reflect His character and communicate with Him in a loving relation-ship. What a stunning honor God has given you and I!

Our Creator formed us within our mothers with just as much detail as He did with Eve and Adam. A king from ancient days wrote this, "You formed my innermost being,

11. Gen. 1:28 (Voice)

shaping my delicate inside and my intricate outside, and wove them all together in my mother's womb."[12] Think about it! God was present at the very moment you were conceived. You and I were planned and chosen by Him long before the heavens and earth were created.[13]

Like God, we're designed to speak words that generate an atmosphere of well-being and happiness. Because we are spiritual beings, we will live forever, even when our earthly bodies die. *Where* we live forever, is a decision we will make here on earth. The Creator of the universe has invited us to be adopted back into His family — a family of kindness, forgiveness, and belonging. We can freely accept this invitation or reject it.

You might ask, "If God purposed in His heart for humans to live happily ever after, then what in the world happened? Why did God allow murder, rape, abuse, and sickness in the first place? If God created families and friendships to be blessed, then why do our relationships fall apart?" Those are very good questions.

God designed people with choice power. We aren't created to be mindless, robotic followers. We are intentionally formed with freedom to choose. What actually took place to spoil this perfect existence, was the result of the decisions our first ancestors made when they listened to, believed in, and acted on a lie.

---

12. Ps. 139:13 (The Passion Translation)
13. Eph. 1:4 (Amplified Bible Classic)

artwork by Jan Louis

*"He gives families to the lonely
and releases prisoners from
jail, singing with joy!"*

Ps. 68:6 (TLB)

Chapter 3

The Grinch Factor

*"A thief has only one thing
in mind — he wants to steal,
slaughter and destroy."*

John 10:10a (TPT)

If you have ever watched the movie *The Grinch Who Stole Christmas*, you'll agree that the Whos from Whoville weren't bothering anybody. They were happily going about their business, enjoying life as they should be. But according to the story, the Grinch was angry with their happiness. He was so jealous; he decided to steal Christmas and attempt to destroy their contented community.

In a similar way, the Bible tells us that a bitter, jealous being wanted to destroy humanity and separate them from the Creator's love. He couldn't stand the fact that God created human beings in His likeness, to reflect His goodness, and live a cherished, productive life.

21

Satan was initially created an angelic being. At some point he decided he wanted to *be* God, instead of living contentedly with the perfect plan designed for him. When satan rebelled against his Creator, he took on a dark nature of evil, death, and destruction.

This vile persona *hated* human beings and came uninvited into the garden paradise designed for the human family. Satan entered this beautiful atmosphere with the intent of deceiving humans into giving up their God-given authority. He wanted to be top dog, because he desires the worship and glory only our Creator deserves.

The devil brewed a clever concoction of lies mixed with truth and served it to Eve. Adam was standing right there with her![14] The serpent slyly suggested to them that their Creator didn't have their best interests at heart. Satan's strategy has never changed! He still uses lies to con people into doubting the goodness of a loving God.

Sadly, many people have swallowed these same defective thinking patterns. They believe God is behind catastrophes like hurricanes, tornadoes, disease, and destruction. There are those who believe God is an angry being who loves to punish the humans He created. Nothing could be further from the truth! God did not send His Son into the world to condemn the world. He came to be our *rescuer*.[15]

Because Eve and Adam believed the deceiver, their garden paradise was ruined. Now *everything* would change. Instead

14. Gen. 3:4,5 (English Standard Version)
15. John 3:17 (English Standard Version)

of kicking out the one who trespassed on their soil, the first two people opened the door wide to fear and chaos. The One they once trusted and knew as a loving Parent; the One who hung out with them each day in their gorgeous garden; this is the One they doubted and walked away from. The first people on earth chose to listen to a stranger's voice, instead of their Creator's.[16]

When this poison of sin and death entered the human spirit, our downward spiral began. The first family forgot where their real DNA came from. Instead of the blessing designed for them, they experienced the curse. Adam and Eve shared the consequences of their wrong choices when they rebelled against God. Now that satan was the ruler, disease and destruction swept over the landscape. Instead of loving kindness, abuse and jealousy contaminated the human family. Violence and suffering became the norm.

Thankfully this was not the end of the story. Even when the first humans hid from God's presence, He came looking for them — not to harm, but to help them. Of course, God knew where they were when He called out, "Where are you?" His heart's cry really was, "Why have you left My side and broken My heart?"

To put it bluntly, Eve and Adam divorced themselves from the parenthood of God! Danny Silk describes this sense of loss like this: "the false identity we must unlearn is the orphan

---

16. John 10:5–10 (English Standard Version)

identity. This is the identity we form apart from relationship with God."[17]

> **When we choose badly, there are consequences, but that doesn't mean the consequences have to last forever.**

For the first time, Eve and Adam were afraid of God and ashamed of who they were. The Creator's bright presence that clothed them was gone. They knew they had lost something irreplaceable. But God didn't turn away from their distress. He actually *redressed* them with clothing He personally made from animal skins. God is a hands-on Creator! In the midst of our biggest failures, He's present to help us get back on track.

If you have experienced this feeling of orphan identity, you are not alone. John Newton, who wrote the song "Amazing Grace," penned these words, "I once was lost, but now am found, was blind but now I see." A loving Father *always* looks for children who are missing. He never stops searching until He finds them.

Because we are created in God's image, we have the power to choose. Unfortunately, we sometimes make very wrong choices. When we choose badly, there are consequences. But that doesn't mean the consequences have to last forever! We can turn around and follow the Creator's plan. He is

---

17. Danny Silk quote, FB, May 4, 2019, "Loving on Purpose,"

always working to bring us back to the full and complete life He designed.

Right there in the garden, God declared that a woman's offspring would destroy satan's hold on the human family. God told satan, "I will make you and the woman enemies to each other. Your descendants and her descendants will be enemies. Her child will crush your head and you will bite His heel."[18]

This very prophecy came to pass over two thousand years ago when Jesus was born of a virgin named Mary. Because this teenager said *yes* to God,[19] you and I have a hope and a future! Do you see how valuable girls and women are? Miracles will happen when *anyone* of us gives God our yes!

The Bible tells us when the right time came, God sent His Son, born of a woman,[20] to rescue those trapped in sin and restore them to their true child of God selves. Jesus crushed satan's rule by taking our place and dying on the Cross. When He rose from the dead, Jesus took back our freedom keys and gave them to all who believe in His Name.

How inspiring that God chose Mary to carry the hope of the world in her womb. He entrusted her with His own Son. This was the highest honor anyone on earth, present, past, or future, has *ever* been given. It's no wonder there is a huge assignment against women and unborn children today.

---

18. Gen. 3:15 (International Children's Bible)

19. Luke 1:38 (English Standard Version)

20. Gal. 4:4 (English Standard Version)

A woman's womb is a sacred place. Think about it, Jesus, the Son of God, came from a woman's womb!

Don't let your voice be stolen!

Together as a sisterhood, we can rediscover and celebrate our infinite worth. You and I are not a problem. We are not to be used and abused. We are not an afterthought. Females are the finishing touch of God's creation.

Don't let your voice be stolen! You and I can use our words and influence to help encourage our sisters instead of competing with them. All throughout history, the Creator of the universe chose women to do astounding things to bring blessing and help to humanity. *You* are one of those women!

artwork by Charlene Douglas

"He sent me to heal the wounds of the brokenhearted, to tell the captives, "you are free,"..."

Isa. 61:1 (TPT)

Chapter 4

From Chaos to Completeness

*"Bring your broken heart to the One
who has all the missing pieces."*

Shelley M. Christian

We have all grown up hearing fairy tales where the girl is rescued by the prince and ends up happily ever after. But in reality, some of us have been waiting for that rescue for a very long time. The facts are, bad things don't just happen to mean people, they happen to nice ones as well.

Life isn't always fair. Some of us have been abused and crushed by those we trusted. It's a known fact that young girls are being trafficked right now in North America by the age of thirteen or fourteen. Have you ever wondered why this is happening?

You and I were created for relationship. Every one of us desperately wants to belong and to be loved. As females, we may crave this acceptance so much that we let our guard down and start to develop harmful behaviors. Those who come from abusive homes are even more at risk, because the ones who should be protecting them have failed. There can even be those close to us who say they love us just to get something from us; but that is *not* genuine love.

Love never forces us against our will.

Love never abuses us and then says it's our fault.

Love never insults us and tells us we are nothing.

Love never sells us for its own gain.

At this moment, you may be experiencing emotions of despair or are struggling with memories of abuse. You may even feel like giving up. Let me urge you *not to give in* to that impulse! There is a light trying to pierce through your darkness. There is a *real* Prince of Peace.

There is an actual future filled with hope for you and I. Dare to believe it's true.

Jesus came to earth for the express purpose of putting our lives back together. We can bring our broken hearts to the only One who can make us whole again. God came in human skin to take the weight of our hopelessness upon Himself and bring us to a safe place. He wants to lift you up, not put you down. Our Creator says, "…I know the plans I have for you… plans for good and not for evil, to give you a future and a hope."[21]

Do you believe there is an actual future filled with hope for you? Put your hand on your heart; breathe in grace and breathe out trust. Dare to believe it's true.

---

21. Jer. 29:11 (The Living Bible)

You may have watched those around you fail, but *no one* is born to live a defeated life. You and I don't have to repeat the failures of others. We can begin a brand-new family history! When you see yourself the way God sees you, a sense of peace will start flooding your being. Remember the red geraniums in my window? That mass of blooms caused a young woman to believe *her life mattered*. She realized she was more precious than the flowers in my window. If I cared for those geraniums and nourished them, how much *more* does your Creator care for and want you to flourish?

We must understand something. Jesus *did not* come to set up a religion. In fact, He stood against those who put heavy burdens on the people. The religious teachers of Jesus' day taught that God was a demanding, angry god, who was not approachable. They modelled a god who was not touchable. Jesus came as a human being to expose these lies and reveal His Father's compassionate heart.

You may have heard of a famous East Indian leader named Mahatma Gandhi. In all sincerity, he wanted to help his fellow citizens. Gandhi thought all religions were alike and asked, "What difference does it make if we follow different routes, provided we all arrive at the same destination?"[22] We all know this is a popular worldview, but the question is, is it a *truthful* one? In the book, *What's Wrong With Religion*, Skye Jethani brings a more accurate observation. He brings to light that instead of ending at the same place, all religions *start* from the same place. Mr. Jethani said, "Religions are

---

22. Mahatma Gandhi (aquotes.org)

how people in every culture respond to a world confused by chaos, plagued by scarcity, and corrupted by injustice."[23]

Have you believed that if you just do the right things and perform all the right rituals, that somehow God will help you? This is the deception of religion in every culture. God *always* wants to help you and I! He isn't a pawn in a chess game we control by ceremonies we perform or the good things we do. He is the Creator and we are the created. God chose to reach out and freely give us His Son. Jesus is the only One who lived a life without sin, so He is the *only* One who can rescue us.

In Canada, where I live, some religious leaders of the past joined with government to forcibly remove indigenous children from their homes. They placed these traumatized children in residential schools and foster care. Many of these institutions tried to remove the identity of these children and make them feel ashamed of who God designed them to be. This is abuse of the highest nature! Not everyone treated the children badly. But many of them experienced severe abuse by church leaders who said they represented our Creator. *They did not!*

None of these actions were born of God's love. Instead, they were spawned through prejudice and unbelievable arrogance. God did not create any people group to dominate over another. Those who could have stopped this insanity looked the other way. Fred Rogers, who created a much-loved children's program said, "We live in a world in which we need to share responsibility. It's easy to say, 'It's not my child, not

23. Skye Jethani, *What's Wrong With Religion* (Wheaton, IL: SkyPilot Media, 2017), pg. 15,16

my community, not my world, not my problem.'"[24] Together we can change this! You are my sister and I am yours. I will not look away from your pain. You and I can choose to be a lifeline for someone else!

I want you to know God *didn't look the other way* when you were suffering. You are not unseen. Jesus came to turn the religious tables upside down and expose those who attempt to control people through fear. Jesus stands up for those who are mistreated. And those who really follow Him will stand up for you as well. No matter what circumstance you are facing, God is *for* you, not against you.

Our loving Creator had the cure for our pain and confusion long before Eve and Adam turned away from Him. All humans are initially flawed by the nature of sin. To rescue us, "God took the sinless Christ and poured into Him our sins. Then, in exchange, He poured God's goodness into us."[25] This is complete and radical love in action. You are that valued!

One of my mentors said, "If we can break away from the condemnation programmed into you and I from childhood and come into the free, beautiful atmosphere of restoration... the love relationship with God as partners and friends... then God can move freely in and through us." [26] This is the life we were born for!

---

24. Fred Rogers, Fred Rogers Center, October 11, 2017, Facebook

25. 2 Cor. 5:21 (The Living Bible)

26. Dr. T. L. Osborn, Anointed and Appointed for Action, message on YouTube, July 4, 2019

LOVING

artwork by Jan Louis

"*...you will know the truth and
the truth will set you free.*"

John 8:32 (ESV)

Chapter 5

Love + Truth = A Person

"We're not defined by the likes of many,
we're defined by the love of One."

Pastor Sammy Rodriguez

In high school, I thought truth was a set of ideals you believed from childhood. In my first year of college, I realized almost everyone had a different version of the truth. Some would say, "It's okay to cheat if you really need to." Others would say, "If it feels good, do it." But when I started reading God's perspective in the Bible, I discovered Jesus said something *totally* the opposite. He said "... you will know the truth and the truth will set you free."[27] I began to see there was only one definition of truth and that was the *God-kind*. If anyone receives this truth, it will set them free in every way.

I read another staggering thing Jesus said about Himself. He announced, "I am the Way, I am the Truth and I am the

---

27. John 8:32 (English Standard Version)

Life…"[28] Could it be that truth has a name? Not just words on a page…not just someone's religious ideas about life? Yes, truth is a Person, and His name is Jesus.

Jesus is the complete expression of God wrapped in human skin. Amazingly, our Creator humbled Himself by coming as a baby from a carpenter's home to live like you and me. Jesus mended broken people, healed the sick, fed the poor, and lifted both women and men to their true dignity. God doesn't just have love, He *is* love!

God doesn't just have love, He is love.

We know that religious leaders in Jesus' lifetime were not representing the loving character of God. That is why Jesus *chose* to live among us, so we could experience for ourselves that God is touchable, inclusive, and inviting. He took children in His arms and blessed them. Jesus restored people's faith in His Father's kindness and gave them a place to belong. You may not feel like you belong anywhere, but you do! You and I have a reason to live. How do we know this? Because what Jesus did next in the recorded history of His life, is the most amazing thing of all.

The Son of God so identified with our pain and failure, He took our place and our punishment in the ultimate sacrifice. He was tortured and then died a horrible death on the Cross for our sin. He was bruised for the healing of our

---

28. John 14:6 (The Passion Translation)

trauma.[29] Jesus took away the keys of death and hell from the devil, crushed his authority, and rose from the dead as our Champion. This is *good news* to all who believe in Him.

If you have heard a different version of God our Creator; if you have heard He is unreachable, untouchable, and wants to harm you, then you have heard the wrong story.

Throughout human history, God has been misrepresented by all kinds of people who don't have a personal knowledge of His compassion for the hurting. Jesus always lifted women to their true potential. He defended women who were abused and treated with prejudice and bigotry. There is a recorded incident in the Bible where religious leaders wanted to kill a woman because she broke their law. This terrified woman was dragged to Jesus and thrown at His feet.

The religious crowd wanted Him to condemn her, but Jesus demanded they search their own hearts first. He said, you who've never sinned, go ahead and cast the first stone. One by one, all her accusers slunk away because they knew they had done far worse things than she. I believe Jesus smiled at the woman when He said, "Woman, where are they? Has no one condemned you?" She whispered, "No one Lord!" He replied, "Neither do I condemn you; go, and from now on sin no more."[30]

You are *not invisible* to the eyes of your Creator and Friend. When Jesus lived on earth, He was drawn to the bruised and bleeding. He often scolded His followers, because they looked at

---

29. Isaiah 53:4,5 (Amplified Bible Classic)
30. John 8:2–11 (English Standard Version)

a person's outward appearance instead of their heart. Everyone that came to Jesus was loved and healed by Him. *Everyone!*

When Jesus rose from the dead, the only thing satan had left to use against us was the power of a lie. It's no surprise that deception was exactly what he used on Eve and Adam in the beginning.

Guess what? You and I don't have to believe those lies anymore! When we make the choice to welcome Jesus and become God's own child, the devil no longer has the right to mess with us and bring confusion. In fact, our Creator sent His Spirit to strengthen us to stand against every lie. We can tell the devil to get lost by using the Word of God against him. Jesus brings us well-timed help, coming just when we need it![31]

All of these powerful promises are in the pages of God's written story. It's vital to understand the Bible is not an old-fashioned, dusty book. It's not a list of do's and don'ts. Throughout its pages, God shines a spotlight into our inner beings and reveals the truth that frees us. It's stunning when we discover the original plan for the human family. It's also shocking how our rebellion can impact our lives forever, if we choose to reject Jesus' beautiful sacrifice for us.

No manner how many times we walk away, our Creator never gives up on His dream to bring us back to the family table. Because God so loved the world, He sent His Son so we could be restored as beloved children. You are worth God's Son. That makes you priceless. Will you say that with me? *"I...am...priceless!"*

---

31. John 14:16–18, Heb. 4:12–16 (English Standard Version)

artwork by Jan Louis

*"...love your neighbor as well
as you love yourself."*

Luke 10:27b (TPT)

Chapter 6

Loving Your Own Self

"Don't treat yourself the way
others treat you, love yourself
the way GOD loves you."

Shelley M. Christian

Do you feel loved and celebrated for who you are? If not, your opinion of yourself will be based on the words and actions of others. And sometimes these words and actions are brutal. If you have lived in a dysfunctional home, you might have heard these ugly put-downs:

"I wish you had never been born."

"You weren't planned, I never wanted you."

"Nobody likes you, so get lost."

"Why can't you be like your sister?"

"You're good for nothing!"

"You don't deserve anything...you don't deserve to live."

"You're ugly."

"You're fat."

"You're scrawny."

"Nobody loves you and they never will."

"I hate you."

These cruel expressions are *not* who you are. They are spoken by people who have never understood a healthy family and are strangers to the Father's love. Whoever talks like this is broken and damaged themselves. These words are not truth words. They are whispered by the deceiver whose chief purpose is to wreck our lives!

I shouted with joy the day you were born and bragged about you to the angels.

God speaks to us *exactly the opposite* of the deceiver, He says:

"I planned for and chose you as My own before the earth came into being."

"I shouted with joy the day you were born and bragged about you to the angels."

"Every good thing I created is to bless you."

"I came to give you life that is full and overflowing."

"I will always love you in spite of your flaws."

"You are beautifully made."

"I like you just the way you are!"

"Even on your worst day, My love for you never changes."

"I will never tell you I love you and then abuse you."

"I will correct you to help you, not to hurt you."

"No one is hopeless because I am your Helper."

Every fiber of our being was designed for peace and joy. We were created to be addicted to only one thing; the pure love of God. Until we discover and receive this extravagant love through Jesus, we will look for happiness in everything else, but find nothing gives us what we crave. Medicating our pain with alcohol, food, drugs, and casual sexual encounters only leaves us empty and wounded.

I was someone who didn't esteem myself. At a crucial age I went through a year of severe bullying. It *seemed* most of the high school had turned against me, but now I know that wasn't true. I was shunned and called names that made me feel as if I'd been punched in the gut. At one point I was physically assaulted. As a result, I certainly didn't love who I was.

When any of us goes through this kind of abuse, we usually turn on ourselves and ask, "What's wrong with me? After all, it *has* to be me. If I were loveable, then those around me would like me, too. Why was I even born?" The absolute truth is that you and I were born *on purpose*. You and I need to speak to ourselves like we would to someone we love.

There is a world of difference between loving yourself and being self-absorbed. When we love who we are, we will not put ourselves down or deny our worth. It takes courage to look in the mirror every morning and say, "I am miraculously and wonderfully made. I am born for an excellent purpose." You may find this tough to do, but I challenge you to say it until you believe it's true!

There are many reasons why we struggle with accepting our own value. Those who live through abuse are sometimes told to keep secrets that were *never* meant to be kept. Like friends of mine, you may be skilled at sensing danger, because you had to be on high alert to someone's moods in your childhood. Have you lived life at a heightened stress level? If so, you may struggle with sharing your real feelings because hiding them was essential to protecting yourself.

When you hear the word *thrive*, it might be hard to grasp right now. And that's okay. When our lives have been lived in survival mode for so long, it takes a while to discover the freedom God intended for us. But don't stay stuck in that rut! It's possible for you to go from barely surviving, to actually thriving.

One of the ways you can get unstuck, is to let go of abusive relationships that attempt to control or demean you. There are helplines across North America where you can text or call. There are safe houses for women and teenagers in almost every city. There are godly people in your community who will stand beside you until your broken wings can fly.

How do you know if someone is controlling or abusive toward you? Here are some vital signs:

You can only talk freely when that person is out of earshot.

You can't ever be yourself in that person's presence.

You blame yourself for the abuse you are suffering.

You are depressed and anxious most of the time.

You try to please the other person, even when what they ask is against your will.

A crucial thing you can do to untangle yourself from an abusive relationship, is to create a step by step action plan to follow with numbers to call if you're in danger. Write this

THE RED GERANIUM SISTERHOOD

down and keep it in a safe place. If you can, have a mobile device with you at all times and gather a support network where you can safely get shelter.

Another way to get unstuck is to stop blaming others. When life is unbearable, do we think God is the source of our trouble? Blaming Him for what's wrong may seem logical. Some of us wouldn't want to admit it, but at times we may have shaken our fist at God and shouted, "If You are really loving, why did You let these things happen to me? Where were You when I needed You most?"

I want to assure you of something. Your loving Creator is not on a holiday. He was and is working hard to get help to you. That is why you are reading this book today, because you are *that* valuable.

When we recognize we're stuck in harmful cycles or thought patterns, we have a decision to make. We can stay a victim or we can choose to break free and start living again. God is ready to help us. Our Creator is a loving parent who only wants the best for our lives. In fact, the Bible tells us that Jesus is praying for you and I right now.[32]

Do not believe you are inferior and damaged because someone in your past or present doesn't believe in your worth. What is our worth anyway? It is so much more than a human evaluation. No rejection or abuse can hold you prisoner when you believe the *God evaluation* of who you are. Your value is in the shape of a Cross!

---

32. Heb. 7:25 (English Standard Version)

**Our worth is so much more than
a human evaluation. Believe the
GOD evaluation of who you are.**

Looking back on the worst times of my life, I know
God was trying to show me my worth in so many ways.
Throughout my childhood, I was shown unconditional love
by my parents and siblings. All around me on our farm, there
were signs of God's goodness. At times I would run to the
pasture and bury my head in the horse's mane and just cry.
God knew I needed that comfort. I encourage you to get
back to nature — to take a walk somewhere that gives you
joy. Why not ask a friend and go for a bike ride or picnic?
Take the time to gaze at a sunset while it dips beneath the
horizon, or grow your own beautiful flowers and put them in
your window!

God is never finished with shaping our lives. He can
orchestrate a rescue plan in the most unusual ways. After
that painful year of bullying, God created a way through my
sewing club for me to enter a modelling competition. I was
still so insecure; I was sure this would be painful! But it was
during this event, coinciding with a concert by a Christian
band, that I heard about the *real* Jesus, the One who gave
His life for me. I was given the chance to hang out with teens
who liked me for who I was. They were kind and showed
me what true sisterhood was about. That week of my life
was transforming!

You might be saying to yourself, "I never had anybody care
for me like you're describing. Nobody seems to care whether

I live or die." I hear you. Some of us haven't had a loving family or a supportive community behind us. But I'm asking you, please don't measure your value based on what *they say*. It's what *Jesus says* that matters! He is working behind the scenes to rescue you. He is the Shepherd who runs after the one who is lost, who can't find their way back to safety. He can bring you to the right people who value and esteem you. If Jesus did it for me, He will do it for anyone!

You and I are not invisible to Him. There is a story in the Bible of a woman named Hagar who was the servant of a wealthy couple.[33] Hagar was treated so harshly by her female boss, that she ran into the desert, desperate and broken. She felt as if no one in the world cared for her. While she was crying bitter tears, *God Himself* came and spoke encouragement to her heart. He told Hagar He had a plan for her and that all would be well. In wonder and gratitude, she named Him: *The God Who Sees Me*. You really are seen by the One who loves you best.

I'd like to share a similar kind of encounter I had where Jesus healed me from the effects of bullying. To be honest, I didn't know I still needed healing, but Jesus did! This unusual encounter happened when my husband and I were attending meetings in Alberta, Canada. The speaker was sharing from the Bible, how God sees and loves us the exact way He sees and loves His Son, Jesus.

While the minister was speaking, a remarkable thing happened. God's Spirit opened my eyes into another realm where

---

33. Gen. 16:5–14 (English Standard Version)

I saw myself as a teenager on one of the worst days of my life. On this occasion, I'd been selling raffle tickets to raise money for our small town's fund-raising efforts. The end result I hoped for, was winning the title of Carnival Queen. Unfortunately, this very public event happened to collide with the year I was bullied.

My competitors at this event were skated onto the ice by their boyfriends while we waited for the results. Since most of my peers didn't want to associate with me, I had to ask my own brother to be my escort. He was kind enough to say yes. To further my embarrassment, I couldn't wear skates because of a bad injury to my knee. As a result, I had to hobble around the ice on boots while the rest of the girls skated gracefully around the arena. Believe me, if I could have escaped that day I would have.

But now, in this unusual vision I was experiencing, everything about that humiliating day began to change! Jesus Himself skated onto the ice surface and asked me to sit down on a chair at the center of the arena. He took off the ugly boots I was wearing that night and fitted me with a spotless pair of ivory skates. To my shock, He even laced them up for me. Next, Jesus wrapped a purple robe around my shoulders and placed a jeweled crown on my head. Then He stood me up, offered His arm with a smile, and skated me around the arena with great pride and joy.

When you detox your thinking with the way God sees you, you won't have to fit into anyone's box.

As I stood there in that church watching this scene, tears of gratitude flowed down my face. I realized that all the heartache we go through is *not* the end of the story! I discovered that God longs for you and I to see our worth in His eyes. Jesus is present to heal you right now. He desires us to be whole and to enjoy life. You and I are loved and loveable, no matter what we may feel at this very moment. Just take a minute, close your eyes, and see yourself seated in the inner circle of God's love. Ask Jesus to reveal His happiness in loving you and the open invitation He brings. Thank Him for helping you see yourself the way He sees you.

There is so much pressure on us females to conform to an image which hides our true selves. We cannot find our worth by how others might view us. Our joy in living only comes when we remember *who* we belong to. Only then will our eyes be wide open to the reality of who we really are. When you detox your thinking with the way God sees you, you won't have to fit into anyone's box. You can learn to love yourself and celebrate the life you've been given.

artwork by Jan Louis

*"The King's daughter is all
glorious within; Her clothing
is interwoven with gold."*

Ps. 45:13 (NASB)

Chapter 7

Keeping Your Colors

*"Your personal boundaries protect
the inner core of your identity
and your right to choices."*

Gerard Manley Hopkins

Finding out who we really are as unique creations of God, empowers us to thrive, not just survive. The key to this discovery is simple. We must no longer believe what "The Grinch" throws our way. Instead, we must believe the Truth Person who gave His life for us. As we talked about earlier, we can't love ourselves until we come to terms with what we believe about God and what He believes about us. In other words, it is critical to understand our *core identity*.

If we believe we are created like animals, we will act like animals. If we believe no one loves us, we will develop a victim mentality and wrongly decide that *everyone* and *everything* is against us. We will lash out and be jealous of others and end up destroying our own lives and others in the process.

All of us need to understand that hating ourselves is the opposite of God's beautiful design for our lives.

I want you to do something unusual right now. Use your imagination and picture with me a special wall in heaven. On this wall are numerous photographs of God's beloved family members. I want to ask you something. Do you see yourself pictured in a stunning frame on that wall? If you said *no*, then you need to ask yourself, *why not*?

Why wouldn't you see yourself in that collage of God's family photos? Maybe the reason is, you believe the welcome mat is only laid out for those who perform well. Thankfully, God's acceptance of us is not based upon our ability. He is never in a bad mood, because His love is not conditional on you and I always doing everything right.

You and I may see our weeds, but God our gardener, sees our *seed potential*. Inside every tiny seed are the possibilities of what that seed can become. We have these creative possibilities built into us, too. But we need to believe they are there!

Surprisingly when we fail, God doesn't see us as failures. He will never abandon us, even at our worst times. He will show us what we need to change without threatening or demeaning us. In fact, you and I were handpicked to receive Jesus' kindness while we were still in darkness and engaging in harmful behavior toward others as well as ourselves.[34] All that God is asking, is that we embrace His Son Jesus, so we can live our lives from this new core identity.

34. Eph. 1:4,5; Eph. 2:4,5 (English Standard Version)

There is a heartbreaking story in the Bible about a young woman who let go of her core identity after suffering a sexual assault. Her name was Tamar (meaning *palm tree*). She began life in an extremely wealthy family. In fact, it was a royal family. She was given a stunningly colored robe, embroidered with gold. This coat identified her as a king's daughter who was clearly loved, esteemed, and honored. Tamar wore that exquisite robe with dignity and happiness, never dreaming anyone would want to harm her.

But Tamar's fairy-tale existence was snuffed out in one brutal, selfish act of rape by her stepbrother. She fought against him to stop the assault, but tragically, he overpowered her. Like the coward and bully he was, her stepbrother blamed her for his wicked act.

Tamar's father, the king, was very angry with his son, but did *nothing* to punish him or do anything to restore his daughter's dignity and worth. Tamar's father acted like a coward as well. As a result of her grief, Tamar tore her coat of many colors into pieces and lived the rest of her life as if she was damaged goods. Tamar made a disastrous decision to let go of her core identity and believe her life was over.[35]

What happens to you, does not have to define you.

It is extremely important for you and I to believe that what happens *to* us does not have to *define* us. Your experience in

---

35. 2 Sam. 13:6–20 (English Standard Version)

life may be one of abuse and rejection, but that is not the blueprint God designed for your future. Even if your family or so-called friends fail or mistreat you, Jesus never will! He has a perfect plan to lift you up and give you an excellent purpose on earth. You were designed and embroidered in your mother's womb with distinct colors revealing gifts, abilities, value, and worth.

If we have been sexually, physically, or emotionally assaulted or bullied, there is a strong tendency to let go of our personal boundaries and let the abuse continue. We may even enter high-risk lifestyles, or develop addictions which strip us of esteem in our own eyes.

You have the right to your skin and who touches it. You have the right to demand respect when you say *no* to someone. You and I have the right to get the help needed in overcoming abuse, to be safe in our own skin. We have choice power! We need to practice saying *no* out loud. Go ahead, try it right now. Say *No* to abuse!

No one has the right to rip away your coat of many colors. They may try, but you and I must hold fast to our high value and worth. These colors can only be ripped away when we believe the lies and give ourselves to something beneath us.

The palm tree, which is the meaning of Tamar's name, is an unusual tree. No matter how much it has been battered by storms, the fruit only grows sweeter. The palm tree cannot be uprooted from its place of security, because the branches and trunk do not break, they only bend. You are that palm tree! You can be healed of your past when you see your roots firmly planted in God's acceptance and affection. It is crucial you find out who you *really* are and never forget it. We must not allow the trauma we have suffered uproot us from our wonderful personhood. Our identity comes from our Maker. He believes in our worth and never uses or abuses us.

Dr. T.L. Osborn said is his book *The Message That Works*, "Nothing is more vital to a person's self-esteem than to discover their own value. Every human is a creation of God. People are the product of divine love. That is why hatred and fear are so destructive in human lives."[36]

I want to relate a stunning rescue that took place in a young woman's life when she believed in her own value. My husband shared this woman's extraordinary story with me to the best of his memory. We will call her "Joanna" to protect her identity. While Dr. Joanna was examining our dog, she asked my husband what he did for a living. When Jim told her we were ministers, the vet put her schedule aside and described her shocking experience in detail.

When Joanna was a young teenager, her stepfather began molesting her. He became so obsessed that he eventually abducted Joanna, taking her to a rural area. This wicked man basically kept her as a prisoner in his house. Joanna wasn't allowed to go back to school and was threatened with harm if she tried to escape. Eventually, Joanna became pregnant through repeated sexual abuse and had two children while still in her teens. Anguish and hopelessness overwhelmed this young woman, because she *believed* her life would always be this way.

---

36. Dr. T.L. Osborn, The Message That Works, OSFO publishers, 2011;

What our friend didn't know was that behind the scenes, God was at work to rescue her. One day someone in the area managed to place a New Testament Bible in Joanna's hands. She knew there was something precious about its contents, so this gift was carefully hidden from her tormentor.

Each night after her kidnapper went to sleep, our friend would sneak out of bed and hide in an upstairs closet where she had stashed a lawn chair and a flashlight. Under cover of darkness, Joanna began to read about God's amazing love plan for the human race. When she realized Jesus died on a Cross to save her, Joanna wept with joy.

Day by day, hope began to ebb its way into her battered heart. These newfound truths began to outgrow Joanna's fear of her abuser. She realized no person had the right to threaten and dominate another human being. Joanna discovered her core identity! She believed words from the Bible that said, "...you will know the truth and the truth will set you free."[37]

One remarkable morning, Joanna's courage overruled her fear. She confronted this man and told him she was leaving. So fierce was she in her determination, that her stepfather became *afraid of Joanna* and let her go!

Joanna left that awful place with her small children and began an amazing journey. She knew the Bible clearly said that God's plans for her were good,[38] so she confidently went back to high school and completed her GED test with one of the highest marks in her class. Next, she attended university

---

37. John 8:32 (English Standard Version)

38. Jer. 29:11 (English Standard Version)

and graduated with distinction as a doctor from the College of Veterinary Medicine. After defying all the odds against her, Joanna became a successful veterinarian in a Canadian city.

What is extraordinary is that Joanna was able to trust a man again — trust this person enough to love and be loved in return. God gave her a husband who cherished Joanna and believed in her worth. Her new husband showed his wife the kindness she never had. They treated one another as equals in the eyes of God.[39]

Nothing is impossible when you and I discover our worth and esteem. Our Creator didn't design us to be miserable and depressed. He didn't bring you into this world to be caught in a trap of abuse, addictions, and hopelessness. From the very beginning we were designed in the image of God. The devil came to rob us of this core identity. But Jesus came to restore it and give us a future filled with promise. Will you believe it?

---

39. Gen. 1:26, 27; 1 Pet. 3:7 (The Passion Translation)

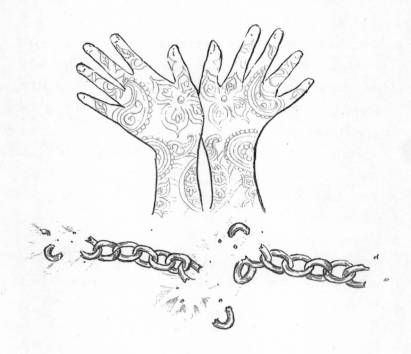

artwork by Jan Louis

*"Forgive us the wrongs we have done,
as we ourselves release forgiveness
to those who have wronged us"*

Matt. 6:12 (TPT)

Chapter 8

Forgiving the Unforgivable

"She has been forgiven all her many
sins. This is why she has shown
me such extravagant love..."

Luke 7:47 (TPT)

Something in your past may be eating at you like a cancerous sore. You may be deeply hurt. You may have built walls around yourself so high and so strong, no one has been able to penetrate them. It may also be you've done something you are terribly ashamed of, something you can't forgive yourself for. If you are filled with hatred and self-loathing, I want to assure you that you don't have to live another day in that hell and isolation.

There comes a time in our lives when we must decide whether living in bitterness is more important than our own freedom and personal peace.

Unforgiveness is a deep, ugly root growing just beneath the surface. Many people wrongly believe that holding on to bitterness is a strength. In fact, families and people groups are so full of rage with injustices they have endured, they camp there for *generations*. If we allow it, the root of bitterness will sap our lives until we're reduced to an empty shell.

When most people hear the word forgiveness, they mistakenly believe that forgiving someone means what they did to you is okay. But that is not true! Forgiveness isn't ignoring the wrong someone has done. Forgiveness is a God-given remedy for *your* benefit, not the other person's. It removes the poison slowly seeping into and destroying you. Until we forgive, we are giving permission for someone to keep us frozen in the past, instead of moving forward with joy into our future.

We must decide whether living in bitterness is more important than our own freedom and personal peace.

An American woman, Elizabeth Smart, was fourteen years old when she was abducted at knifepoint by a crazed maniac. This man, with the help of his equally wicked wife, chained, terrorized, and raped Elizabeth repeatedly for nine months. When she was finally rescued and returned safely to her family, Elizabeth's mom spoke words that gave her the courage to let go of a victim mentality and embrace the future. She said, "Elizabeth, what these people have done to you is terrible, and there aren't words strong enough to describe how wicked and evil they are. They have stolen nine months of your life away from you that you will never get back.

"But the best punishment you could ever give them is to be happy, is to move forward with your life, to do all the things you want to do. Because by feeling sorry for yourself, by holding onto the past, by reliving it, that's only allowing them to steal more of your life away from you. And they don't deserve that, they don't deserve a single second more..."[40]

Elizabeth did just that! She grew up to be a strong, confident, happy woman. Elizabeth married a kind, loving man and they have a precious family. She is sought after around the world as a keynote speaker. Elizabeth learned that as long as you hang onto bitterness, you give power to the perpetrator. Forgiving someone *does not* give them permission for your trust to be betrayed again. You have the right to your boundaries and do not have to allow abusers back into your life. Releasing forgiveness takes the chains from your own neck, so *you* can walk away free![41] Like Elizabeth, you can choose to be happy and take steps forward to live the life you were designed for.

There was a teenager in the Bible who was abducted as well. Joseph's story is found in the book of Genesis.[42] Like Tamar, he was also greatly loved and given a coat of many colors signifying his worth. One night, Joseph had a dream

---

40. Brandy McDonnell, features writer, "Interview: Elizabeth Smart still tries to live by her mother's advice," *The Oklahoman*, Nov. 9, 2015.

41. Isa. 52:2 (English Standard Version)

42. Gen. Chapters 37-45 (English Standard Version)

which he mistakenly shared with his older stepbrothers. Because the dream involved being promoted above his brothers, they reacted with jealousy and threw Joseph in a deep pit.

With hatred in their hearts, the brothers took their jealousy a step further and sold Joseph as a slave to the Egyptians. The stepbrothers ripped up Joseph's multicolored coat and soaked it in blood to convince their father that wild animals had killed him. To top it all off, later in Joseph's life, he was imprisoned for a crime he did not commit.

If anyone had a right to be bitter and vengeful it was Joseph. But instead of nursing his bitterness, Joseph drew strength from God's love and kindness. Because he was honorable and had integrity in everything he did, God brought about Joseph's release from prison and gave him such favor he was promoted to the highest position in government, right next to the ruler of Egypt.

Through a series of events, Joseph's own brothers were forced to get help from Egypt during a time of famine. When Joseph saw his brothers for the first time since they had sold him, anger and revenge surged through his being. But he made a very difficult choice. Even though it was agonizing, Joseph *chose to forgive* his brothers and decided to bless them instead.

From the ashes of the fire that brought you to your knees, comes the strength to rise and dream a new dream.

How was Joseph able to forgive such a crime against him? I believe Joseph realized that even in the darkest pit, God had *never* abandoned him. Joseph understood that no one has to stay a victim of their circumstances. His brothers humbled themselves and bowed down before Joseph, just like his dream as a teenager. When you and I refuse to drink the poison of unforgiveness, we keep our colors of dignity and can start to dream again!

Do you realize that Someone has already forgiven the unforgivable in you and me?

All of us have fallen short of the goodness of our Creator. We were all born sinners. Each of us has harmed someone else by our words or actions. That is why Jesus came to die in our place, so we could be forgiven and have our sins thrown as far as the east is from the west.[43]

When we accept Jesus as our King and Rescuer, He comes into our hearts and washes us clean. Jesus said powerful words when He hung bleeding on the Cross. He said, "Father, forgive them. They don't know what they're doing."[44] God will always bring about justice, but He is also compassionate, forgiving, and full of grace.

Yes, it is a real struggle to forgive others. But God made us in His image, which means we have choice power. If we freely decide to forgive, Jesus will give us the ability. We just have to ask! Forgiveness is a choice, not an emotion. If you and I make the choice to forgive, the day will come when

43. Ps. 103:12 (English Standard Version)
44. Luke 23:34 (God's Word)

the memory of the abuse will no longer harm or hold you captive. I speak from personal experience about this. From the ashes of the fire that brought you to your knees, comes the strength to rise and dream a new dream! God is the One who inspires these good dreams for our lives.

However, there may be one person you never thought of forgiving. One of the healthiest things you can do after receiving God's forgiveness is to *forgive yourself.*

Several years ago, I became friends with a woman in a small community. We were hanging out on the front step one day, enjoying the summer weather. I shared with her how Jesus took my failures and wrongs on the Cross and that she could receive His forgiveness, too. My new friend broke down weeping in despair. She said, "God could *never* forgive me!"

I held this woman in my arms as her body shook with sobs. I assured her, "There is no sin that God cannot forgive! That is why Jesus came, because we *all* need a Savior. We cannot save ourselves." I shared with her that I had also done things I was ashamed of. If we are going to be a true sister-hood, we need to be honest with one another.

Courageously, my friend told me about two abortions she had had as a teenager. Every day of her life she had deeply regretted these choices. I helped her receive God's gift of for-giveness and she was set free from the weight of that guilt! My friend then made a powerful choice to forgive herself, because she realized Jesus was holding *nothing* against her.

It was a wonderful day when this lovely woman let go of self-hatred and received the grace God offers every one of us.

Maybe you have already forgiven others, but like my experience, there could be someone you know who is struggling with bitterness and regret. You too, can be a conduit of God's love and help them experience that same freedom.

God has not let you and me down. If you feel He is the One who has stolen from you, then you are believing a lie. The devil is the one who hates us. He is a thief and the source of all lies. God sent His Son to destroy the works of the devil.[45] Jesus came to restore us to a life of peace with Him and with one another. He offers us a fresh start without shame. We can begin this journey from brokenness to wholeness today.

---

45. 1 John 3:8b (English Standard Version)

artwork by S.M. Christian

"Rise up in splendor and be radiant,
for your light has dawned."

Isa. 60:1 (TPT)

Chapter 9

Brokenness is Not Your Address

"Although the world is full of suffering,
it is also full of the overcoming of it."
Helen Keller

Everything in life comes down to a choice. We can allow ourselves to be buried by life's circumstances or we can choose to believe in our incomparable worth and rise above those same challenges.

There is an ancient fable describing this choice power. One day, a donkey fell into an old well in a farmer's field. The animal brayed for hours while his owner tried unsuccessfully to get him out. Finally, the farmer gave up and decided his old donkey wasn't worth saving. He got a shovel and started filling in the hole. The donkey kept up its cries, but gradually became silent. After an hour of shoveling like crazy, the farmer looked in to see how it was going. To his amazement, he saw his old donkey jump out of the well with a kick and run away!

You see, when the donkey first saw the dirt being piled on him, he panicked. Then he realized the stuff being dumped on him could also be used for his escape. As each shovelful hit his back, the donkey would shake it off and step up on the growing mound. Eventually, the pile grew high enough for him to jump out and run free!

We can get through life's deepest challenges by shaking off the setbacks and stepping up to the plate with courage.

You know what? No matter who we are, life is going to shovel dirt on us. And those who are supposed to help us, may decide we aren't worth their time. That's why it's crucial we believe in our own value. We will get through life's deepest challenges by shaking off the setbacks and stepping up to the plate with courage. You and I don't have to become part of the dirt pile!

If we look again at Joseph's life from the Bible, we discover he encountered setbacks again and again. People falsely accused him of wrongdoing and guilt was heaped upon him. But Joseph had something beautiful happening in the midst of it all. He had a relationship with his Creator. He knew God was *with* him and would never leave him to rot in a pit. That knowledge empowered Joseph to shake off the injustice and rise to his true destiny.

Were you given a rough start in life? A good friend of mine had tons of *dirt* piled on her from an early age. She wrote a letter describing her struggle and how God's amazing grace drew her up and out of that horrible place. With her permission, I am sharing the contents of her letter with you.

As a young girl, my friend was filled with such deep guilt and shame that it consumed every aspect of her life. It began at the age of five when her father sexually abused her. Through the continuing years of abuse, she learned to conceal the pain, so much so, that even her mom and younger siblings had no clue of the deep hurt and confusion she was struggling with. My friend tried to live a normal life as a young First Nations girl, but on the inside, she was screaming for help. The only peace she had was attending church with her grandparents. It was there she learned about the *real* Jesus.

This beautiful child found comfort in writing poetry to God and being able to talk to Him freely. She discovered in God's Word that He knew *everything* about her, even the number of hairs on her head.[46] Finally, she had Someone with whom she could share her deepest secrets and innermost fears! But, as the years progressed, this precious teenager felt trapped by the continued abuse of her father. She felt her heart slowly shatter into a million pieces. Some days she felt like brokenness was her identity.

But God had not forgotten about her. When she became a young woman, she heard powerful teachings from God's Word that began a deep cleansing of her soul. One of these

---

46. Luke 12:6,7 (The Passion Translation)

freeing truths gave her the ability to shake off the pain, forgive her father and step up to her true identity as God's child. In this verse she read, *anyone* who belongs to Christ has become a new person. "The old life is gone; a new life emerges!"[47] When my friend read these healing words, her eyes were opened and she saw that new meant *new*! Not fixed up. Not refinished like an old chair. She said, "I was *brand new*...a creation that never existed before. When I came to Christ, the old me passed away and I became new!"

Further on in that same set of verses, my friend saw that God no longer counted her sins against her. Instead, He cancelled them and restored her to favor and a new family. This realization gave her the strength to finally forgive herself. You might ask why she would have to forgive herself when she was the victim? Tragically with sexual abuse, something unclean can come into a child's life. When very young, victims of abuse will sometimes act out upon others what they themselves have suffered. After years of shame, my friend realized she was forgiven and no longer condemned with this guilt. God's Word reprogrammed her thinking and she was totally set free!

One of my friends and mentors, Dr. LaDonna Osborn, said this, "Having a renewed mind is the greatest challenge for many. It's not easy. From childhood our thinking has been continually shaped by family, culture and the atmosphere of sin's rule. In Christ, all things are new and that includes our thinking. How? Through knowledge of the Word of God. Don't settle for only knowing what others tell you about

47. 2 Cor. 5:17b (The Message)

God's will. Read the book for yourself! The bible is a book of transformation. It answers everything!"[48]

Jesus nailed our sin to the Cross with Him. He never deserved our sin, just as we didn't deserve His free gift of everlasting life. Because of His love for you and I, Jesus made the *great exchange* to give us right standing with Him. Now we can receive what our Creator has always planned for us.

You can talk to God right now and receive His love. Just whisper out loud, "Jesus, thank You for taking all my pain and shame on the Cross and rising from the grave to give me life. Thank you for forgiving all of my wrongs and giving me a fresh start. Help me to forgive others as You have forgiven me." If you prayed that and believed it, you are now a child of God. Welcome to the family table!

My beautiful friend wanted to share her favorite Psalm with you, describing her freedom as a beloved daughter of the King:

I love the Lord because He hears my prayers and answers them.
Because He bends down and listens, I will pray as long as I breathe!
Death stared me in the face - I was frightened and sad. Then I cried, "Lord save me!"
How kind He is! How good He is! So merciful, this God of ours!

Psalm 116:1–5 *The Living Bible*

---

48. Quote by Dr. LaDonna Osborn, from FB, July 23,2019

EMBRACING

artwork by Jan Louis

*"I give thanks to you, because
I have been so amazingly and
miraculously made."*

Ps. 139:14 (GW)

Chapter 10

The Camouflage of Comparison

"No one can make you feel
inferior without your consent."

Eleanor Roosevelt

Comparing ourselves with others is one of the most destructive things we can do to our mind and emotions. When we copy someone else, we camouflage the beauty and uniqueness of our own personhood. Camouflage, according to the dictionary, is an attempt to disguise ourselves, so we blend in with our surroundings. Why do we do that? Why do we want to hide who we are and shrink to someone else's box?

The answer is simple. We often value our peers' opinions, far more than what God has spoken over our lives. Women especially struggle with body image. We are much more aware of what we don't like about ourselves than what we do. We females often view a magazine's airbrushed image as the goal we should aspire to. This constant comparison corrupts the image of our distinct self. It's very natural to want people to like us. But when that desire becomes the focus of our happiness, we sell ourselves short. Friends who are authentic will never pressure you to be someone you are not. Choose your friends wisely.

After experiencing bullying in my school, I made a very wrong choice. Promising myself I would never be unpopular again, I made an inner vow to do what it took to gain acceptance. I often hid my beliefs and the qualities that made me who I was, in order to make others happy. In essence, I became a people pleaser. Was I at peace with myself? Not at all. The sad result of being a people pleaser, is that you become cowardly.

Friends who are authentic will never pressure you to be someone you are not.

In my grade 12 year, I believed I had finally achieved the popularity I had been striving for. I was very excited to be chosen as our class valedictorian. On the surface it appeared everything was coming together for me. However, behind the scenes, a drama was unfolding which truly revealed what I'd allowed myself to become.

You see, there was a girl in my class who isolated herself from others. As her classmate, I was kind to this girl, but had not befriended her. I was aware of the difficulty of her home life, but wasn't concerned enough to help her with what she faced. In my quest to have the approval of my peers, I turned a blind eye to her suffering. So much so, I had no idea she was forbidden to take part in our graduation celebration. I was totally ignorant of the fact she was kept in her house that day. This was how self-absorbed I had become. By living someone else's life, I had become hardened to the hurts of others.

The end of this story is a good one. But it had nothing to do with me making the right choices that year. It was actually three of my classmates who became the heroes at our grad. These students took the other girl under their wing. They found out she was forbidden to come to grad and didn't have a dress to wear. My amazing classmates pooled their resources and somehow came up with a lovely gown. Then they hatched a plan to go out to this girl's farmhouse and knock on the door. While one of them kept her dad busy chatting, the other brave friend helped my classmate escape through her bedroom window. They quickly hid her under blankets in the car and hustled her off to our graduation.

My three classmates embraced their friend and gave her the dignity and esteem she deserved. Their example is the heart of *The Red Geranium Sisterhood*. How were they able to risk their own safety to do so? Because at the young age of seventeen, they knew who they were and had stopped comparing themselves to everyone else. They didn't care about what others thought.

I heard this statement and wholeheartedly agree: "When we walk confidently into a room, not thinking we are better than others, but realizing we don't have to compare ourselves at all, that is real freedom." You and I can celebrate others and their gifts without feeling jealous and inadequate ourselves. Why? Because we have been given our own unique qualities that *no one else* on earth possesses!

God delights in originality. As a gardener, I've observed there are no two flowers that bloom exactly alike. As well, astronomers tell us there are no two stars that glow exactly the same.

Do you realize that some of the most famous, well-loved women in history, cared little for the perfect body that consumes so many females' lives? These exceptional women had inner core values that made them irresistible: kindness, courage, intelligence, humor, to name a few. While it's important for each of us to be physically fit and glowing with health, any good thing can become so obsessive that it consumes our minds and takes the joy out of living. True beauty comes from within and radiates to our outer being. Think about it, when people look back on our lives, will they talk about our body weight or whether or not we had a six-pack? What they will do, is celebrate what we did in creating a better world and how we enriched our families and communities. *This* is the legacy that counts.

Every culture has female heroes, past and present, who inspire us to live the life we were born for. One of these Canadian heroines was a First Nations Ojibwa woman named Nahnebahwequay (Nah-nee-bah-we-qua) which means *upright woman*. Her English name was Catherine Sutton. Because Catherine believed in God, in her dignity, and in the worth of her people, she took on the Canadian government back in 1857 to right a wrong.

At that time, First Nations peoples were denied the right to purchase their own land already granted to them by law. Nahnebahwequay fought for her family and her people to be given back their rights. She was able to sail to England and ask the Queen for help, because a group of concerned Christians paid for her voyage and did everything possible to make her journey a success. These Christians helped her like they would someone in their own family. That is what a *true sisterhood* does!

Through her bravery and skill in communicating, Nahnebahwequay won the right from Canada's government to buy back her family's land. When she returned to Canada, she kept on working for her people. We need to remember she did this during a time when women didn't even have the right to vote. We need *more* courageous women like Catherine Sutton in our midst. You and I can be those women!

Another fearless woman we can model our lives after is Harriet Tubman. She was an African American, born into slavery in the U.S.A. A powerful movie has been released about her astounding life called *Harriet*. As a child, Harriet was beaten, whipped, and deprived of life's simplest pleasures. She said she "grew up like a neglected weed, ignorant of liberty, having never experienced it."[49] Some of you may feel like that in your present circumstances. You may have lived with abuse for so long it seems normal, but it's not!

---

49. Harriet Tubman Historical Society, harriettubman.org

As Harriet grew older, she knew no human should ever suffer the hell of slavery and abuse. She longed for freedom and drew near to Jesus in her suffering.

Finally, Harriet was able to escape. Using the North Star and her strong faith in God, she was guided safely through rivers and dangerous terrain. Throughout her journey, there were compassionate Christian women and men from the south who helped Harriet. These godly white people opened their homes and helped the slaves on their way to freedom, even risking being arrested themselves. What matters is not the color of our skin. What *really* matters is the color of our hearts — the color of love! This is the essence of true sisterhood.

After Harriet experienced the taste of freedom, she still wasn't satisfied. Enjoying her new life of happiness no longer filled her soul. Harriet knew deep within herself that other slaves had to be saved. Harriet heard the shrieks and cries of agony of those being beaten. She had heard their groans and prayers. She said in her own way of speaking, "I was free, and dey should be free also."[50] Harriet went back time after time and brought hundreds of others to freedom with her.

But Harriet didn't stop there. She fought for women's rights, established a home for the elderly, and even took part as a Union spy in defeating Confederate troops during the Civil War in the States. Harriet knew who she was created to be and was determined to influence the culture around her.

---

50. Harriet, The Moses of Her People by Sarah H. Bradford, George R. Lockwood and Son, 1886. pg. 32

**Refuse to be swallowed by the
culture of cowardliness around
you. Instead, leave a trail of
kindness wherever you go.**

Another wonderful friend of mine was raised on a First
Nation reserve in Alberta, Canada. As a young person she
experienced the reproach of society against her and her
people. She saw herself as a victim of other people's domination and choices. But there came a day when Jesus became
her Liberator! He freed my friend from a victim mentality
because she chose *not to allow* the past to define her any
longer. She read in the book of Joshua, Chapter 5, that her
shame had been rolled away. She realized no curse could stay
on her. Why? Because she believed Jesus *reversed* the curse
and blessed her when He became a curse for humanity on
the Cross.[51]

My friend discovered she didn't need to lay claim to cultural things to get approval from others. Instead, she found
that God's goodness followed her because she embraced
Jesus and was now a child of God. My friend is proud of
her First Nations heritage and has never looked back! She
simply stopped comparing herself to others. This confident
woman went on to receive her master's degree and then her
doctorate. Now she travels across North America, sharing
the truths of the Creator's love plan for all who will listen

---

51. Gal. 3:13 (English Standard Version)

and believe. We can follow in her footsteps and let Jesus "rewrite our history."[52]

I challenge you not to shrink to the expectations of others. I challenge you not to allow fear to be an overriding factor in your decisions. Fear is a paralyzing force that stops us from realizing our dreams.

Yes, there will be opposition. It won't be easy. Others who are insecure in themselves, will always try to press you into their mold. But when you know your worth in God's eyes, you can embrace and live this new life in all of its fullness.

Why not be brave and ask God to bring to your community those who will stand with you? Introduce yourself to those who are bullied or rejected and welcome them into your circle. When you have genuine friends at your side, they will strengthen you. They will walk with you through obstacles you encounter and challenge you to live a life of courage and kindness.

Be everything God has designed you to be. You are not a weed. You are not a problem. You were born to thrive like a sunflower nourished by the sun. You were created to be whole: spirit, soul, and body.[53] Once you step into your freedom, then go and lift someone else's head above water and bring them back to shore.

In my case, I can't go back and erase what I didn't do to help my fellow classmate or others that I failed. But I can

---

52. Dr. Velma White, from the speech "Your reproach has been rolled away" Jan. 24, 2019

53. 1 Thess. 5:23 (English Standard Version)

make the choice *today* to pour God's goodness into those around me. So can you!

Never allow the cruelty of others to make you cruel or afraid to stand for justice. Be inclusive of others. The true mark of character is refusing to be swallowed by the culture of cowardliness around us. Instead, you and I can leave a trail of kindness wherever we go.

artwork by S.M. Christian

*"I will not abandon you or leave you
as orphans in the storm
— I will come to you."*

John 14:18 (TLB)

Chapter 11

A New Family Album

*"Our photos were all stashed away
and so we didn't see, the truth about
the treasure, the start of you and me."*

Author Unknown

Let's visualize something together. I'd like you to picture yourself as a model being photographed for a well-known fashion magazine. You've been told your images will be seen by *hundreds* of *thousands* of people. Would you feel self-conscious? Would you try to hide your self-perceived flaws, go on a crash diet, and work out like crazy? No doubt all of us would say, "Are you kidding? Absolutely!" "Let's grab the false eyelashes and get a makeover!"

Now form a mental image of yourself standing before your Creator and Designer. In His presence, you and I don't have to be self-conscious and hide. We don't have to try to make ourselves into someone we are not. The One who formed you with great love in your mother's womb doesn't compare you to others or expose you to ridicule.

You and I don't have to be intimidated by anyone! If God Himself loves us completely in spite of our imperfections, why should we let others tell us we don't measure up? Our Creator sees the end from the beginning and shapes our life story with care. He knows how to fix our mess and bring us to wholeness. The colors He paints us with are a dancing prism that would astonish us if we would just let our eyes be opened!

The blood that poured from Jesus on the Cross is an unusual substance. His blood contains the power to wash us totally clean. When we grab hold of God's lifeline through Jesus our Rescuer, the stains of our old life are completely wiped away. Our old, shameful nature no longer exists. We are reborn as new creations!

The tough thing is, our memories have *not* been erased. All of us have snapshots in our subconscious of past experiences. Some are good, some even wonderful. Sadly, many are painful. Some of these vivid pictures may be abuse, rejection, or abandonment. If these images play over and over in your mind, they can keep you in a prison of self-loathing and fear. These memories can also send us into emotional turmoil where we react in harmful ways to others as well as ourselves. Don't you think it's time to have these past scenes removed from the video replay in your mind?

When a painful memory of an abusive parent plays through our thoughts, you and I can make a conscious decision to mentally *peel it out* and replace it with our Creator's kind words and safe embrace. This is what a friend of mine did with the ugly memories he had of an alcoholic parent's abuse. One day he was reading a verse in the Bible[54] that describes God's intense love for every human being. As he reread that verse again and again, he felt his frozen emotions begin to thaw and for the *first time* he experienced the warmth of God's love.

My friend, Dr. David Eckman said, "Oftentimes, as people from an unhealthy home proceed through adulthood, they do so with regret. They realize that they did not have the opportunity of having a childhood...what many of us miss from childhood is an experience of encouragement and sympathy."[55]

When you and I believe the truths of Jesus Christ, we can enter this new reality and be re-parented by God. It's powerful to experience being loved unconditionally!

Have you ever been betrayed by someone? Unfortunately, most of us have. When tormenting scenes of a friend or husband's betrayal push themselves into your thinking, ask God for His ability and strategy to deny them power to mess with your mind. Day by day, you will see a new picture of your priceless worth emerge from the pain.

As we read Bible accounts of Jesus showing His friendship and love to those beaten down by society, let's *place ourselves* in the story and receive that same acceptance and healing!

---

54. Eph. 2:4 (English Standard Version)

55. David J. Eckman, Creating a Healthy Family (Pleasanton: Becoming What God Intended Ministries,1996), pg. 26-27

This may not happen overnight. It's a process we must commit ourselves to, until wholeness comes. Jesus will stick closer than a brother to you. He promises *to never betray* or *abandon us.*[56] He was betrayed by His closest friends when He went to the Cross, so He understands our deepest wounds. You and I can trust Him with our hearts.

I have a close friend who experienced temporary abandonment by her parents when she was seventeen. One winter's night after a terrible fight with her sister, my friend ran into the cold and wandered weeping through the streets. She peered through windows and saw families enjoying each other around the supper table. How she longed to place herself on the inside of these happy families! What my friend didn't know, was that the One who loved her best, was planning to fulfill her deepest longing.

My friend met the man of her dreams who introduced her to the Man who would fulfill her dreams, Jesus Himself. She discovered her worth as God's beloved daughter when she invited Jesus to become her Savior and Friend. The pain and trauma of that year dissolved as she saw herself welcomed at the family table, enjoying her Heavenly Dad's unconditional love.

As we pore over the pages of Jesus' life on earth, we see a vivid picture of what God is really like. He is a good Father who always wants to protect His children. A good father never leaves His child alone to fight for themselves. Even

---

56. Prov. 18:24; Heb. 13:5 (English Standard Version)

when we do things wrong, He corrects us in a way that is loving and gentle.

You and I are painted with the colors of kindness, compassion, acceptance and worth.

I would like to share an experience from my childhood that describes this kind of love. When I was sixteen years old, my dad lent me his brand-new three-quarter-ton truck for the evening. It was a beauty! I was so excited to take it to a meeting in town, that it slipped my mind our heavy water tank had been removed from the truck box. Forgetting that information would come back to bite me.

I left our farm and sped off on the gravel road, already late for the meeting. About two kilometers from town, I suddenly lost control of the truck. Fear paralyzed me as my foot froze on the gas pedal. I began fishtailing back and forth because there was no weight from the water tank to hold me steady. Eventually, the inevitable happened. I slid off the road at an incredible speed and rolled the truck over and over until it landed on its wheels *opposite* to the direction I was going.

I sat there stunned, in awe I was still alive. I knew beyond a doubt that God had somehow saved my life, even though I didn't deserve it. Running to a farmer's house just a few hundred meters from the crash, I breathlessly explained what had happened. Our neighbor walked back with me to the crumpled mass of metal and muttered under his breath, "Shelley" he said. "There is no way you should have walked out of that vehicle." He then called my dad and told him he was bringing me home.

I dreaded the moment when I had to face my father and tell him I had totaled his new Ford truck. My parents had often purchased used vehicles because of budget restraints on the farm. This was the first new truck they had owned in many years. When we arrived at our house, I didn't want to get out of the car. I was sure my dad would be furious!

But as I opened the door and placed one foot on the ground, I looked up and saw my dad standing in the doorway. That image will stay with me as long as I live. There was my father, arms opened wide, beckoning me to come to him. I ran into his arms sobbing and asking forgiveness. As Dad's arms held me close, he said words that disabled my fear and shame. "Shelley," he whispered hoarsely, "I can buy a thousand trucks, but there is only one of you! I'm so thankful you're alive...we will get through this together."

You see, even though my father wasn't perfect, he was used at that critical moment to demonstrate what our Heavenly Father is really like. When I mess up as God's child and feel I can't approach Him because of my shame, I am reminded of my earthly father. And if my earthly father can forgive and shelter me, how much more will my Father in heaven forgive and restore me? There is a wonderful verse in the Bible that describes this perfectly. It says, "So now we come freely and boldly to where love is enthroned, to receive mercy's kiss and discover the grace we urgently need to strengthen us in our time of weakness"[57]

57. Heb. 4:16 (The Passion Translation)

Remember me describing the worst day of my life as a teenager? When Jesus rewrote that day, He created a new scene and washed the shame of that memory from my consciousness. He painted me with the colors of kindness, compassion, acceptance, and worth. From that moment on I decided to "set up camp" on who *God* said I was. And that choice needs to be made every single day.

Family counsellors and mental health therapists tell us that our lives will move in the direction of our strongest thoughts. A mentor of mine, Dr. Daisy Washburn Osborn said, "No woman can rise above her own thoughts and words. If she talks defeat, failure, worry, sickness, inferiority and unbelief, she will live life on that level."[58] We need to ask ourselves, "What level do we want our lives to be lived on?" Only you can make that decision for yourself!

Let your words be ones your Heavenly Father has spoken over your life. We find these life-giving words in the Bible. When we let God shape our lives from the inside out, instead of letting others mold us from the outside in, we will experience transformation, just like a butterfly emerging from its cocoon.

Our new family album must be taken off the shelf again and again, to remind us that we are not orphans...that we are not alone. You and I are children who are planned for, protected, and loved. Our new identity as beloved daughters must seep into our consciousness until it pours out every fiber of our being.

---

58. Dr. Daisy Washburn Osborn, *The Women Believer*, osborn.org

artwork by Charlene Douglas

Chapter 12

The Sisterhood of the Red Geranium

"Life is not about the capital I or me. Life is about us and we."

Eva Olsson (Holocaust Survivor)

Contrary to popular culture, our existence is so much more than Snapchat, Twitter, Instagram, or our eyes locked on our phones. These ways to interact are great for keeping in touch, but even a good thing can become harmful if we don't set boundaries.

Spending actual time in one another's presence and engaging in laughter and conversation, is the friendship glue that holds us together. When we go through trauma, the existence of a genuine friend can pull us from the brink of self-harm and suicide. God created us to form these *happiness relationships*.

Some young superstars in the entertainment world are burning out. A few have admitted in interviews that their addiction to Instagram was controlling their lives. Because of this, many of these celebrities have chosen to distance themselves from some of their social media. A survey conducted by the Royal Society for Public Health, asked fourteen-to twenty-four-year-olds in the United Kingdom, how social media has affected their health and well-being. The results showed that Snapchat, Facebook, Twitter, and Instagram all led to "increased feelings of depression, anxiety, poor body image and loneliness."[59] Could it be that without face-to-face or verbal interaction, we are not fully experiencing the relationships God designed for us to be healthy and happy?

A well-known advocate for children said, "...in appreciating our neighbor, we're participating in something truly sacred."[60] I believe every life is sacred, because each one of us is given breath from God. Every female has been placed on earth for a divine purpose that *no one else* can fulfill. But none of us can achieve this in and of ourselves.

Every life is sacred, because each one of us is given breath from God.

We were created for *relationship*. Making small connections every day is a way for people to battle isolation and low self-esteem. Sometimes the difference between an awful day or an awesome one, is simply reaching out with the encouragement we need ourselves. How about opening a

59. Rachel Ehmke, "How Using Social Media Affects Teenagers," Child Mind Institute; childmind.org.

60. Fred Rogers, Commencement Address at Middlebury College, May, 2001

door for someone who is coming into the mall after you? Or giving a genuine complement to a friend? Why not smile at people instead of avoiding them? How about gathering some friends around a campfire and enjoying the sights and sounds together? When we truly love ourselves, we won't find it hard to love our neighbor.

We can reawaken our passion for life by stepping outside and looking at the world like we did when we were kids. When was the last time you invited a friend to go for a swing in the park or a hike by a river? When did you stop making snow angels or drink in the beauty of the moon at dusk? A simple red geranium in my window during a cold winter, was a sign to a young woman that someone possibly cared. Something so small can mean the world to someone else.

This chapter starts with a quote about life not being about the capital *I*. When thinking about writing this book, *i* asked God to confirm whether or not *i* should go ahead with it. The next day, while driving down a snowy street, a passerby near my car keeled over unconscious. I slammed on the brakes and pulled over to where this teenager lay in the snow. A teacher who was walking by helped me get her out of the snowbank. This frightened young woman told us she was on extremely high medication for depression and bipolar disorder. She was in grade 12 and voiced the fear of failing her final year.

I knew God placed me at that specific location to be a *sisterhood* to her. My new friend left her cell number on my phone and we exchanged encouraging texts as long as possible. This intelligent and sensitive teenager came from a culture that believed most white people were prejudiced against them. That broke my heart, because *i* understood the history of why she might think that way. My heart grieved for her, because she shared that she couldn't live with her parents and that she was alone except for an auntie. I knew this young woman needed someone to show her how valuable she was. Every person deserves a chance to live the beautiful life God planned for them. Do you believe that?

The idea of sisterhood is demonstrated in the following story. During World War II, long before most of us were born, people of Jewish heritage became the focus of mass murder by the Nazi regime. There was really nowhere for these precious families to escape. Human beings were herded like cattle by the Nazis and crammed into unheated railway cars in brutally cold weather.

One of the people in these railcars was a Jewish teenager. The account of how he survived a night of freezing temperatures without nourishment or blankets for survival is astounding. Sitting next to the boy on this train, was an elderly man whom the teenager recognized from his neighborhood. This man was shivering uncontrollably. The teenager put his arms around the old fellow and began warming his limbs, face, and neck. The youth pleaded with the gentleman to hang on throughout the seemingly endless night.

The teen was starting to succumb to the extreme cold himself, but he never stopped creating heat by massaging the elderly man's body. Finally, night passed and morning light stole its way through cracks in the car. The young man looked around to see how the other prisoners were doing. To his complete horror, all he could see were frozen bodies lying everywhere. That's when he realized they were the *only two* who had survived! The old man survived because someone cared enough to keep him warm. The teenager survived because he chose to warm someone else. This is the secret to life! When we choose to look beyond our own problems and bring hope to someone else, encouragement and healing will flow like a waterfall back to us.

You may have noticed *i* chose not to capitalize the word *I* in this chapter. This was done on purpose. The English language is the only one that capitalizes the pronoun *I*. I find that startling! It is my opinion that this change began when our culture became *me* focused instead of *others* focused.

We are not created to be self-absorbed. Science has proven that when we reach out and are kind to others, beneficial hormones are released that improve our well-being. God is so amazing because He created us to function this way. Our health and welfare can only be sustained when we become a neighborhood of friends.

This world is not always a safe place, but you and i can join forces to be atmosphere transformers. With a common purpose, we can break down walls of prejudice, hatred, and jealousy that try to swallow our worth and keep us suspicious of one another. There is a proverb that says, If you search for good, you will find favor; but if you search for evil, it will find you![61] When a friend was teaching in our city, he said this, "Look for the gold in somebody, anybody can see the dirt. It takes no gifting to see the negative in someone's life."

---

61. Proverbs 11:27 (English Standard Version)

My hope is that we take the single threads representing our lives and allow them to be woven into a *sisterhood*. Instead of *I* and *me*, let's become a community of *us* and *we*. Together, we can participate in God's esteem for us until it moves into every sphere where women gather. It's time to take our coat of many colors off the hanger...to *wear it* for the world to see! Let's boldly place geraniums in our windows and let someone know their life has significance. Together, we are the *Red Geranium Sisterhood*.

CONCLUSION

artwork by Jan Louis

Growing a Culture of Kindness

"*If we have no peace, it is
because we have forgotten that
we belong to each other.*"

Mother Teresa

Growing a culture that values others, begins with a decision. A decision to lay aside envy and competition and become the kind of friend who reaches out on purpose with kindness.

But, how does this become a reality? Sometimes we start out with good intentions, but they can quickly fizzle out unless we have clear direction of where we're going together.

Whoever we are, no matter our age or culture, we are going to influence a life in a positive or negative way. We can see the landscape change from depression and isolation to one of wholeness and hope, if we choose to cross every barrier and take steps forward.

Through embracing the love of Jesus, we can be influencers for miracles! With the goal of sisterhood in mind, you and

I can encourage a hurting soul by shining our own light until others clearly see their own worth and dignity.

One way to remind ourselves of these truths, is by having a buddy system. Just like we were told to never go swimming alone, why not team up with a friend and be a sisterhood to someone new? And how about keeping a daily journal as you watch your community come alive as you practice these things? As well, you can start a book club of *The Red Geranium Sisterhood* and invite others to participate. Create your own ideas and watch them flourish. You can be the answer to someone's prayer.

When we get together with other women, let's look for something to compliment, instead of something to criticize. There is gold in everyone! When you and I offer encouragement, it's amazing how quickly kindness will come back to us. There are far too many movies and books about females gossiping about and bullying each other. Let's change that. Let's draw a bigger circle to include others.

The illustrations in this book give you a visual of what our lives are designed to be. If you like, buy some pencil crayons and color them for your own therapy. There are intrinsic healing qualities in art that have benefited all cultures throughout history. When you read the bible verses with each drawing, I encourage you to say them out loud and know they are speaking directly to you. *Make it personal!*

Another way to make progress, is to have a truth manifesto posted in your room or on your mobile device. But most importantly, choose to imprint these realities upon your heart. The truth proclamations on the next page will help you experience and live out your worth, even on your most difficult days. Speak them to yourself and *believe* them as you do. And why not write down your own manifesto on the extra page?

I know that together, you and I can fulfill the unique plans our Creator desired for us from the beginning. *The Red Geranium Sisterhood* is more than an idea, it's a transformation of hearts. As a sisterhood of friends, we can redesign our world with kindness and compassion. Are you ready?

artwork by Jan Louis

The Red Geranium Manifesto

My Creator lovingly shaped me with exquisite detail in
my mother's womb.
Jesus chose me before the world was formed, so
I was always wanted and planned for.
I am worth the price of God's Son
— that makes everyone, including me, priceless.
When I begin each day, I choose to embrace the Creator's
love for myself and others.
Each of us is unique and one of a kind
— so we can celebrate each other.
I am a work of art, designed with dignity in the
image of God.
I will shake off the shame and rise to my true destiny.
God spoke the world into existence,
so I speak life and blessing into my day.
No one has the right to strip away my coat of many colors,
so I will wear it with joy.
I refuse to believe the lies and give myself to something
beneath me.
I am an esteemed daughter in God's royal family.
I choose to believe the Truth that sets me free.
I choose to look for the gold in others as well as myself.
As a sisterhood, we can transform our world with kindness,
compassion, and red geraniums in our windows.
It starts with me today!

Create Your Own Red Geranium Manifesto

Acknowledgements

All of my relationships, both in heaven and on earth,
have inspired the writing of this book.
I am thankful for:
My relationship with my Creator and Savior, Jesus, Who
welcomed me to the Father's family table.
And for the Holy Spirit, who is the true Writer
and Revelator.
My relationship with my loving husband, Jim, our precious
children, grandchildren, and my amazing mother and family.
My relationships with excellent mentors, dear friends, and
fellow writers who offered insight and prayed for me through
this journey. Thank you in particular to Nyla Wiebe for poring
over the manuscript with proofreading and suggestions.
My relationships with the women who shared their stories with
me. You are the sisterhood who give hope to others by living
out your identity as cherished daughters of God. I salute you!
My own sister, Jan Louis, who did most of the illustrations
in this book. Her art depicts the beauty of her soul and her
own journey to restoration.
Charlene, Robyn, Amy, Joel and Katharina, thank you for
your creative advice and extra set of eyes.

About the Author

For over twenty years, Shelley M. Christian has been a speaker at women's conferences in Canada and other nations, where she empowers women from all cultures to believe in their excellence and esteem through God's eyes. In addition to *The Red Geranium Sisterhood*, Shelley has published a healing devotional co-written with her husband, titled *Healing Nuggets*. She also self-published a summer curriculum for children called *Metamorphosis*, which teaches children how to overcome low self-worth, develop esteem for themselves and others and discover the love of Jesus.

Shelley lives in Saskatoon, Saskatchewan, Canada with her husband, Jim. Presently, she travels throughout Canada teaching the truths from *The Red Geranium Sisterhood* and speaking on Spirit, Soul and Body Wholeness. Shelley enjoys hiking, growing gorgeous blooms, and hanging out at the lake with her family and friends.

For further information or booking engagements,
you can reach Shelley at:

www.shelleymchristian.com

Copyright

 FriesenPress

Suite 300 - 990 Fort St
Victoria, BC, V8V 3K2
Canada

www.friesenpress.com

ISBN
978-1-5255-8881-5 (Hardcover)
978-1-5255-8880-8 (Paperback)
978-1-5255-8882-2 (eBook)

1. Religion, Christian Living, Women's Issues
2. Religion, Christian Living, Personal Growth
3. Self-Help, Motivational & Inspirational

Distributed to the trade by The Ingram Book Company

MW01120603

Humber College Library
3199 Lakeshore Blvd. West
Toronto, ON   M8V 1K8

160201

Power without Law

The Supreme Court of Canada, the *Marshall* Decisions, and the Failure of Judicial Activism

ALEX M. CAMERON

McGill-Queen's University Press
Montreal & Kingston • London • Ithaca

© McGill-Queen's University Press 2009

ISBN 978-0-7735-3583-1 (cloth)
ISBN 978-0-7735-3610-4 (paper)

Legal deposit fourth quarter 2009
Bibliothèque nationale du Québec

Printed in Canada on acid-free paper that is 100% ancient forest free
(100% post-consumer recycled), processed chlorine free

This book has been published with the help of a grant from the
Canadian Federation for the Humanities and Social Sciences, through
the Aid to Scholarly Publications Programme, using funds provided by
the Social Sciences and Humanities Research Council of Canada.

McGill-Queen's University Press acknowledges the support of the
Canada Council for the Arts for our publishing program. We also
acknowledge the financial support of the Government of Canada
through the Book Publishing Industry Development Program (BPIDP)
for our publishing activities.

Library and Archives Canada Cataloguing in Publication

Cameron, Alex M
    Power without law : the Supreme Court of Canada, the Marshall
decisions, and the failure of judicial system / Alex M. Cameron.

Includes bibliographical references and index.
ISBN 978-0-7735-3583-1 (bnd)
ISBN 978-0-7735-3610-4 (pbk)

    1. Political questions and judicial power – Canada. 2. Canada.
Supreme Court. 3. Micmac Indians – Legal status, laws, etc.
4. Malecite Indians – Legal status, laws, etc. 5. Marshall, Donald,
1953– – Trials, litigation, etc. I. Title.

KE7709.C34 2009   342.7108'7209716   C2009-903050-0
KF8205.C34 2009

Typeset by Jay Tee Graphics Ltd. in 10/13 Sabon

To Mum and Dad
For their courage and wisdom

Contents

Acknowledgments   xi

Introduction   3

1 The Canadian Constitution   14

2 Judicial Activism and Its Critics   23

3 The Legal Background to *Marshall (No. 1)*   44

4 *Marshall (No. 1)* in the Trial Court   48

5 The Court of Appeal   71

6 The Decision of the Supreme Court of Canada: *Marshall (No. 1)*   75

7 Fire on the Water, and *Marshall (No. 2)*   82

8 Rewriting Nova Scotia History   89

9 Judicial Levitation: The Hovering Treaty Right   105

10 Trade, Treaties, and the Constitution   112

11 Fundamental Laws: The Rights of British Subjects and a "Promenade Down Barrington Street"   118

12 After the *Marshall* Decisions: Legal Uncertainty and Government Response   127

13 *Stephen Marshall/Bernard*   132

14 The Failure of Judicial Activism   143

Appendix   *R. v. Marshall (No. 1)*   152

Notes   215

Index   241

Acknowledgments

I am grateful to my employers at the Nova Scotia Department of Justice and the Nova Scotia Public Prosecution Service for enlisting me to work on the very interesting issues that gave rise to this book. I am indebted to Stephen Poole, who would only accept a bottle of whisky (not paid in advance) for his many suggestions to improve the manuscript. Cathy and Carolyn typed and retyped the manuscript with infinite patience. I am especially thankful to Roger Martin of McGill-Queen's University Press, who discovered my manuscript and patiently guided me to improve it. Kyla Madden and Joan McGilvray shepherded it to publication and Lesley Andrassy carefully copy-edited. Most of all, I thank my wife for encouraging me, and my "team" for interrupting my "law-work" when it was time to play.

POWER WITHOUT LAW

Introduction

On an August morning six years ago the appellant and a companion, both Mi'kmaq Indians, slipped their small outboard motorboat into the coastal waters of Pomquet Harbour, Antigonish County, Nova Scotia to fish for eels. They landed 463 pounds, which they sold for $787.10, and for which the appellant was arrested and prosecuted.

On an earlier August morning, some 235 years previously, the Reverend John Seycombe of Chester, Nova Scotia, a missionary and sometime dining companion of the Governor, noted with satisfaction in his diary, "Two Indian squaws brought seal skins and eels to sell". That transaction was apparently completed without arrest or other incident.

So begins the judgment of Justice Ian Binnie, writing for the majority of the Supreme Court of Canada in the case of *R. v. Marshall (No. 1)*, [1999] 3 S.C.R. 456.[1] Justice Binnie went on to decide that the Maliseet, Passamaquoddy, and Mi'kmaq of the Maritime Provinces have a constitutionally protected treaty right to hunt, fish, and gather for the purpose of making a moderate livelihood.

One need only read these opening paragraphs to divine the ultimate decision. They colourfully and sympathetically describe an innocent pastoral scene: fishing in tranquil coastal waters. They link that activity with what Justice Binnie characterized as an equally innocent transaction over two centuries earlier: Mi'kmaq women selling a few eels to a "man of the cloth." The tenor of these paragraphs suggests that Justice Binnie thinks it unfair to convict native people for fishing and selling a few eels,

something that in another era was "completed without arrest or other incident." The two paragraphs are written very much in the tradition of Lord Denning, an English judge and arguably the most famous judge of the last century. He would begin a decision, for example, like this: "summertime cricket is the delight of everyone";[2] and it would be clear that the fellow hit by a ball while standing near the cricket grounds would lose his lawsuit.

But while they are graceful and evocative, Justice Binnie's opening paragraphs contain a significant mistake. Reverend Seycombe's purchase of eels violated Nova Scotia law. He should have been arrested and charged.

In March 1760 the Nova Scotia House of Assembly enacted a statute entitled *An Act to prevent any private Trade or Commerce with the Indians.*[3] The purpose of the statute was to "prevent private persons from carrying on any separate Trade Commerce or Dealings whatsoever" with Indians. Indian trade was to be confined to government-run trading posts, "truckhouses," and persons licensed by the government. Accordingly, no one in Nova Scotia could buy or sell "any kind of provisions, goods or Merchandize whatsoever," from Indians. The statute provided for a stiff fine of fifty pounds. Reverend Seycombe broke the law in buying skins and eels from natives.[4] There was good reason for this law. In both New England and Nova Scotia, in the 1600s and 1700s unregulated trade between natives and English traders had typically involved the purchase of furs with liquor. The result was very often tension and open hostilities. In another diary entry, not mentioned by Justice Binnie, Reverend Seycombe records, "Indian squaws brot mink skins + a large Bear skin, sold for a quart of wine."[5] Having only just arrived from Boston a few weeks before, Reverend Seycombe was probably not aware that his trade with native women was unlawful. But then, as now, ignorance of the law was no excuse for failure to comply with it. It is perplexing that Justice Binnie missed this point; the 1760 statute was squarely in front of the Court in *Marshall (No. 1).*[6] In fact, one of the expert witnesses in the case testified that Reverend Seycombe broke the law.[7] Already the decision is suspect. One would reasonably suppose

that the treaty right to catch and sell eels implied by Justice Binnie would have as its foundation evidence – perhaps extensive evidence – of a lawful historic trade in eels. In fact, there was no other evidence of any eel trade between natives and non-natives.[8]

This mistake is noteworthy for what it portends. The Court's decision in *Marshall (No. 1)* exhibits a worrisome inattention to historical and legal detail and to fundamental constitutional principle. In fact, the evidence in *Marshall (No. 1)* and the constitutional law relevant to it are contrary to the decision rendered by the majority. Yet the enduring result of the decision has been to dramatically reorient the legal landscape in the Maritime Provinces. This decision reflects serious problems with our judicial system.

But none of this was apparent when, in October 1999, the Supreme Court of Canada issued its decision. The decision was celebrated in jubilant native communities throughout the Maritime Provinces. Canada's highest court had confirmed a constitutionally protected native treaty right to "hunt, fish and gather" for the purpose of gaining a "moderate livelihood." In other words, the court said that the treaties between native bands and British colonial authorities in the period 1760–61 gave the Mi'kmaq, Maliseet, and Passamaquoddy natives in the Maritime Provinces constitutionally protected economic rights to harvest the region's resources.

The decision sent shock waves through many resource-dependent, non-native communities. There had never been a suggestion of any such "treaty right" in the 250 years since British settlement of the Maritime Provinces had begun. Communities that had, for generations, depended for their economic survival on the fishery and the forest felt threatened by the *Marshall (No. 1)* decision, the uncertainty that surrounded it, and the bold claims advanced by native leaders and native communities through reference to it. Moreover, the Court's reasoning in *Marshall (No. 1)* was bewildering. While the Court confirmed that native people had a treaty right, no treaty document recorded any such right. Instead, the Court relied on a document of discussions prior to the treaty. But that document did

not describe any such right either. Rather, the Court surmised what native "concerns" must have been and what British promises must have been made in those discussions. So the foundation for an apparently sweeping treaty right was judicial conjecture.

The result was uncertainty, insecurity, incredulity, and resentment in the non-native community, heightened expectations among natives, and violence. At Burnt Church, New Brunswick, and Saint Mary's Bay, Nova Scotia, Natives seeking to assert "treaty rights" clashed with Fisheries officers. Boats rammed boats, boats were sunk, rocks were thrown, lobster pots were smashed. Tensions rose between native and non-native communities. Shots were fired. Armed native "warriors" gathered. There were ugly demonstrations, and "one of the worst race riots in Canadian history."[9] Natives were pitted against non-natives in communities that had co-existed peacefully for centuries. All as a direct result of the court's decision.

Unfortunately, the *Marshall (No. 1)* decision has wrought more harm than the fractiousness and violence it brought to peaceable communities. It has frustrated the non-native community. It has cost Canadian taxpayers hundreds of millions of dollars as the federal government entered into agreements with local native communities that arose from their demands post-*Marshall (No. 1)*. It has introduced uncertainty into the already troubled economic climate of the Maritime Provinces.

I became involved in these issues in early 2001. At that time, I was a lawyer with the Nova Scotia Department of Justice where I practised civil litigation. In Nova Scotia, there is a clear separation between the Public Prosecution Service (PPS), which prosecutes violations of criminal and provincial laws, and the "civil" side of the Department of Justice, which provides legal advice to government and represents government when it sues or is sued. In 1999, when the Supreme Court of Canada released its decision in *Marshall (No. 1)*, the PPS had its hands full with a case known as *R. v. Stephen Marshall*. The charges in that case resulted when Mi'kmaq activists took to the woods, cutting logs on Crown lands, claiming that commercial logging was protected by the same treaties dealt with in *Marshall (No. 1)*, and also claiming

that the Mi'kmaq people retained aboriginal title to (in other words, ownership of) the whole or much of Nova Scotia.

Nova Scotia had been caught flat-footed by both the *Marshall (No. 1)* case and the *Stephen Marshall* case. For years prior to these cases, native rights claims had been brewing, but Nova Scotia had done nothing to prepare to meet them. *Marshall (No. 1)* was a federal prosecution and Nova Scotia stayed out of it. When the case was appealed to the Nova Scotia Court of Appeal, Nova Scotia did not intervene. When it went on appeal to the Supreme Court of Canada, New Brunswick intervened, but Nova Scotia did not. In 1998 it was suggested in the Nova Scotia House of Assembly that Nova Scotia intervene. The Minister of Fisheries advised the House that "we have concluded that it is totally a federal issue."[10] As it turned out, the decision in *Marshall (No. 1)* would become very much a provincial issue. But the comment was telling, reflecting a lack of expertise and failure to prepare the necessary historical materials to examine and respond to native claims of aboriginal rights. This same lack of preparation plagued the provincial Crown prosecutors who were responsible for the *Stephen Marshall* prosecution. Only a remarkable effort, at trial, by those prosecutors and the experts they hired established the necessary historical evidence that ultimately allowed the prosecution to succeed.

In March 2001 the Nova Scotia Provincial Court convicted the native loggers, dismissing their claim to aboriginal title and to treaty rights to log. The natives appealed the decision, and the Appeal Section of the Public Prosecution Service approached me to ask whether I would take charge of the appeal. I had certain reservations about the project. I had not been involved in the trial, and preparing for the appeal meant intimately understanding thousands of pages of evidence, as well as learning whole bodies of aboriginal law. Also, failures in high-profile prosecutions – the Westray and Regan prosecutions are examples – had often led to harsh criticism of the prosecutors involved. Nova Scotia's lack of preparation for the *Stephen Marshall* logging test case did not bode well for the outcome in such a significant case. Moreover, although the Provincial Court

judge had dismissed the native claims, the decision of the Supreme Court of Canada in *Marshall (No. 1)* seemed to be a strong endorsement of native treaty rights, so that sustaining the convictions in the appeal courts looked as though it would be a very steep uphill battle. But the challenge was too attractive to resist. Aboriginal rights law is very much in its adolescence. The case would involve legal argument at the cutting edge of the law. No matter how it turned out, the case held great significance for Nova Scotia. It involved legal and historical issues very similar to those in *Marshall (No. 1)*. It was not unlikely (as in fact happened) that the case would be appealed all the way to the Supreme Court of Canada, and the opportunity to argue an important case in that court was irresistible.

Another factor, which becomes relevant to this story later on, made the case attractive. By law, the PPS in Nova Scotia is independent of government. Politicians and bureaucrats cannot dictate to prosecutors whether or how to prosecute a case. Prosecutors prosecute as they see fit, subject, of course, to legal and ethical constraints, but entirely free of political influence. So the legal arguments that would be advanced in the case would be my responsibility jointly with the lawyer from the Appeal Section of PPS who was assigned as my colleague in the appeal. Nova Scotia's position on native treaty claims and native title claims would be based strictly on law and evidence. No one would dictate to us the positions we would argue. We alone would be responsible for the success or failure of those positions.[11]

Over the succeeding months and years of reviewing the law and sifting through the mountains of evidence relevant to the logging prosecution and *Marshall (No. 1)*, I gradually formed some very disturbing conclusions. The decision of the Supreme Court of Canada in *Marshall (No. 1)* was wrong. Not only was it wrong, it was wrong in a way that causes fundamental concern for the administration of justice in this country. Mistakes were made in the adjudication of the case, both in the trial court and at the Supreme Court of Canada. Of course, everyone makes mistakes and mistakes can be corrected. But the Supreme Court of Canada has preferred to sidestep its mistakes. More-

over, in deciding as they did in *Marshall (No. 1)*, the Supreme Court of Canada disregarded procedural impropriety, compelling evidence, and well-established legal doctrines that were inconsistent with the court's decision. The decision, in my view, is not merely a collection of mistakes; it reflects a judicial attitude that inclines to a result, and is too quick to overlook law and evidence inconsistent with that result. In my view, the decision reflects an approach that threatens the rule of law in this country and reveals serious flaws in our judicial system: the vast powers that have been vested in judges and lawyers by our Constitution, the consequent diminution of democracy, the ability of government to avoid democratic responsibility by purporting to defer to the judiciary, the failure of the judicial system to respond to its mistakes, and, perhaps of greatest concern, a judicial system in which fundamental constitutional law and principle is too malleable to personal judicial predilection. Centuries ago, in the cauldron of England's constitutional crisis and civil war, when our modern parliamentary constitution was forged, an English King warned of the exercise of "power without law." In my view, the decision of the Supreme Court of Canada in *Marshall (No. 1)* reveals an exercise of judicial power, hardly restrained by law or evidence. It should cause us deep concern.

From time to time in this country, a debate erupts regarding the role of the judiciary. A judicial decision or appointment will prompt the suggestion that the decision reflects "judicial activism" or that the judge is an "activist" judge. For some, the comment is an endorsement, a suggestion that the judge is entitled and willing to develop the law or be creative. For others, the comment is a criticism of overly creative judges straying beyond their mandate. Very often, the criticism of "judicial activism" is met with the answer that judges merely apply the law and the Constitution. What happened in *Marshall (No. 1)* should serve as a warning of the dangers of judicial activism, or at least a particular manifestation of it, and the threat to the rule of law and our system of government that it represents.

In the nearly thirty years since Prime Minister Pierre Trudeau engineered great changes to the Canadian Constitution, the

Supreme Court of Canada has considered and decided many controversial cases. Canadians have grown accustomed to court rulings on highly contentious issues. Of course the media weighs in when the Supreme Court of Canada renders a particularly controversial decision. But media analysis tends to be fleeting and superficial. Yesterday's decisions soon become yesterday's news. The media usually do not have the time, the resources, or the expertise to provide informed critiques of judicial decisions. In many law journals lawyers and academics provide detailed analysis of judicial decisions. But these publications are obscure and are not widely available to the public. Moreover, the doctrinal discussions they generally contain are of limited value in analyzing a decision such as the *Marshall (No. 1)* decision, whose basis is largely historical. When the Supreme Court of Canada released its decision in the *Marshall (No. 1)* case, the media acted as it usually does, with an initial barrage of reporting and editorializing, which petered out after several months.[12] Predictably, there has been a flurry of academic writing discussing the *Marshall (No. 1)* decision. Much of it is uninformative, discussing as it does abstract legal theories and doctrines of aboriginal law. None of it examines the 4,300 pages of testimony and hundreds of pages of historical documents that are critical to an understanding of the case.

This book was written with one basic idea in mind. When a judicial decision results in violence, when it pits entire communities against one another, when it fundamentally affects the economic interests of those communities, and when it reorients the legal landscape, the public is entitled to know how and why the decision was made, whether or not the decision was the right one, and what the decision tells us about our judicial and constitutional system. The analysis in this book is a legal analysis. It does not suggest that the Supreme Court of Canada was wrong for policy reasons. It may be, for example, that natives should be given special access to resources on the East Coast for reasons of social and economic policy. Indeed, the plight of many native communities would seem to warrant carefully tailored measures. But policy is the realm of elected governments. Judges

are not meant to decide "policies." So the analysis here is a legal analysis of the evidence, the legal arguments, and the law that relate to the decision in *Marshall (No. 1)*. Government policy will be discussed only to show how that policy has been driven by the decision in *Marshall (No. 1)*. When the *Stephen Marshall* case was argued at the Supreme Court of Canada, Nova Scotia raised many of the points discussed in this book and argued explicitly that *Marshall (No. 1)* was wrongly decided. The government of Nova Scotia was lobbied, unsuccessfully, in an attempt to prevent those arguments. In its decision in *Stephen Marshall*, the Supreme Court of Canada sidestepped those arguments in a profoundly troubling way. It chose, instead, to read down or limit its decision in *Marshall (No. 1)*. But in doing so, it merely exacerbated its own earlier mistakes and, in my opinion, avoided its constitutional responsibility.

A great many issues arise from the points raised in this book: the structure of our judicial system, the scrutiny of judges who preside over it, and the method by which cases proceed through the courts, to name a few. I will not attempt to address those difficult issues. My purpose is simply to provide an analysis of a judicial decision that has had a profound impact on the Maritime Provinces and the people who live here. Judicial decisions, such as that in *Marshall (No. 1)*, can be very complex. Critical legal analysis can be equally complex, as well as obscure. My attempt here is to provide the reader with enough detail and explanation to be informative and accurate, while at the same time limiting the analysis to the major interesting issues presented by the cases. Any failure in this or in any other aspect of the book is, of course, my own, as are the opinions expressed throughout.

A few final introductory points need emphasis. First, this book is sharply critical of the decision of the Supreme Court of Canada in *Marshall (No. 1)*, but is in no way intended to be disrespectful of Justice Binnie or the Justices of the Supreme Court of Canada who endorsed his decision. Judges are not elected. If they make a decision that is wrong, we cannot vote them out of office. All we can do is point out firmly and clearly why they were wrong. Debate in courts of law, and in democratic society

at large, should be vigorous and forceful. It is, after all, directed at the noble goal of discerning justice and the truth and what is right. Vigour must not be confused with disrespect. Indeed, it is my hope that by scrutinizing *Marshall (No. 1)*, this book will highlight the failures of excessive judicial activism and ultimately assist in guarding against such excess. Second, the criticism expressed in this book must in no way be taken as a criticism of the native people to whom the *Marshall (No. 1)* decision applies. Some, perhaps many, among the Mi'kmaq, Maliseet, and Passamaquoddy peoples of the Maritime Provinces perceive injustice in their historic relations with non-native society and think the decision in *Marshall (No. 1)* went some way to make things right. They will be disappointed in the critique of that decision advanced here. But if our constitution is to promote reconciliation between native and non-native society, as our courts have said it should, then the legal and historic founda-tions of that relationship need to be closely examined and care-fully described. It is my hope that the discussion in this book will promote that reconciliation by disabusing misconceptions of obligation and entitlement, and by recalling a foundation for reconciliation that is solidly rooted in the historic record of Nova Scotia, that was noble and inspiring, in 1761 as it is today, and that our courts would do well to honour.

Neither should anything that is contained in this book be taken as a criticism of Donald Marshall, Jr. The story of Mr Marshall is well known. His wrongful conviction, his incarcera-tion for a murder he did not commit, his subsequent release, and the Public Inquiry in Nova Scotia that dealt with those things are grave and complex issues. The imprisonment of an innocent man is profoundly troubling. On an institutional level, it raises pointed questions about the criminal justice system. On an indi-vidual level, it speaks to anguish, despair, and the strength of the human spirit in enduring harsh unfairness. But it is not relevant to the focus of this book that it was Donald Marshall, Jr, and not another native person in the Maritimes, who decided in August 1993 to go fishing for eels. That simple event triggered the judicial proceedings that led to the Supreme Court of Can-

ada decision in *Marshall (No. 1)*. But it is in a sense ironic that it was Donald Marshall, Jr, whose fishing triggered the *Marshall (No. 1)* decision. Mr Marshall's incarceration had come to symbolize much that was wrong with our criminal justice system. The decision that takes his name, in my view, reflects much else that is wrong with our judicial system.

Yet while neither aboriginal communities generally, nor Donald Marshall, Jr, in particular, are the focus of this book, it is legitimate to ask whether the special status that has been accorded to Maritime native communities by virtue of the *Marshall (No. 1)* decision is warranted. Equally, it is legitimate to ask whether the expectations of native communities and the rhetoric of native rights and demands, which have been pitched higher since the release of the *Marshall (No. 1)* decision, are justified. Finally, it is legitimate to explore the frailties of the judicial process and the failures of the activist approach to judicial decision-making that led to the decision of the Supreme Court of Canada in *Marshall (No. 1)*.

I

The Canadian Constitution

To understand the Supreme Court of Canada decision in the *Marshall (No. 1)* case, it helps to have a basic understanding of Canadian constitutional law. To some who have happened to glance at one or other great, long, and complex decision of the Supreme Court of Canada in a constitutional case, this might sound intimidating. To others who might have suffered through uninspiring high school courses in history or political science, it might sound boring. It is neither. The story behind the Canadian Constitution is fascinating.

When most Canadians think of the Constitution, they might think vaguely of the BNA Act or the Charter. These are important parts of the Canadian Constitution, and are relevant here, but they are only part of the Constitution. Other equally important parts were forged in the civil war, dynastic struggle, and religious quarrels of England, over three hundred years ago.

THE GLORIOUS REVOLUTION OF 1688 AND THE PRINCIPLE OF PARLIAMENTARY SOVEREIGNTY

Canada's Parliament and provincial Legislatures are fundamental institutions of our government. They take as their template the British Parliament in London. So to understand the role of our Parliament and Legislatures, we need to look overseas for a

little English history. It's a gripping story of clashing ideas, liberally laced with ambition and bloodshed. It may seem strange that a significant part of Canada's Constitution is found in English history. But the parliamentary principles that arise from that history are as much a part of our Constitution as the better known Charter and they are no less important.

While the full story of the Stuart Kings, the English Civil War, the Commonwealth, the Restoration, and the Glorious Revolution that spawned those principles is beyond the scope of this book, a thread of the story needs to be examined here. It begins in the Middle Ages. Gradually a Parliament evolved. Eventually its consent was required to enact laws. But when Charles I became king of England and Scotland on the death of his father, King James, in 1625, the relationship between the king and his authority through the Royal Prerogative on the one hand, and Parliament and its authority to enact laws on the other, was not well settled. For a decade, Charles I ruled without a sitting Parliament; in effect, he was a dictator, an "absolute monarch." During these years of Personal Rule, he relied on claimed prerogative powers to govern without summoning Parliament. When circumstances forced King Charles to summon Parliament in 1640, it was flooded with petitions denouncing the king's imposition of taxes (Ship Money) through the prerogative, the king's invasion of liberties through the prerogative courts (the notorious Court of Star Chamber), and other arbitrary measures.[1] While complex financial, religious, and social ferment boiled in England in this period, those who challenged Charles I were challenging the Crown's prerogative: "if there was one single institution, one single concern, which emerges as paramount in their actions, perhaps even more emphatically than in their words, it is the institution of monarchy, and the urgent need to define its powers in such a way that the subjects' 'liberties' – above all their right to a regularly heard voice in their own government – would henceforth be assured. And in practice, this entailed ... a prolonged, ruthless and at times breathtakingly successful campaign against the royal prerogative: those particular

powers which the monarch exercised personally, and which collectively constituted much of his effective authority as king."[2]

When the rift between Charles and Parliament widened into Civil War in 1642, the ultimate issue in the words of one Parliamentarian was: "Whether the King should govern as a god by his will, and the nation be governed by force, like beasts, or whether the people should be governed by laws made by themselves and live under a Government derived from their own consent."[3] Parliament's army, led by Oliver Cromwell, swept all aside. Charles I surrendered. But now, the army was master and it purged those in Parliament who did not support it. They were arrested or barred from their seats. The "Rump" that remained demanded the king's trial. He was charged with, among other things, "tyranny" and making war against Parliament, and tried in the House of Commons.[4]

Charles, for his part, contended that his judges had no legal authority to try him. The transcript of the charges levelled against him and his answer to those charges have been preserved. They record his retort to his accusers that they were exercising "Power without Law": "For if power without law may make laws, may alter the fundamental laws of the kingdom, I do not know what subject he is in England that can be sure of his life or anything that he calls his own."[5]

Charles' complaint was directed at the authority – more precisely, the lack of authority – of the House of Commons to try him. "I see no House of Lords here that may constitute a Parliament ... a king cannot be tried by any superior jurisdiction on earth."[6] Charles was on firm ground in challenging the jurisdiction of his adversaries. Parliament was not properly constituted by the House of Commons alone, and in the tradition of the British Parliament, could not enact law without the House of Lords and the king. The House of Lords had refused its consent to the prosecution of the King. This is different from the criticisms raised in this book concerning the Supreme Court of Canada and *Marshall (No. 1)*. The Court undoubtedly had authority to hear the case. But the principle Charles raised in his defence is broader than the narrow jurisdictional point. His

remarks remind us that there are "fundamental laws" in our legal tradition, and those laws must be respected. Law made without proper regard for those fundamental laws is not legitimate law. It is, rather, an exercise of sheer power, and power alone provides no assurance of "life or property." It lacks legitimacy and is undeserving of respect. Power alone, uncontrolled by law, is the very tyranny that Charles was accused of.

The words of King Charles still resonate. They force us to recall that power and law are two very different things. They recognize that institutions of state can exercise power unlawfully. They acknowledge that there are fundamental laws that the powerful must honour. What makes these words particularly appropriate is that they were uttered in a period when the constitutional relationship between Parliament and the king was being forged. Soon after Charles' trial Parliament's role would be confirmed as fundamental law. That law applied to Nova Scotia in 1760 and operates to this day. Yet, in *Marshall (No. 1)*, the Supreme Court of Canada disregarded this fundamental law.

Charles' defence availed him nothing. Power triumphed. He was beheaded on 30 January 1649. The House of Commons had done away with the king. It also did away with the House of Lords. Then, in 1653, Cromwell did away with the House of Commons: "you have sat long enough unless you had done more good ... I will put an end to your prating."[7] His soldiers emptied the Chamber. England was then ruled by one man and his army until Lord Protector Cromwell died in 1658.

Cromwell's death left the future government in doubt. Civil war threatened again. But now a new Parliament was elected. It sent for Charles I's son, who had been waiting in exile since his father's death. The Crown and Parliament were restored. But the issues that began the conflict were still not settled. When Charles II died childless in 1685, his brother James became king. James II was a converted Catholic in a country that had broken away from the Roman Catholic church in the reign of Henry VIII. Like his father, he determined to rule without Parliament and override its religious laws. Once again, the Royal

Prerogative clashed with the law made by Parliament. As noted English historian Hugh Trevor-Roper put it, the English under James II feared "popery and slavery."[8] Again, civil war loomed. But leading men threw their support to a Protestant grandson of Charles I. Dutchman William of Orange and his wife Mary landed in England in November 1688. The army abandoned James. He fled, and spent the rest of his life in exile.

The great issues that had occupied England for a century were now resolved. When William and Mary ascended the throne in 1689, they accepted a Declaration of Rights, later enacted in a "Bill of Rights," that limited the Crown's prerogative powers. The preamble to the Declaration of Rights accused King James II of endeavouring to "extirpate the Protestant religion and the laws and liberties of this kingdom," and it went on to declare a number of "ancient rights," many of which were directed at controlling the prerogative and confirming the role of Parliament:

1 That the pretended power of suspending of laws, or the execution of laws by regal authority, without consent of Parliament, is illegal.

2 That the pretended power of dispensing with laws, or the execution of laws, by regal authority, as it hath been assumed and exercised of late, is illegal.

4 That levying money for or to the use of the Crown by pretence of prerogative, without grant of Parliament, for longer time, or in other manner than the same is, or shall be granted, is illegal.

9 That the freedom of speech and debates or proceedings in Parliament ought not to be impeached or questioned in any court or place out of Parliament.

13 And that for redress of all grievances and for the amending, strengthening and preserving of the laws, Parliaments ought to be frequently held.[9]

This Glorious Revolution settled the great constitutional questions of seventeenth-century England. "The Revolution did make Parliament Supreme."[10] The Crown could not rule without

Parliament. Parliament made laws. The king could not alter them or suspend them, or make his own. These constraints on the Crown prerogative migrated overseas to the colonies. While there were said to be differences in the Crown's authority to rule by its prerogative depending on whether a colony was obtained by conquest or treaty, or was settled, once the Crown authorized a colonial assembly, "the King preclude[d] himself from the exercise of his prerogative legislative authority."[11] A valuable summary of this constitutional law is found in the evidence of Dr Stephen Patterson, who discussed its implications for Native treaties and trade regulation in colonies with legislatures, in the *Stephen Marshall* case:

> Q: What authority, if any, did these individuals who negotiated the treaty [have] to deal with trade or did they have any authority?
>
> A: They didn't have authority to establish the rules and regulations that would govern trade. They had authority to do other things, but they realized that trade is something that is regulated by a legislature ... As the Crown accepted constitutional limits on its authority, especially in the period of the glorious revolution that took place in England.
>
> Q: What is the 'glorious revolution'?
>
> A: 1688. 1689. It is really a kind of bloodless revolution in which Parliament asserts its authority over the king ... The really significant thing ... comes from an assertion of the power of Parliament. Parliament has rights. Parliament has responsibilities. And the king can't intrude in what those rights are.[12]

All of this is as fundamental to the Canadian Parliament and provincial Legislatures today as it was to England in 1689. Parliament and the Legislatures enact legislation. Such legislation becomes law with the assent of the Crown, given through the governor general in the case of laws enacted by Parliament, and through lieutenant-governors in the case of laws enacted by

provincial Legislatures. The prerogative power of the Crown does not extend to making laws. This was fundamental to Nova Scotia in the 1760s, the period considered in the *Marshall (No. 1)* decision. It is fundamental law that the Supreme Court of Canada failed to apply. That failure appears to have been due, at least in some part, to two things: the unfortunate procedure adopted in the trial court, and a shift in position by Mr Marshall at trial. The consequence was that evidence of the limits on the Crown's ability to make laws, such as the passage quoted above from the *Stephen Marshall* case, was not elaborated, although, as we will see, a careful review of the historic record reveals the point.

Of course, much remained to be done after 1689 before our present system of government evolved. The vote had to be extended to a broader electorate. The "administration" had to be weaned away from the monarch and made answerable to Parliament. The prime minister and his office were yet to evolve. All of that lay in the future. But the fundamental role of Parliament was finally settled by 1689, and that settlement is the bedrock of our Constitution to this day.

THE CONSTITUTION ACT, 1867

The Constitution Act, 1867, or as it used to be called, the British North America Act, was a statute passed by the British Parliament to establish Canada in 1867. It is another fundamental part of our Constitution. Most Canadians are aware of the story of Confederation. While that, too, is a fascinating story, it is not terribly important to the issues discussed in this book. There are, however, a couple of points worth mentioning.

First, the *Constitution Act* contemplates both provincial Legislatures and a federal Parliament. As noted, these institutions are modelled on the British Parliament. Second, the Constitution Act provides for the "Division of Powers" between the federal Parliament and provincial Legislatures. Jurisdiction is allocated to one or the other. Section 91(24) deals explicitly with jurisdiction over native Canadians; exclusive legislative

jurisdiction over "Indians and lands reserved for the Indians" is given to the federal Parliament. Similarly, jurisdiction over fisheries is largely that of the federal Parliament. Accordingly, the law Donald Marshall, Jr, was charged with violating was a law of the federal Parliament. Forests, by contrast, are largely the responsibility of the provinces, and so the native loggers in the *Stephen Marshall* case were charged with violating provincial laws.

THE CONSTITUTION ACT, 1982, AND SECTION 35

In 1982 Canada experienced a "revolution" that was no less profound than the Glorious Revolution of 1688. But it was very different. Whereas the Glorious Revolution had confirmed the powers of Parliament, the Canadian "revolution" of 1982 dramatically increased the powers of judges at the expense of Parliament and the Legislatures.

This point is key to an understanding of the *Marshall* (*No. 1*) decision. Before 1982 Canada's Constitution was modelled on the British Constitution. The central pillar of the British Constitution is Parliament. Parliament is supreme. Parliament can pass whatever law it likes, and that law is the "law of the land" until Parliament decides it should be changed. Judges cannot change that law. They cannot overrule it. They can only interpret and apply the laws that Parliament enacts. This is not to say that under the British Constitution, judges are not important. For example, questions often arise as to what Parliament intended by passing particular laws, and such questions are decided by judges. But under the British Constitution, Parliament has the supreme power in deciding what the law will be. Nobody but Parliament can challenge Parliament or change what Parliament has done. If Parliament thinks judges have not properly interpreted laws, Parliament can pass another law setting things right.

An important difference between England and Canada is that Canada has provinces with their own Legislatures. England never had other Legislatures, only the Parliament at Westminster in London. As mentioned, the Constitution Act divides

legislative jurisdiction between Parliament and the provincial Legislatures. But before 1982, within their respective jurisdictions, Parliament and the Legislatures were supreme.

All of this changed in 1982 with the adoption of the Canadian Charter of Rights and Freedoms. The rights and freedoms set down in the Charter are constitutionally guaranteed. By reference to those rights and freedoms, judges can strike down laws made by Parliament or the Legislatures. In a very real sense, judges, not Parliament and the Legislatures, are now supreme. Therein lies danger. Elected representatives in Parliament and the Legislatures are accountable to the electorate. Judges are accountable to no one but themselves. In applying the Charter, they wield enormous power without accountability.

Among the rights guaranteed when the Charter was adopted in 1982 was section 35.[13] It contains this key phrase: "35(1) The existing aboriginal and treaty rights of the aboriginal peoples of Canada are hereby recognized and affirmed."

Notice that s.35(1) refers to "treaty rights." As interpreted by our Courts, the section gives treaty rights constitutional protection. Laws that interfere with native treaty rights in a way that government cannot justify can be struck down by the courts. This was the basis for Donald Marshall, Jr's victory in *Marshall (No. 1)*. The court found that he had a treaty right to fish. The federal laws that he violated by fishing interfered with that treaty right. The treaty right had constitutional protection under s. 35. The constitutional protection of Mr Marshall's treaty right overruled Parliament's fisheries laws. Mr Marshall had violated those laws, but the Supreme Court of Canada said he was constitutionally entitled to do so.

2

Judicial Activism and Its Critics

After the adoption of the Canadian Charter of Rights and Freedoms in 1982, and after a number of early Charter decisions, a debate gradually emerged concerning the new role of the judiciary in Canada's democracy. Critics suggested that "activist" courts were pre-empting legislatures and the executive, making decisions that were properly the decisions of elected officials, not unelected judges. Critics were disturbed that because these decisions were constitutional law, they could not be overruled easily – and sometimes not at all – by legislatures. Others responded by saying that judges are not "activist," but are merely applying the principles set out in the Charter, an obligation imposed on them by the Constitution.

JUDGE-MADE LAW AND LEGISLATIVE REFORM IN AN EARLIER ERA

The often rancorous modern debate over judicial activism did not arise exclusively because of the Charter, although the powers vested in judges in consequence of the Charter have raised the stakes of the debate. Rather, the debate has roots in a long-running controversy concerning the attitude and role of the judiciary. One does not have to dig too deeply into the historical record to find examples of controversial judge-made laws that required legislative correction. In the late 1800s, for example,

judge-made laws collided with the efforts of the emerging trade union movement to improve the wages and working conditions of working people through collective action.[1] Legislative change was necessary to balance the interests of workers against the interests of employers.

A good example is the notorious judge-made "common employment" rule. In the mid-nineteenth century, in the midst of the onrushing industrial revolution, and long before the days of workers' compensation, the courts decided that an employee who was injured at work due to the negligence of another employee could not sue the employer for compensation.[2] Since fellow-workers would rarely be worth suing for compensation, this ruling was a significant hurdle to injured workers seeking redress for on-the-job accidents. Yet the mines and factories of nineteenth-century England, where the rule was developed, were hazardous. In 1854, for example, it was reported that in a three-year period 3,000 fatal accidents occurred in the mines. None was compensated.[3] The mines in nineteenth-century Pictou County, Springhill, and Cape Breton, Nova Scotia, were no less dangerous. In the Pictou coal fields alone, hundreds lost their lives.[4] In the limited circumstances where injured employees could sue, the courts refused to award compensation to injured workers if they were partly to blame for their injuries. These rules reflected a judicial reluctance to expand liability for industrial accidents. One famous judge lauded the law: "there was never a more useful decision or one of greater practical and social importance."[5] The usefulness of the law might have been less apparent to a maimed employee. At the turn of the century, legislatures began to intervene to establish workers' compensation schemes authorizing compensation for workplace injury without reference to judge-made rules governing liability and recovery.

Another example is found in the 1930s, when the Canadian Parliament attempted to respond to the economic crisis of the Great Depression with legislation governing minimum wages, hours of work, and employment insurance. Courts created roadblocks by striking down federal legislation imposing national standards.[6] The Courts were criticized for disabling Parlia-

ment's efforts in a time of national economic crisis.[7] In the case of unemployment insurance, a constitutional amendment was required in 1940 to establish a national program.[8] These examples can be regarded as illustrative of unyielding judicial dogma at variance with societal demands that required corrective legislative action. Alternatively, they can be characterized as proper judicial adherence to legal precedent, despite resulting hardship or unfairness, recognizing that the authority to modify or modernize the law rested with the elected legislature. But whether judge-made law should be characterized as regressively unyielding or dictated by precedent, the fact remains that it is the legislatures and not the Courts that have borne the historic burden of law reform. The statute books are full of examples of legislative reform of judge-made law.[9]

In the field of human rights, the judicial experience with the Canadian Bill of Rights, enacted by the federal Parliament in 1960, is instructive. The Bill of Rights was an ordinary federal statute that enshrined certain human rights and fundamental freedoms. As a federal statute, the Bill of Rights was subject to amendment or repeal by Parliament at any time and could operate only in areas of federal jurisdiction. It did not have the constitutional clout that the Canadian Charter of Rights and Freedoms would later have. In only one case was a statute overruled by reference to the Bill of Rights.[10] The Court restrained itself, reluctant to "deny operative effect to a substantive measure duly enacted by a Parliament ... exercising its power in accordance with the tenets of responsible government."[11] In other words, in applying the Bill of Rights, the Court was very careful to respect the will of the elected representatives of the people, which was reflected in the legislation under challenge.

The American experience, which has a 200-year tradition with a constitutionalized Bill of Rights, illustrates the fundamental problem. Constitutional principles are very much at the mercy of judicial inclinations. To take a striking example, in 1857 the American Supreme Court relied on the Fifth Amendment of the United States Constitution, which prohibits deprivations of "life, liberty or property," to prevent the

emancipation of slaves.[12] While it is hard to square a constitutional guarantee of "liberty" with slavery, the Court held that
slave-owners were constitutionally guaranteed their property.
Most of the judges on the Court came from slave-owning states.
As Peter Hogg, a leading Canadian constitutional author, says,
describing the American Supreme Court of the 1950s under
Chief Justice Warren: "The Warren Court decisions vindicated
values then current among American liberals whereas those of
the [previous] era vindicated values then current among American conservatives. Judicial activism can take any political direction depending in large measure on the political predilections of
the judges."[13]

The interpretation of Bills of Rights, the same author suggests, "varies with changes in the attitudes of the judges who
have to apply it."[14] In a democracy, the attitudes of our elected
representatives have a greater claim to legitimacy than the political predilection of judges and until the Charter, the will of those
elected legislators was predominant. In this context, it is not
surprising that a debate has erupted over the role of judges after
the adoption of the Canadian Charter.

JUDGES VERSUS LEGISLATORS AFTER THE CHARTER

Early Charter cases signalled a sea-change compared to the judicial approach to the Canadian Bill of Rights. Whereas the
approach to the Bill of Rights had been cautious and restrained
and respectful of the will of Parliament, now the Court determined to give the Charter a "large and liberal," "broad and generous" interpretation.[15] A series of controversial decisions by the
newly emboldened court has ensued and these decisions have led
to increasingly vocal criticism of the Court's new-found "activism" and an equally vocal defence. The cases range over a wide
field of issues. They include, for example, a series of decisions
that have read in "sexual orientation" as a prohibited ground of
discrimination in the Charter, leading ultimately to same-sex
marriage;[16] a decision striking down Quebec's prohibition on

private health-care insurance, effectively opening the door to two-tier health care;[17] a decision striking down Canada's Sunday closing law, effectively ending the common day of rest;[18] a decision allowing the court to order the executive arm of government to appear before the courts and report on its conduct, dramatically altering the relationship between the executive and the judiciary;[19] and a decision extending the constitutional right to freedom of association to include collective bargaining.[20]

The changes wrought by these decisions and others like them cannot be minimized. As applied by the Supreme Court of Canada, not to mention lower courts and tribunals, the Charter has effected fundamental and far-reaching changes to Canadian government and society. But it is far from clear that these decisions flow inexorably from the Charter. Does the Charter really mandate judicial ascendency in territory so laden with moral and political choice? Or is the judiciary dabbling in matters that are properly the concern of our elected representatives, making dubious social and economic policy choices in the guise of rights? If so, how can their choices be corrected when their decisions have the veneer of constitutional permanency? Is democracy being diminished by an overreaching judiciary?

Some critics have made no bones about it. The Courts, they say, have used the Charter in a "dazzling exercise of self-empowerment"; they have "succumbed to the seduction of power."[21] The contention is that the Courts are unelected, undemocratic, and elitist. The Court and the "Court Party," their coterie of dependents, including lawyers, law professors, and interest group litigants, have used the rhetoric of law and legal rights to arrogate authority over significant fields of public policy to the Courts. Decisions that should be the subject of negotiation, debate, and compromise among our elected representatives have been pre-empted by authoritarian judicial rule. Judges are dictating policy. All of this is "deeply and fundamentally undemocratic."[22] It has, for example, been suggested that the Court has contradicted the "original legislative understanding" of the Charter by reading in rights that were adverted to but excluded from the Charter during its conception in 1982.

Furthermore, it has been argued that the Court has repudiated its own precedents in pronouncing Charter rights, an approach that is inconsistent with the traditions of the rule of law.[23]

There have been vigorous responses to these criticisms of the Court. Against the assertion that judicial activism is undemocratic, it has been argued that the Court plays a significant role in the protection of minority rights that is "a vital component of a true democracy" and that, in any event, our parliamentary system is" anti-democratic" because "policy-making in Canada is largely removed from our elected representatives and placed in the hands of the executive." Against the charge that judges are too activist, it has been argued that the Courts are obliged to apply the Constitution and that they are restrained by nature ("an unlikely habitat for revolutionaries"). It is said that Charter decisions constitute a "dialogue" with the legislature as a result of which laws are more carefully crafted to respect Charter values. Against the charge that judges have illegitimately expanded their role from adjudication of the disputes of litigants to presiding over the policy contests of interested interveners, it is said that the complexity of modern legal problems requires that the Court hear a full range of perspectives. The Courts, it is argued, have done a "good job" in interpreting the Charter in a way that "fairly balances competing interests" but also promotes the values embodied in the Charter.[24]

The strongest of these points is the simple answer that the Courts have been vested with the Constitutional obligation of applying the Charter and they must apply it in a meaningful way. But there is fundamental merit in the reply that in a parliamentary democracy, substantial – very often overriding – respect must be accorded to the democratic will of elected legislators, particularly given the reality that Courts do not, historically, have a strong record of tempering justice to suit contemporary needs and given that Charter law is so heavily dependent upon the attitudes of judges who have to apply it.

It is, ultimately, the attitude of judges who are charged with applying the Charter that dominates the development of Charter law, and there is no better summary of the activist judicial atti-

tude than the following comment by Justice Rosalie Abella, now a judge of the Supreme Court of Canada, in a speech in 2000:

> With the arrival of the 1990s, a few abrupt voices were heard to challenge the Supreme Court, voices in large part belonging to those whose psychological security or territorial hegemony were at risk from the Charter's reach. As the decade advanced, so did the courage and insistence of these New Inhibitors, most of whom appeared to congregate at one end of the ideological spectrum. While their articulated target was the Supreme Court of Canada, their real target was the way the Charter was transforming their traditional expectations and entitlements. They made their arguments skillfully. In essence they turned the good news of constitutionalized rights, the mark of a secure and mature democracy, into the bad news of judicial autocracy, the mark of a debilitated and devalued legislature. They called minorities seeking the right to be free from discrimination "special interest groups" seeking to jump the queue. They called efforts to reverse discrimination "reverse discrimination."[25]

The remarks are both disturbing and instructive. They are disturbing because they reflect an intolerance of genuine criticism, darkly attacking the motives of the critics. The motives of the critics should not be dismissed as sinister. The criticisms are more often founded in a genuine concern for the democratic process, not self-interested entitlements, or insecurities. Neither is it accurate to characterize all those who disagree with judicial activism as cranky right wingers. But the comments are instructive for identifying, though inadvertently, the division between judicial activists and their critics. The critics, in the minds of the activists, are the "New Inhibitors" retarding legitimate minority demands for equality. On the other hand, the overriding mandate for judicial activists, as they conceive it, is to reverse discrimination, as they define it, and their pursuit of that goal is *un*inhibited. The very long judicial tradition of caution, restraint, and deference to democratic and legal principles is lost sight of.

There is no need to repeat the disagreements between activists and their critics over the many other controversial decisions that divide them. Instead, this book deals solely with the decision of the Supreme Court of Canada in *Marshall (No. 1)*, and its aftermath. But the analysis here digs deep into the evidence, argument, and law – material that serves as the foundation for any judicial decision and is often inaccessible to the proponents and opponents of activism whose debates are handicapped as a result.

ACTIVISM AND ABORIGINAL RIGHTS

The *Marshall (No. 1)* decision did not appear out of the blue. It arose out of a particular judicial context. In few areas of law has the Supreme Court of Canada been as activist as in the field of aboriginal law. Beginning with the first case to deal with the aboriginal rights provisions of the Constitution, a number of leading cases reflect a tenuous adherence to the language of the Constitution, a disregard for fundamental and long-standing legal principles, and a lack of caution for the implications of the Courts' decisions. In deciding as they did in *Marshall (No. 1)*, the majority may have broken new ground, but the activist path they were travelling was well-worn.

The first of the aboriginal rights cases to reach the Supreme Court of Canada was that of *R. v. Sparrow*.[26] Sparrow was a member of the Musqueam Indian Band in Vancouver. For centuries, the Musqueum had fished salmon in the waters of the Fraser River. In the late nineteenth century, the federal government began regulating the salmon fishery and those regulations became increasingly strict as commercial and sport fishing combined with native fishing to put pressure on salmon stocks. Even so, by the 1970s, the policy of the federal Department of Fisheries and Oceans (DFO) was to give priority to native food fish requirements, subject only to the demands of conservation.[27]

In the late 1970s the Musqueam Band caught about 5,000 fish under their food fishery licence. But by 1982 they caught 58,000; about 400 pounds of fish for every man, woman, and

child in the band.[28] If all ninety-one native bands upstream of the Musqueam were permitted to take the same proportionate amount of food fish, the survival of some salmon species would be jeopardized.[29]

The increased Musqueam fish catch was a consequence of a change made in 1978 when the DFO had begun to permit fishing with 75 fathom drift nets.[30] Now, DFO determined to reduce the fishing power of the Musqueam fishery by reducing the maximum size of the drift nets for the food fishery to 25 fathoms.[31] Sparrow objected to the drift net restriction. He said it violated his rights under s. 35 of the Constitution Act, 1982, and that issue proceeded to the Supreme Court of Canada. This, then, was the first opportunity for the Supreme Court of Canada to discuss s. 35(1). Its approach to the provision would chart the course for aboriginal law.

Before commenting on the Court's approach, it is useful to recall how the 1982 changes to our Constitution were structured. The Charter is the best known of the 1982 constitutional changes. It comprises thirty-four sections. The language of these sections is clear and explicit, "the Canadian Charter of Rights and Freedoms guarantees the rights and freedoms set out in it" (s. 1). The various sections elaborate Democratic Rights, Mobility Rights, Legal Rights, Equality Rights, Language Rights, and Fundamental Freedoms. These are guaranteed. Promised. Obligatory. The Charter describes the only limits to that guarantee. The guarantee is "subject only to such reasonable limits prescribed by law as can be demonstrably justified in a free and democratic society." (s. 1). The structure of this language has been central to the development of the Charter. It mandates a two-step analysis of Charter rights and freedoms. In the first step, those rights and freedoms are given broad definition. In the second step, the question is whether limitations on those rights are justified.

Section 35 reads differently. It is not part of the Charter. It is a separate part of the Constitution entitled "Rights of the Aboriginal Peoples of Canada." It is wedged between the Charter and S. 36 of the Constitution Act, 1982. S. 36 is widely regarded as

merely "aspirational" and not justiciable.[32] S. 35(1) says: "The existing aboriginal and treaty rights of the aboriginal people of Canada are hereby recognized and affirmed."

These rights must be existing. They are "recognized" – their existence is acknowledged – and they are "affirmed." An affirmation is not a guarantee. It is something akin to an "assertion," statement, or declaration, perhaps having some sense of confirmation. But the absolute language of guarantee is absent from s. 35. Instead, s. 35 used a word that is less definitive, connoting lesser protection, and there is no language referencing "justifiable limits" to those rights. There are subtleties of language here, but this is the language of the Constitution. To diligently apply the Constitution, courts must have regard to its language. In *Sparrow*, the Court was scarcely inhibited by the language of s. 35 in contrast to the language of the Charter.

The Court began its analysis in *Sparrow* by rejecting an argument advanced by the federal Crown that, after a century of federal regulation, any Musqueam right to fish had been extinguished. The Court said regulations could not have extinguished the Aboriginal right to fish.[33] "Existing" rights were those that had not been extinguished and the Musqueam right to fish, though heavily regulated, was not extinguished. Significantly, the Court also said that the existing aboriginal right was unaffected by the way regulations might have shaped it before 1982.[34] A century of regulations of the native fishery were irrelevant to the nature of the existing right. The Court was, legitimately, concerned that if rights were defined to incorporate the manner in which they were regulated across the country, the constitutional right would be a "crazy patchwork of regulations."[35] But a reasonable response to that concern would have been to constitutionalize only the aboriginal right to fish, while leaving regulations over fishing methods, seasons, and species outside constitutional scrutiny.

Turning to the "recognized and affirmed" language of s. 35, the Court acknowledged that this language was not absolute,[36] but decided that the section required a generous, liberal interpretation.[37] Furthermore, the Court decided that "any government regulation that infringes upon or denies aboriginal rights"

must be "justified."[38] "Parliament is not expected to act in a manner contrary to the rights and interests of aboriginals and, indeed, may be barred from doing so."[39] So, despite the significant difference in language between the Charter and s. 35, the Court adopted an approach to the analysis of s. 35 that was little different from its approach to the Charter. Judicial memos discussing the case reveal Justice Wilson advocating a robust approach to s. 35, suggesting that any other approach would lead one to wonder "what the Indians got as a result of s. 35(1) for which they fought so hard."[40] One may equally wonder why a constitutional provision outside the Charter should be interpreted like a Charter right.

In the context of the fishery, the Court made the following startling pronouncement respecting the "justification" of federal regulations:

> The nature of the constitutional protection afforded by s. 35(1) ... demands that there be a link between the question of justification and the allocation of priorities in the fishery. The constitutional recognition and affirmation of aboriginal rights may give rise to conflict with the interests of others given the limited nature of the resource ...
>
> The constitutional nature of the Musqueam food fishing rights means that any allocation of priorities after valid conservation measures have been implemented must give top priority to Indian food fishing ...
>
> If in a given year, conservation needs required a reduction in the number of fish to be caught such that the number equalled the number required for food by the Indians, then all the fish available after conservation would go to the Indians according to the constitutional nature of their fishery right. If, more realistically, there were still fish after the Indian food requirement were met, then the brunt of conservation measures would be borne by the practices of sport fishing, and commercial fishing.[41]

So a constitutional provision that merely recognizes and affirms native rights was interpreted to give natives rights to the

exclusion of others, in certain circumstances. Conservation of
fishery resources, which both native and non-native activities
deplete, would be borne by others first and by natives only in
the last resort. Nothing in s. 35(1) really demands such native
priority. The section simply affirms rights. It could reasonably
be said to limit unreasonable native *exclusion* from traditional
native activities. But, the language of s. 35(1) is not, as the
Court noted, cast in absolute terms. A judicial interpretation
that limited native exclusion and encouraged native and non-
native sharing is more consistent with the language of the
section than the absolutist approach of priority and exclusivity.
In a later decision, the Court said that reconciliation of native
society with non-natives was at the heart of s. 35.[42] Exclusivity
is hardly conciliatory.

Moreover, the Court rejected the suggestion that an Aboriginal right to fish, which received constitutional protection, should
be distinguished from the methods used to exercise that right:
"it would be artificial to try to create a hard distinction between
the right to fish and the particular manner in which that right is
exercised."[43] In other words, the Aboriginal right to fish was
simply a right to "get fish." So, apparently, it did not matter
whether the Aboriginal fisher used a 500 fathom drift net or
dynamite. It was for the Crown to prove that prohibiting such
methods was a justifiable restriction on the right. This reasoning
would not have followed from an analysis that recognized that
s. 35 was fundamentally different from the Charter. If s. 35(1) is
more like a statement than a guarantee, it seems to warrant less
protection. The right to fish in *Sparrow* could have been confined to aboriginal methods of fishing, or the method could
have received no constitutional protection at all. Beyond this,
the reasoning is flawed. It ignores a fundamental purpose of
s. 35: to protect aboriginal culture in the wash of Western industrial society that has engulfed it. In light of that purpose, the
method of exercise of an aboriginal right is a crucial modifier of
the right. A native person fishing in a traditional way is engaged
in a cultural practice that is extremely important to many
aboriginal societies. The Constitution rightly protects the prac-

tice. A native person trawling with a drift net is not engaged in a culturally significant activity.

In its first discussion of s. 35, then, the Court started badly. It developed an approach to s. 35 that is not consistent with the language of the Constitution and, in doing so, it adopted the language of priority and exclusivity, an approach that fosters discord rather than native – non-native reconciliation. At the same time, it had little regard for a strong purpose of s. 35, the protection of aboriginal culture. It failed to recognize that constitutionalizing aboriginal rights such as fishing must be limited to culturally significant fishing activities. It suggested, instead, that aboriginal rights such as fishing could be carried on by any means, including, it seems, the most modern industrialized techniques, such as trawling, and it ignored the reality of a century of salmon fishing regulations in defining aboriginal rights that continue to exist. In the view of the Supreme Court of Canada, aboriginal cultural practices were irrelevant to the exercise of a right intended to protect aboriginal cultural practices. The Court sent the case back to trial to determine whether the drift net restriction was justified.[44]

After the *Sparrow* decision, the Supreme Court of Canada grappled with s. 35(1) again in *R. v. Van der Peet*. Ms Van der Peet was a member of the Sto:lo Nation on the Fraser River in British Columbia. She was charged with selling salmon caught under a native food fish licence. She claimed an aboriginal right to sell salmon, protected by s. 35. The case was the Supreme Court of Canada's first opportunity to deal with the definition of the aboriginal rights recognized and affirmed in s. 35(1).

Chief Justice Lamer wrote for the majority. It was his view that s. 35(1) affirmed aboriginal rights for the very simple reason that when Europeans arrived in North America, "aboriginal peoples were already here, living in communities on the land, and participating in distinctive cultures, as they had done for centuries."[45] Section 35(1) was the constitutional framework for the reconciliation of the two.[46] Drawing support from the French text of s. 35(1), which refers to aboriginal rights as "les droits ... ancestraux," he decided that aboriginal rights were the

"crucial elements" of pre-existing distinctive aboriginal societies – the practices, customs, or traditions "integral to the distinctive culture" of aboriginal societies that existed in North
America prior to contact with the Europeans.[47] They were the
"defining features" of aboriginal culture.[48] Where modern native
practices, customs, and traditions had "continuity" with those
of pre-contact times, they were protected under s. 35(1).

This definition of aboriginal rights is laudable. It is true to the
language of the Constitution. It recognizes that what s. 35(1)
helps to protect is the distinctiveness of aboriginal cultures,
threatened as they are by the assimilating forces of the Western
industrial culture that surrounds them. In response to the concern that proving aspects of aboriginal culture at the time of
contact – in some cases hundreds of years ago – would be too
difficult, Justice Lamer directed courts to interpret the evidence
"with a consciousness of the special nature of aboriginal claims
and of the evidentiary difficulties in proving ancient rights."[49]

But, where Chief Justice Lamer's judgment in *Van der Peet*
faltered is in a passage discussing the evolution of aboriginal
rights: "Because the practices, customs and traditions protected
by s. 35(1) are ones that exist today, subject only to the requirement that they be demonstrated to have continuity with the
practices, customs and traditions which existed pre-contact, the
definition of aboriginal rights will be one that, on its own terms,
prevents those rights from being frozen in pre-contact times.
The evolution of practices, customs and traditions into modern
forms will not, provided that continuity with pre-contact practices, customs and traditions is demonstrated, prevent their protection as aboriginal rights."[50]

So, aboriginal rights can evolve. All they need is some continuity with earlier traditions. But, here, Chief Justice Lamer
failed to respect the force of his own logic, and the language
of the Constitution. If aboriginal rights are meant to protect
aboriginal culture, then surely there is a more obvious limit to
their evolution than the vague "continuity" standard that Chief
Justice Lamer described. While aboriginal practices should not
be confined to their "primeval simplicity," surely modern aborig-

inal practices cannot "evolve" to the extent that they indistinguishably adopt the practices of non-native culture. As in *Sparrow*, then, the Court refused to recognize the need for cultural limits on a provision of the Constitution that is meant to protect native culture.

The consequence of the Courts' approach is most apparent in the later decision of *R. v. Sappier & Polchies*.[51] There, a native logger in New Brunswick removed timber from Crown lands using a skidder, a hydraulic loader, and an 18-wheeler logging truck for processing at a sawmill to build a timber-frame house. Despite its ruling in an earlier case that logging was "not a traditional" native activity and was, indeed, "inimical" to the native traditional way of life,"[52] the Supreme Court of Canada upheld all of this as the valid exercise of a constitutionally protected aboriginal right to harvest wood for domestic use. Traditional native cultures in New Brunswick were incapable of harvesting mature timber.[53] It is unclear what native cultural practices were reflected in the accused's activities. Indeed, it is difficult to imagine a better example of native assimilation to practices wholly foreign to native culture. The result in the case is fairly attributable to unrestrained judicial activism.

By the mid 1990s the Court began to turn its attention to the concept of aboriginal title, making declarations of law that are both sweeping and puzzling. In *R. v. Adams*[54] the Court held that aboriginal title was a distinct type of aboriginal right given constitutional protection under s. 35(1). Strangely, the Court has never grappled with the question of why it should have interpreted aboriginal rights in s. 35(1) to encompass aboriginal title when it has interpreted the Charter to exclude the protection of property rights.[55] Then in *Delgamuukw v. British Columbia*,[56] the Court elaborated its doctrine of aboriginal title.

Delgamuukw involved the claims of the Gitksan and Wet'suwet'en peoples of British Columbia, some six or seven thousand in number, to own fifty-eight thousand square kilometres of the Province. The trial of the case lasted some 374 days. The Supreme Court of Canada decided that because the trial judge had failed to properly consider the oral histories of the native

claimants, there should be a new trial. Ordinarily, that should
have concluded the Court's judgment. But Chief Justice Lamer
went on to make bold pronouncements about the law of aboriginal title, noting that the Court's jurisprudence on aboriginal
title was "somewhat underdeveloped."[57] *Delgamuukw* has
become the leading case on aboriginal title, yet the legal doctrines advanced by the Court to describe aboriginal title – that it
is a "unique" interest in land that is communal and inalienable
and cannot be put to "irreconcilable" uses – are questionable.

Significant in the discussion of aboriginal title in Canada is
the proposition in the pre-Charter case of *Calder v.* AG (BC)[58]
that "when the settlers came, the Indians were there, organized
in societies and occupying the land as their forefathers had done
for centuries."[59] It is a proposition of fundamental fairness that
where native peoples occupied land historically, where they
remain in occupation of that land and their right to do so has
not been removed or limited, the law should protect their occupation. Yet, to say that native title "is held communally" and
"cannot be held by individual aboriginal persons"[60] is to con-
strain all native societies in this country to a romantic Utopian
collectivist ideal that is economically disadvantageous, historically questionable, and inconsistent with common law. Among
native peoples of the east coast of Canada, for example, it has
been suggested – albeit controversially – that lands were owned,
and that they were owned privately by family groups and
descended from generation to generation through the male
heir.[61] If this is correct, and if, as Chief Justice Lamer said in
Delgamuukw, aboriginal title must take into account the
"aboriginal perspective,"[62] then it may be that the aboriginal
title of some native groups in Canada was *not* communal. Without evidence of the landholdings of native groups across Canada, Chief Justice Lamer ought not to have made such sweeping
statements as to the "communal" nature of aboriginal title.

Similar is Chief Justice Lamer's assertion that lands that are
subject to aboriginal title cannot be used in a way that is "irreconcilable" with native "occupation of that land and the rela-

tionship that the particular group has had with the land."[63] Native land cannot, for example, be "strip mined" or paved for a parking lot without first being surrendered to the Crown.[64] The common law never applied such constraints to lands owned outright by their owner. This limitation of native ownership of aboriginal title lands is fairly characterized as a policy choice made by the Supreme Court of Canada, one that acts as a significant brake on native peoples wishing to merge their economies into the modern economy. Chief Justice Lamer said in justifying the rule that the historic native relationship to the land "should not be prevented from continuing into the future."[65] All well and good, but if traditional native reliance on the land in modern times has left many native communities in abject poverty, it is a policy that has little to commend to it. Moreover, the suggestion that native land cannot be used "in such a fashion as to destroy its value" for traditional uses perpetuates the stereotypical "myth of the ecological Indian."[66] It is, however, intellectually compatible with the Utopian communal ideal of traditional native society.

Yet another characteristic attributed to aboriginal title in *Delgamuukw* is its purported inalienability. According to Chief Justice Lamer, native lands "cannot be transferred, sold or surrendered to anyone other than the Crown."[67] It is true that as a matter of policy, to protect native people from improvident transactions, the Royal Proclamation of 1763 prohibited non-native purchase of native lands and that policy has been continued by legislation ever since.[68] But in Nova Scotia, where the relevant part of the Royal Proclamation of 1763 never applied,[69] native people were free to sell lands to non-natives. In 1762 Nova Scotia's legislature attempted to invalidate such purchases, but the bill did not receive the governor's assent.[70] In Nova Scotia, at least, it appears that native sale of land was lawful. Elsewhere, native sales were prohibited by policy and enactment. It was, accordingly, too sweeping for Chief Justice Lamer to suggest that aboriginal title is inalienable. The suggestion is, in effect, legislative in nature rather than the judicial application

of common law or constitutional rules.[71] It is also severely restrictive of the liberties of native people who are constrained in their ability to sell or mortgage their lands.

In *Delgamuukw*, the Court rejected the suggestion that aboriginal title was simply common law "fee simple" title held by native people. It rejected the sensible, time-tested doctrines of the common law, preferring instead its own creations – communality, irreconcilability, inalienability – all of which are of dubious legitimacy and doubtful merit. The Court's comments concerning the extent of aboriginal title also deserve mention. Discussing native claims to ancestral lands, Justice LaForest suggested that "vast tracts of territory" were involved.[72] Chief Justice Lamer, similarly, suggested that aboriginal title encompassed extensive territories: "the development of agriculture, forestry, mining and hydroelectric power, the general economic development of the interior of British Columbia, protection of the environment or endangered species, the building of infrastructure and the settlement of foreign populations ... can justify the infringement of aboriginal title."[73]

Expansive aboriginal title claims encouraged by this language were reflected in the later cases of *R. v. Stephen Marshall* and *R. v. Bernard*.[74] There, the claims advanced were, effectively, for the whole, or much, of Nova Scotia and the better part of New Brunswick. The Supreme Court of Canada ultimately rejected these claims, using much more cautious language respecting the extent of aboriginal title.[75]

The foregoing cases illustrate judicial activism at work, fashioning aboriginal rights of unwarranted breadth while disregarding long-established common law doctrines. The case of *Haida Nation v. British Columbia*[76] is another example.

The Haida people of the Queen Charlotte Islands, or "Haida Gwaii," off the British Columbia coast, have claimed aboriginal title to all of those islands and the surrounding waters. But, when they went to court in 2000, it was not to press their claim for aboriginal title. Rather, it was to demand that they be consulted respecting the grant of tree-farm licences to forestry companies on the Queen Charlottes. They won. More than that, in a

decision that has hamstrung governments and bureaucratized decision-making from coast to coast, the Court said that whenever unproven claims of aboriginal rights are asserted, and whenever activities may infringe asserted rights, governments have a duty to consult with native people and perhaps accommodate their concerns. In other words, native people need merely claim rights – not prove them – to trigger a government duty to consult. On the facts of the case, the Court held that the BC government was obliged to consult with the Haida respecting the tree-farm licences. Given the untold hundreds of thousands of similar authorizations given by provincial, municipal, and federal governments across Canada annually – exploration licences, mining permits, building permits, to name just a few – this decision has imposed a huge burden on government decision-making.

Yet the legal basis for the duty to consult is doubtful. The Court said that it arose from the "honour of the Crown," whose "historical roots" suggest that it must be "understood generously."[77] Not one case cited by the Court to sustain either the "honour of the Crown" or the duty to consult pre-dated the inception of the Charter and s. 35 in 1982. The Court relied on its own post – 1982 jurisprudence as the basis for the duty to consult. The "honour of the Crown" was originally conceived as a principle of interpretation of treaties and statutes to ensure that promises to native people were fulfilled and to preclude appearances of "sharp dealing."[78] It is an enthusiastic approach to the law to fashion a sweeping and previously unknown duty to consult and accommodate from a mere principle of interpretation. Beyond this, the Court linked the duty to consult to s. 35: "Section 35 represents a promise of rights recognition, and 'it is always assumed that the Crown intends to fulfill its promises' ... This promise is realized and sovereignty claims reconciled through the process of honourable negotiation. It is a corollary of s. 35 that the Crown act honourably in defining the rights it guarantees and in reconciling them with other rights and interests. This, in turn, implies a duty to consult and, if appropriate, accommodate."[79]

It is true that s. 35 promises "rights recognition." But it says nothing about a "duty to consult." It says merely that aboriginal and treaty rights are "recognized and affirmed." Moreover, the "promise of rights recognition" in s. 35 is a constitutional promise. How it is, as a matter of law, a "corollary" of s. 35 that the Crown must consult respecting the claimed s. 35 rights is far from clear.

In *Haida*, the Court argued powerfully that it was simply not fair for governments to unilaterally exploit claimed resources pending judicial resolution of claimed aboriginal rights. Native heritage could be "irretrievably despoiled" before a claim succeeded. Consultation and accommodation can serve to temper this. The point, in some circumstances, is very strong. But, it is, at bottom, a policy argument that has been reworked by activist judges into our constitutional law.

Undoubtedly, these four leading cases reflect a genuine judicial response to the plight of many native communities in this country. But the institutional capacity of judges to properly respond to that plight is very limited. While the approach is well intended, what these cases also reflect, in my respectful estimation, is a pattern of judicial incaution in the realm of native law – too little regard for either the language of the Constitution or the long-established rules of the common law and insufficient inhibition in the development of judge-made rules. That pattern would be repeated, and taken a step further, in *Marshall (No. 1)*.

In the debate over judicial activism, some have attempted to identify principles that should serve to limit the enthusiasm of excessively activist judges. For example, Chief Justice Beverley McLachlin has spoken of the "discipline" of the case whereby courts "stick to the issue raised by the case," thereby avoiding unnecessary digressions.[80] Justice Claire L'Heureux-Dubé, who signed the majority reasons in *Marshall (No. 1)* said, in response to critics of judicial activism, that those critics "ignore the process of legal reasoning and justification that forms part of every legal decision. Legal interpretation requires a judge to use arguments and sources that are acceptable within the legal community and justify that decision with regard to those values ... The

need to make arguments and justify a result in accordance with the principles of legal reasoning prevents the mere imposition of the judges' preferences."[81]

These are strong points. If they were respected, they would serve as a legitimate, recognized check on the judiciary and its application of the Charter. But *Marshall (No. 1)* reveals that determined judicial enthusiasm to "reverse discrimination" can and does lead judges to go well beyond "the issue raised" and abandon accepted principles of legal reasoning. What the record in *Marshall (No. 1)* reveals is a decision made in the face of contrary evidence, in the face of contrary law, despite patent procedural impropriety and despite binding and contrary fundamental legal principles. The majority decision was "uninhibited" by those safeguards that are meant to control judicial decisions. As such, it was everything that critics of judicial activism have railed against, an assertion of judicial power outside the proper role of the judiciary, which disrespected the authority of legislatures and Parliament and was, consequently, undemocratic.

In an address some years ago, Chief Justice Beverley McLachlin expressed confidence that "between the extremes of excessive judicial activism and judicial timidity we will find solutions that will serve Canadians well."[82] It is my hope that the critique advanced here will assist in that endeavour, revealing errors in judicial approach that are not consistent with accepted and recognized standards of judicial approach. Recognizing the problem is the first step to its mitigation and may help temper zealous activism while yet allowing the Charter to thrive as a strong and meaningful source of rights for all Canadians.

3

The Legal Background to *Marshall (No. 1)*

Native rights in Nova Scotia are a relatively recent judicial development. In earlier periods, native rights claims were given short shrift by judges. Perhaps the best example is the 1928 case of *R. v. Syliboy.*[1]

Mr Syliboy was the Mi'kmaq "Grand Chief" in Nova Scotia. He was charged in Inverness County, Cape Breton, with possession of muskrat and fox pelts, in violation of the provincial Lands and Forests Act. He claimed that under a treaty with the British governor of Nova Scotia in 1752, Mi'kmaq Indians were permitted to hunt and trap at any time. The judge said, correctly, that the 1752 treaty applied only to a small band of Mi'kmaq at Shubenacadie and could not have applied to Mr Syliboy, who was from Cape Breton. But he went on to say that the Treaty of 1752 was not a treaty at all. The Mi'kmaq, he said, were "uncivilized people or savages" and therefore were unable to have a proper treaty. Today, such language and analysis are unacceptable. Characterizing native peoples as "savages" is offensive and irrelevant. A deal is a deal and if a deal was struck and kept,[2] it ought to be honoured. But the case reveals the attitude of the courts to native claims in an earlier period.

In the 1970s the judicial attitude began to change. In 1975 the Nova Scotia Court of Appeal dealt with the case of *R. v. Isaac.*[3] Mr Isaac was an Indian. He was charged with possession of a rifle on a road in the Chapel Island Indian Reserve in Cape

Breton, in violation of the province's Lands and Forests Act. He was acquitted. The court said the provincial statute could not apply to prohibit an Indian hunting on an Indian reserve.[4] But the case was limited to Indian reserves. It did not extend beyond those reserves. Two years later the same court convicted a native person who was hunting eight miles from his reserve without a licence as required by the provincial Lands and Forests Act.[5]

In 1982, when Canada changed its Constitution to provide constitutional protection for "aboriginal and treaty rights," the pace of change to aboriginal rights law quickened. In 1985 the Supreme Court of Canada heard the case of *R. v. Simon*.[6] Mr Simon was a Mi'kmaq Indian and a member of the Shubenacadie (Indian Brook) Indian Band. He was caught on the highway near his reserve with a rifle and shells, without a hunting licence, in violation of the Nova Scotia Lands and Forests Act. He argued that under the Treaty of 1752 he had "free liberty of hunting and fishing as usual" and was therefore not subject to the provincial statute.

Remember that 50 years before, in the case of *R. v. Syliboy*, a County Court judge in Nova Scotia had said that the "savages" of 1752 were not capable of having a treaty. Understandably, the Supreme Court of Canada was having none of that. The court said the treaty had been validly created and that it protected hunting by natives who were covered by the treaty. In *R. v. Syliboy*, Mr Syliboy had been a Cape Breton Mi'kmaq, but Mr Simon was from the same Shubenacadie Band that had signed the 1752 Treaty. The Supreme Court of Canada said his treaty right to hunt could not be restricted by the provincial Act. Mr Simon was acquitted. Importantly, the Supreme Court of Canada also said in the *Simon* case that there was not enough evidence before the court to conclude that the 1752 Treaty had been terminated by hostilities. This issue would resurface in the *Marshall (No. 1)* case ten years later, where it would be partly responsible for the confusion and failures in that case.

The next significant case in Nova Scotia was the Court of Appeal decision in *R. v. Denny*.[7] Mr Denny was a Mi'kmaq and a member of the Eskasoni Indian Band. He was charged with

fishing salmon without a licence, in violation of the federal Fisheries Act regulations. He had been fishing in the Bras d'Or Lakes in Cape Breton, near the Eskasoni Indian Reservation. The Court of Appeal said that fishing for food was Mr Denny's aboriginal right, and he was acquitted of the charge. But the court very carefully limited its decision. It said that Mi'kmaq aboriginal rights extended "beyond the strict perimeter of Reserve lands to the waters incidental and adjacent to the Reserves." The *Denny* case had a ripple effect. As it was making its way through the courts, Mi'kmaq organizations in Nova Scotia organized a moose hunt in the Cape Breton Highlands, far from any Mi'kmaq reserve. The hunt ignored the Nova Scotia Wildlife Act, and a group of hunters was charged. But part way through the trial the Court of Appeal rendered its decision in the *Denny* case. The Crown gave up the fight, and the Mi'kmaq hunters were acquitted. Soon after, Nova Scotia changed its policy towards native hunters. Mi'kmaq hunters were now permitted to hunt on Crown lands.

Similarly, in the early 1990s, after the *Sparrow* decision of the Supreme Court of Canada relating to native fishing rights in British Columbia,[8] the federal government began permitting native bands in Nova Scotia to fish for food.

By the early 1990s, then, native rights claims had made significant advances. Nova Scotia courts had decided that natives could hunt on and fish near reserves without violating federal or provincial laws. But these cases did not suggest that natives had aboriginal rights to hunt or fish commercially. A native treaty right to hunt commercially had been given some support in the *Simon* case, but the case dealt only with the 1752 Treaty which applied to only one native band, and the court left open the question of whether that treaty had been terminated by hostilities. As a matter of policy, governments had begun to permit native hunting and fishing for food and social purposes.

The law in New Brunswick was in many respects similar to that in Nova Scotia. In the early 1990s the federal government began allowing native bands in New Brunswick to exercise a limited food fishery.[9] The same Supreme Court of Canada deci-

sion that prompted the federal government to open a native food fishery in Nova Scotia and New Brunswick was taken by New Brunswick courts to permit native hunting.[10]

A peculiar development of the law in New Brunswick involved the Treaty of 1726. New Brunswick courts have said repeatedly that the treaty entitles Maliseet Indians to hunt and fish, even where so doing violates provincial game laws.[11] Strangely, prosecutors in New Brunswick do not appear to have seriously contested the point. In contrast, the courts in Newfoundland have ruled that the 1726 Treaty was terminated by subsequent wars, and therefore cannot be a source of native rights.[12] In a very controversial decision in 1996, two New Brunswick judges in the lower courts took the 1726 Treaty farther. They ruled that the 1726 Treaty authorized native commercial logging on provincial Crown lands.[13] The New Brunswick Court of Appeal eventually overturned the lower court rulings.[14] But native expectations had been elevated by the lower court decisions, and the rulings created "turmoil, anger and the possibility of violence in the forests of New Brunswick."[15] One of the lower court judges was a self-described "activist" judge.[16] His decision and the fall-out from it was a harbinger of what would come when the Supreme Court of Canada announced its decision in *Marshall (No. 1)*. It all started in August 1993, when Donald Marshall, Jr, went fishing for eels in the waters of Pomquet Harbour, Nova Scotia.

4

Marshall (No. 1) in the Trial Court

The Provincial Court in Antigonish, Nova Scotia, where Mr Marshall's case was tried, is an unassuming building, located next to some fast-food outlets just down from the Exhibition Grounds. In November 1994 two small groups assembled before Provincial Court Judge John Embree, a former Crown prosecutor, to deal with the charges against Mr Marshall. Mr Marshall was represented by Bruce Wildsmith, a very talented professor at Dalhousie Law School, who had carved his name by pursuing native rights claims in Nova Scotia's Courts. His advocacy on Mr Marshall's behalf was impeccable. He was assisted by Eric Zscheile, an able advocate hailing from Kansas. They would call two expert witnesses to testify: Dr John Reid,[1] a transplanted Scot and professor of History at St Mary's University in Halifax; and Dr William Wicken, who was employed by the Union of Nova Scotia Indians and Confederacy of Mainland Mi'kmaq as a researcher and historian. The federal Crown was represented by Michael Paré, a very capable Crown lawyer, and his assistant, Ian MacRae. They would call one witness: Dr Stephen Patterson, a professor of History at the University of New Brunswick in Fredericton.

THE TREATY OF 1752, AND THE HALIFAX TREATIES OF 1760–1761

By the time Donald Marshall, Jr, began fishing for eels in August 1993, native people in the Maritime Provinces were relatively

free to fish and hunt to feed themselves. But hunting and fishing to make money was something quite different. Courts had not countenanced any aboriginal rights to hunt and fish commercially, although such a right under the 1752 Treaty was hinted at in the *Simon* case. The language of the 1752 Treaty could be argued to constitute a commercial right. This is what it said: "It is agreed that the said Tribe of Indians should not be hindered from, but have free liberty of hunting and Fishing as usual and that if they shall Think a Truckhouse needful at the river Chibenaccadie or any other place of their resort they shall have the same built and proper Merchandize lodged therein, to be exchanged for what the Indians shall have to dispose of, and that in the mean time the said Indians shall have free liberty to bring for sale to Halifax or any other Settlement within this Province, skins, feathers, fowl, fish or any other thing they shall have to sell, where they shall have liberty to dispose thereof to the best Advantage."

In *Simon*, the Supreme Court of Canada said this clause "appears to contemplate hunting for commercial purposes."[2] Donald Marshall, Jr, had caught 463 pounds of eels and sold them for nearly $800. This was more than a food fishery. This was a commercial fishery. It was also a violation of federal laws; he was fishing without a licence in a closed season with illegal nets. The federal Crown prosecuted him. And when Donald Marshall, Jr's trial began in 1994, it is not surprising that his lawyer, Bruce Wildsmith, advised the court that Mr Marshall's defence would rely on the 1752 treaty. The *Simon* case, which had discussed that treaty, was the only decided case Mr Marshall's lawyer could point to that might be said to endorse a commercial right to fish or hunt. But not only did Mr Wildsmith advise the court that Mr Marshall's defence would rely on the 1752 Treaty he also indicated that this was the *only* treaty that the defence would rely on. On the very first day of the trial, he said this: "we know about the treaties in 1760 and 1761 ... and ... we say despite those documents, the operative treaty today for our purposes, is the Treaty in 1752."[3] This advice, and the Crown's reaction to it, is one of the keys to understanding the subsequent failure of analysis at the Supreme Court of Canada.

It is normal procedure, in aboriginal rights cases, for the Crown to lead evidence establishing that the offence took place; for example, that the accused was fishing at a particular place and time in violation of a statute or regulation. Once that is established, it is then up to the native defendant to show that he has a constitutional right that shelters him from that statute or regulation. For example, if the defendant wishes to establish a treaty right, he would normally have historians testify about the treaty he relies on. The Crown can then call its own historians to respond to, and perhaps disagree with, the defendant's historians.

In Donald Marshall, Jr's case, there was no real dispute that he had caught and sold eels in contravention of federal fisheries regulations. The question was, could he show that he had a treaty right to shelter him from those regulations. But this is where Crown prosecutors made a regrettable decision. They agreed to call their expert witness first. As they explained to the trial judge on the first day of the trial, "we have agreed to call our historian, notwithstanding the fact that we haven't heard their side of the story. That is an accommodation to the defendants and it would allow us to at least get the ball rolling. We ask the court to keep in mind that we're doing that in the absence of knowing the documents that will be relied on by the other side and their theses."[4]

Already, on the very first day of trial, the stage was set for a disaster. The Crown understood that the thrust of Mr Marshall's treaty defence was the Treaty of 1752, and the Crown agreed to call evidence from its expert historian before the defendant's historians testified. Based on Mr Wildsmith's representation, the focus of the evidence of the Crown's expert historian was the Treaty of 1752. But as it turned out, Mr Marshall eventually abandoned his reliance upon that treaty, and switched his focus to the Mi'kmaq-British treaties of 1760–61. Mr Marshall's lawyer advised the court of this change of position after Dr Patterson, the Crown's historian, had completed his evidence, and before the defence called his own expert historians to testify.

It is perplexing that this was allowed to happen. The Crown's case was gravely wounded. Some of the evidence necessary for the Crown to respond to the claims that would later be made about the Halifax Treaties of 1760–61 had not been elaborated.[5] Absent the elaboration of that evidence, when the case was heard at the Supreme Court of Canada that court fashioned its own version of the history of Nova Scotia by way of concluding that the Treaties conferred a right to hunt, fish, and gather on Maritime Mi'kmaq. Referring to the Supreme Court of Canada's analysis, Dr Patterson has written that the court's historical analysis "has no evidentiary support that I have ever encountered."[6] To take just one example, when the case reached the Supreme Court of Canada the decision of that court turned largely on the interpretation of *one* document (a document recording Maliseet-British treaty discussions dated 11 February 1760). But in his direct evidence at trial the Crown's expert witness *never mentioned* that document or the documents relevant to it. He did not mention it because no one had any idea that the document would figure significantly. After all, when he testified, Dr Patterson understood that the defence would be based upon the Treaty of 1752 and his evidence largely focused on that treaty. If Dr Patterson had known what the document would be said to stand for, he could have shown that the interpretation of the document that would later be adopted by the Supreme Court of Canada was obviously wrong. When Dr Patterson was cross-examined by the lawyer for Mr Marshall he was never once asked a question about the document.[7] All of this cannot be minimized as a small technical objection. The expert evidence tendered on behalf of Mr Marshall relating to the treaties and their historical context was rejected by the trial judge.[8] Dr Patterson's evidence was preferred, so presumably the trial judge would have preferred his evidence respecting the 11 February 1760 document. That a case so dependent on historical facts should turn against a party, based on a document that the party's witness, an expert historian, was never given the opportunity to explain in his evidence, reveals a serious flaw in the judicial process.

Why did Mr Marshall's lawyers so abruptly change their strategy from reliance on the 1752 treaty to the Halifax Treaties of 1760–61? Very simply, they had very little hope of succeeding under the Treaty of 1752. Mr Marshall was a Cape Breton Mi'kmaq. The Treaty of 1752 was signed by the chief of the Shubenacadie Band for the ninety-odd members of that band, and for no one else. That treaty could not be said to apply to Mr Marshall. But equally important, Dr Patterson testified that the Treaty of 1752 did not survive subsequent hostilities. The British, after all, were at war with the French and Mi'kmaq, including the Shubenacadie Mi'kmaq, after 1752 and for the rest of that decade. It is difficult to think that a Treaty of Peace that predated those hostilities could be said now to survive those hostilities and confer existing rights. The Supreme Court of Canada in the *Simon* case had said that not enough evidence had been presented to show that the Treaty of 1752 had been terminated. Here was that evidence. So Mr Marshall's lawyers prudently abandoned their position rather than have a court state that the 1752 Treaty was no longer relevant. They gambled everything on the Halifax Treaties of 1760–61.[9]

THE "TRUCKHOUSE" CLAUSE

While the evidence and argument in *Marshall (No. 1)* took up many volumes, required forty days of historical evidence, and involved hundreds of historical documents and hundreds of pages of written submissions, the very central issue for the trial court, once Mr Marshall's lawyer clarified that he was no longer relying on the Treaty of 1752, was the effect of a short clause in the Halifax Treaties of 1760–61.[10] That clause, known as the "trade clause" or "truckhouse clause," prohibited native trade with non-natives, except with government-appointed managers of truckhouses, and each of the Halifax Treaties provided that a truckhouse would be established at a particular location in Nova Scotia. "Truckhouses" were trading posts. The clauses were pretty much the same from treaty to treaty, varying only in relation to the location of the truckhouse. Here is the clause of

the Halifax Treaty with the LaHave band which the Supreme Court of Canada considered in *Marshall (No. 1)*: "And I do further engage that we will not traffick, barter or Exchange any Commodities in any manner but with such persons or the managers of such Truck houses as shall be appointed or Established by His Majesty's Governor at Lunenburg or Elsewhere in Nova Scotia or Accadia."[11]

Notice that the clause is written in the negative, as a prohibition. It does not say natives are *entitled* to trade at truckhouses. It says natives will *not* trade *except* with truckhouse managers. The clause says nothing whatsoever about natives having access to the *things* that were traded, for example furs and feathers. But despite the lack of explicit reference in the trade clause to any right either to trade, or to fish and hunt for the purpose of trading, Mr Marshall argued that those rights should be included in the clause.

The federal Crown argued, in response, that no such rights could be implied and that, in any event, since the whole point of the treaties was to receive the submissions of native peoples as subjects of the Crown, any native rights under the treaties were subject to law, then and now. In other words, the natives agreed by treaty to be subject to British law, including the fisheries regulation that Mr Marshall had violated when he went fishing for eels. So even if the treaty did contain an implied right of the sort claimed by Mr Marshall, it could do nothing for him. It was "subject to the overriding legislative authority of the state, the jurisdictional authority of which had been accepted by the Mi'kmaq in these treaties."[12] The constitutional protection afforded to treaties under s. 35 made no difference. One treaty right could not be plucked out for constitutional protection while ignoring other treaty terms that bore on that treaty right.

The trial judge took a very practical approach to these different arguments. He pointed out that the truckhouse clause was built on the assumption that there would be truckhouses.[13] But the truckhouses were wound down by 1762.[14] The trade clause, he said, gave the Mi'kmaq an implied right, "to *bring* the products of their hunting, fishing and gathering to a truckhouse to

trade."[15] But once the government decided to eliminate truck-houses, any native trade rights under the Halifax Treaties disappeared as well.[16]

While the ultimate disposition of the case by the trial judge makes practical sense, some of his comments caused confusion at the Supreme Court of Canada, and others were improperly disregarded in that court.

COMPETING APPROACHES TO HISTORY

It helps to have an understanding of the position of the federal Crown and the position of Mr Marshall on the relevant history, as well as the competing approaches to history, which were in contention at the trial. An appreciation of these positions makes it easier to explain the mistakes that Justice Binnie would ultimately make.

The position of the federal Crown was, in general terms, as follows.[17] Events in Nova Scotia during the Seven Years War marked a watershed in the relationship between natives and British in the province. In the half-century after Britain had won the colony in 1710, British official presence in the colony was limited to neglected outposts at Annapolis Royal and Canso. While efforts were made to treat with native peoples in 1725–26, 1749, and 1752, those treaties came to naught. Native peoples were closely allied with the French and joined with them in conflict with the British in that period. But profound changes were wrought in the decade prior to the Halifax Treaties of 1760 and 1761. Halifax was founded as a British settlement and military stronghold in 1749. In 1752 "foreign Protestants" were settled on the south shore. In 1755, after the outbreak of the Seven Years War, soldiers from New England besieged and captured Fort Beausejour, paving the way for the infamous expulsion that removed thousands of Acadians from the province while others fled into the forests for refuge. Then in 1758 a British naval force and some 13,000 British soldiers captured Fortress Louisbourg. The following year Quebec City itself surrendered to the British after General Wolfe's victory in the Battle

of the Plains of Abraham. In 1760 Montreal would capitulate, signalling the British conquest of New France. Already the first of the New England Planter migrants, some 7,000 of whom would soon settle vacated Acadian lands, were arriving in Nova Scotia.

These events were hard for the Mi'kmaq, Maliseet, and Passamaquoddy peoples of Nova Scotia. They were still reeling from an outbreak of disease in 1746–48 and the resulting "massive depopulation."[18] Now their French ally and provisioner was defeated, their Acadian friends were gone or scattered, British military power was ascendant and British settlements were growing. It was in this context that native peoples in Nova Scotia made treaties with British officials in the period 1759–61. Those treaties, and those treaties alone, described the treaty rights and obligations of native peoples in this region that are relevant today. Under those treaties, native people became subjects of the British Crown and agreed to live under British law equally with other British subjects. The treaties gave them no "special" treaty rights to carry on commerce or have access to resources. All of this is clearly described in the most detailed record of treaty discussions from this period, a document recording the speeches of Lieutenant-Governor Belcher and the Cape Breton Mi'kmaq chief in a treaty ceremony including three other Mi'kmaq chiefs in June of 1761. That document of the Governor's Farm Ceremony is crucial to understanding the Crown's position.[19]

On 25 June 1761 Lieutenant-Governor Belcher, members of his council, senior military officers, and "other officers and principal Inhabitants of Halifax" met with four native chiefs at the governor's farm in Halifax. The lieutenant-governor made a speech. What he said was interpreted by Mr Maillard, a French priest who had ministered to native people in Nova Scotia since 1735 and who was a fluent Mi'kmaq speaker. "I assure myself," he said, "that you submit yourselves to his [the King's] allegiance with hearts of Duty and Gratitude, as to your merciful conqueror." He referred to the power of the king's "mighty fleets and armies." The king would both punish and protect. To

have the king's protection, what was required of native peoples
was "fidelity and obedience" to the king. He referred to their
"vows of obedience." They would be "fellow subjects," "in the
wide and fruitful field of English liberty." They would be protected by British law; "the laws will be like a great hedge about
your Rights and properties." Repeatedly, native peoples were
referred to as "fellow subjects," "under one mighty Chief and
King, *under the same laws and for the same rights and Liberties.*"
They were to be "in full possession of English protection and liberty." The treaty was to apply "to their children's children."

After the lieutenant-governor's speech, the treaties were
signed. Hatchets were ceremonially buried. Only then did the
chief of the Cape Breton Indians speak. There was no "negotiation" whatever. The British proposed treaty terms. The lieutenant-governor spoke. The treaties were signed. There was
no discussion of native rights to "trade" or to have access to
resources. The nearest thing to a discussion about commerce
was the lieutenant-governor's assurance that natives would not
be cheated; "Your Traffick will be weighed and settled in the
scale of honesty."

The speech of the Cape Breton chief, "in the name of all the
rest," is equally telling. He said their "intentions were to yield
ourselves up to you without requiring any Terms on our part."
He thanked the British for their "merciful" behaviour. "We
must have wretchedly perished unless relieved by your humanity, for we were reduced to extremities." This point is emphasized repeatedly; that the British were "generous" to natives
who were in "distressed and piteous circumstances" and were
relieved from great want. He also acknowledged British power
in the region. "You are now master here"... "dispose of us as
you please"... "Receive us into your arms; into them we cast
ourselves." And he confirmed native submission to British law:
"As long as the Sun and Moon shall endure, as long as the Earth
on which I dwell shall exist in the same state you this day see it,
so long will I be your friend and Ally, *submitting myself to the
Laws of your Government, faithful and obedient to the Crown.*"

The ceremony then concluded, "with dancing and singing, after their manner upon joyful occasions, and Drinking His Majesty's Health under three vollies of Small Arms." The language of the speech of the Cape Breton chief is of unequivocal submission. Nowhere is there a hint of negotiations respecting, or special entitlement to, commerce or resources.

The historians who testified for Mr Marshall had an entirely different description of the treaties in this period. Their position was that British control of Nova Scotia at this time was "very tenuous."[20] They suggested that the treaties must be understood in this context. One of these historians, while acknowledging that the British had achieved military success by 1759–60, went so far as to say this: "The military reality, as I understand it, was that these successes for the British remained extremely fragile ... one reason ... that it was entirely conceivable that French naval sea power would very quickly become a factor as was shown quite dramatically in the French seizure of St. John's Newfoundland in 1762."[21]

It is puzzling that this historian should have been allowed to testify to these things. He himself limited the scope of his expertise to the time before 1720. Yet the trial judge allowed him to testify on matters well after that date.[22] The federal Crown should not have allowed his evidence to go unchallenged. Standard histories of the Seven Years War point out that in the fall of 1759 the British navy smashed the French fleet. In late August a French fleet from Toulon in the south of France, seeking to run the British Blockade, was destroyed at Lagos, off Portugal. Then in November another French fleet sailing from Brest suffered the same fate at Quiberon Bay on the west coast of France. "The French had seen their last effective squadron on the Atlantic destroyed."[23] The French navy was "eliminated as a strategic threat" in the Royal Navy's "most decisive victory until Trafalgar."[24]

The following spring, in response to pleas to relieve Quebec, the French could muster only four vessels. Two were captured by British ships blockading the French coast. The other two

were sunk in Chaleur Bay.[25] Its navy crippled, France could only watch helplessly as their colonies fell. British forces at Quebec were relieved by an entire British fleet in the spring of 1760. British forces seized French possessions in India and in the Carribean. It is, quite simply, historically inaccurate to characterize British control of Nova Scotia in 1760 or 1761 as "fragile" because of any threat from the French Navy.

Absent this evidence, the testimony of the historians called by Mr Marshall to the effect that British control of Nova Scotia was "tenuous, " was more forceful than it should have been. This was not fatal to the Crown's case. In fact, the trial judge would go on to reject the description advanced by Mr Marshall's defence of the historical context of the treaties.[26] But more powerful evidence might have dissuaded Justice Binnie from relying on that description, something that should not in any event have tempted him in the light of the trial judge's rejection of it. Mr Marshall's historian went on to testify that the natives, in this period, were "not a beaten people,"[27] and that the terms of the treaties "were not dictated" by the British.[28] Similarly, it was said the British documents of the period, including the treaties, should not be taken to mean what they say. This would be a "eurocentric understanding of the world."[29] For example, a British officer's description of natives as "naked and starving" really didn't mean that they were naked and starving.[30] Several documents describing native peoples as having "capitulated," really did not mean that natives had capitulated."[31] The record of the speeches at the Governor's Farm Ceremony in June of 1761 cannot be taken at face value because the interpreter at the Ceremony must have "smoothed over" the language that appears in the record.[32] Even the treaties themselves did not mean what they said. For ease of reference, here again, is the relevant language of the "Truckhouse Clause" that was central to the case: "And I do further promise for myself and my tribe that we will not ... hold any manner of commerce traffick nor intercourse with them [the French] ... And I do further engage that we will not traffick, barter or Exchange any Commodities in any manner but with such per-

sons or the managers of such Truckhouses as shall be appointed or Established by His Majesty's Governor."

This is what Dr W. Wicken, the historian testifying for Mr Marshall, said about the meaning of the clause under a very capable cross-examination by the federal Crown's lawyer, Michael Paré:

> Q. With respect to the ... truckhouse provision ... you've suggested that the individuals who are affected by this treaty could trade at other places and intended to do so ...
> A. Yes
> Q. Okay, and would that include trading with anyone with whom they wished to trade?
> A. Yes
> Q. Would that include the French?
> A. It might include the French, yes ...
> Q. So are you saying that also in this regard we cannot give any real meaning, or should we, to the plain ... what appears to be the plain reading of those words?
> A. Yes. That's what I am suggesting.[33]

According to Dr Wicken, the truckhouse clause, which prohibits trade with the French and prohibits trade outside truckhouses, meant, rather, that natives were entitled to trade wherever they liked with whomever they liked, *including the French*, and were *not* restricted to trading at truckhouses. His historical analysis was scarcely constrained by the language of historical documents. This historical approach permitted Mr Marshall's expert great interpretive scope. The record of the ceremony at Belcher's Farm in which native peoples were described as "subjects" of the King, "under the same laws and for the same rights and liberties" was not to be taken literally.[34] Even though the Mi'kmaq treaties of this period make no mention of earlier treaties, those earlier treaties were said to have been incorporated in the later treaties.[35]

The competing historical approaches to the treaties were very carefully considered by the trial judge. He rejected the approach

of Mr Marshall's expert, saying "The interpretation offered on behalf of the Defendant of the trade clause and the treaties, placed in the historical context which it suggested as the appropriate one, is not one that I accept." He went on to say, "The general intent of the 1760–61 Treaties would not have been the subject of any misunderstanding by the Mi'kmaq because of language or translation problems.[36] There was "no misunderstanding or lack of agreement between the British and the Mi'kmaq about the essential ingredients of these treaties as they appear in written form before me."[37] In other words, the documents meant what they said.

These conclusions by the trial judge were extremely important. They amounted to a rejection of much of the evidence advanced by Mr Marshall, and they confirmed that the treaty documents were accurate.[38] As a matter of law, all of this should have limited Justice Binnie's approach to the treaties. Instead, the majority decision reveals a lack of caution respecting both the trial judge's comments and the documents.

THE CAPE BRETON TREATY, AND THE QUESTION OF OTHER TREATIES

It is ironic that the Treaty of 1752, which applied to only one Mi'kmaq band and which soon became a dead letter due to subsequent war, later became fixed in the lore of the Mi'kmaq people as a treaty that applied to all Mi'kmaq people in New Brunswick and Nova Scotia and that endures to the present day.[39] For example, a former chief of the Pabineau First Nation in northern New Brunswick recently testified that when he was chief he photocopied the Treaty of 1752 and "gave it to everybody in the community."[40] In contrast, the Halifax Treaties of 1760 and 1761, which finally concluded a peace between the British and several Mi'kmaq bands, were long-forgotten. In fact, not until the 1970s were these treaties rediscovered in the Nova Scotia Archives; and before Mr Marshall's trial, no court anywhere had ever dealt with them.

The "newness" of the Halifax Treaties should have sounded an alarm. Lawyers and judges alike should have been very careful in dealing with these treaties for fear that what they might say might ultimately be unnecessary and inaccurate. This is fundamentally important to our judicial system. Courts are governed by a doctrine of precedent, meaning that lower courts are respectful of the ruling of their peers, and are bound by the decisions of higher courts. But strictly speaking, only the findings and rulings of courts that are essential to their ultimate decisions are binding on other courts. Non-essential comments, called "*obiter dictum*" (literally, comments made in passing) are properly avoided. In other words, courts are meant to decide disputes that are before them, and not things that are *not* before them.

But in the *Marshall (No. 1)* case, all of this was forgotten with respect to a very significant issue. The case involved one Mi'kmaq individual from Cape Breton, who was charged with illegal fishing. The case did *not* involve *any other* Mi'kmaq from anywhere else. Yet the courts treated the case as if Mi'kmaq from every band in the Maritime Provinces and Quebec were involved in the case. Repeatedly in his decision, the trial judge said that all the Mi'kmaq in Nova Scotia had entered into one of the Halifax Treaties of 1760–61. He said "every Mi'kmaq Sakamow (Chief) came to Halifax in 1760 and 1761 and entered into these treaties."[41] But that issue was not in front of him. Donald Marshall was from Cape Breton, and there is no doubt whatsoever that in June 1761 the "Chief of the Cape Breton Mi'kmaq" came to Halifax and signed a treaty with Lieutenant-Governor Belcher. The only question for the court was whether *that* treaty contained the commercial right to fish that Mr Marshall claimed. Whether other Mi'kmaq in Nova Scotia and New Brunswick had a similar treaty was not at issue. But the damage was done. When the Supreme Court of Canada rendered their decision in the *Marshall (No. 1)* case, they repeated what the trial judge had said; that all Mi'kmaq had such a treaty.[42] This comment on an issue that was not before the court raised expectations in every native community in the Maritime Provinces that they too had "Marshall rights."

In the *Stephen Marshall* case, the court was asked to revisit the question of whether all Mi'kmaq had a Halifax Treaty. The court expressed considerable doubt that all the historic bands had such a treaty. One judge, for example, said "it is not clear that all bands had in fact signed treaties,"[43] and pointed to evidence that perhaps only about half the existing Mi'kmaq bands had signed a treaty. The Supreme Court of Canada has now agreed that different treaties were made with different bands.[44] To take an example, one of the documents in evidence in *Marshall (No. 1)*, dated June 1764, says "some tribes who were never here before came from distant parts of the province to make their submissions."[45] Since the entire truckhouse system was dismantled in 1761–62, the treaty with these bands could not have contained a truckhouse clause or the right to hunt, fish, and gather that Justice Binnie annexed to it.

THE "CHAIN OF TREATIES" ARGUMENT

Still another issue respecting the 1760–61 Treaties was dealt with by the trial judge, and would later be mishandled by the Supreme Court of Canada. I need to digress to explain the point. After the British seized control of Nova Scotia in 1710, they attempted at different times to make treaties with native bands. They made treaties in 1726, 1728, 1749, and 1752. Finally, there were the Treaties of 1760–61.[46] There is no real dispute among lawyers and historians that the Treaties of 1760–61 endured, and endure to this day. But what has been controversial is the relevance of the earlier treaties. Here, the views of the natives and the Crown have differed markedly. The Crown says that the earlier treaties are irrelevant; that in each case they were followed by Mi'kmaq-British hostilities, which abrogated them.[47] The natives, on the other hand, say that the treaties form a "chain" so that the earlier treaties were "part and parcel" of what was agreed in the 1760–61 Treaties. They suggest the language of some of the earlier treaties is favourable to their claims to economic rights and to hunt and fish. For

example, the 1752 Treaty said the Indians will have "free liberty of Hunting and Fishing as usual" and "Free liberty" to bring what they have "for sale." The 1726 Treaty said natives "shall not be molested in their persons, Hunting, fishing & Shooting & Planting on their Planting grounds nor in any other their lawful occassions by his Majesty's subjects ..."

In making the argument that the Halifax 1760–61 Treaties incorporated the earlier treaties, Mr Marshall emphasized the first of the Halifax Treaties of 1760. This was the treaty with the Maliseet and Passamaquoddy, native peoples who lived in the St. John River valley and in Passamaquoddy Bay. They had executed a treaty with the British in both 1749 and 1726, and their 1760 Treaty explicitly incorporates parts of those earlier treaties.[48] Shortly after the Maliseet and Passamaquoddy Treaty was signed in early 1760 the British showed it to a Mi'kmaq Chief who said that "all the Tribe of Mickmacks would be glad to make peace upon the same Conditions," and sometime later the governor wrote that he had made peace "on the same terms" with Maliseet and Mi'kmaq. Mr Marshall argued that this meant all Mi'kmaq treaties contained the same terms as the Maliseet-Passamaquoddy Treaty, and those terms include the terms of all the earlier treaties.

All of this was hotly contested at the trial in *Marshall (No. 1)*. Accordingly, the trial judge was careful to deal with the evidence and argument on the point. He decided that the 1760–61 Mi'kmaq Treaties did not renew earlier treaties.[49] They simply don't contain any reference to any earlier treaties. But he said, "Beyond that, the contents" of the Maliseet-Passamaquoddy Treaty and the Mi'kmaq treaties, "are essentially the same." He came to this conclusion after simply comparing the written terms of the treaties. None of this is remarkable, until we come to consider how the Supreme Court of Canada dealt with the trial judge's comments and his reasoning on these things. Suffice it for now to say that the trial judge's analysis was distorted and said to stand for propositions that it simply does not stand for.

THE EMPHASIS ON THE WRITTEN TREATIES

Yet another basis for the failure at the Supreme Court of Canada was laid down very early in the trial of the case. Once again, it was linked to the original position of Mr Marshall, that the commercial right to fish that he was claiming arose out of the 1752 Treaty.

The Crown responded to this by pointing out that treaty rights that Mi'kmaq may have today could not be referable to the 1752 Treaty. Rather, treaty rights that endured to the present day could only arise from the Treaties of 1760–61. This is what counsel for the Crown said on the very first day of the trial: "The operative Treaties for determining Mr Marshall's Treaty rights in this case are the Treaties of 1760 and 61."[50] In saying this, all he was saying was that the Treaties of the 1760–61 period remain relevant, not the 1752 Treaty. But this approach affected the analysis of all the judges and lawyers involved in the case from the trial through to the Supreme Court of Canada. Indeed, there were *formal written* treaties between various Mi'kmaq bands and the governor of Nova Scotia that were discussed and signed at Halifax in 1760–61, and copies of some of those treaties survive to the present day. So the tendency in the case was to focus attention on these *written* treaties and the discussions surrounding them *at Halifax*, as reflecting existing native treaty rights. But when the Supreme Court of Canada turned its attention to the documentary evidence of those treaty discussions at Halifax, in rendering their decision in the *Marshall (No. 1)* case, they failed to consider extremely important historical evidence respecting British-native interactions *outside Halifax* in the months before the Halifax Treaties were signed. As a result, when the Supreme Court of Canada rendered its decision finding that there was a treaty right to hunt, fish, and gather, they got their history wrong. The foundation for their analysis was historically inaccurate. All because of the tendency to take a very narrow view of the relevant historical evidence.

THE CONSTITUTIONAL POSITION OF THE
GOVERNOR OF NOVA SCOTIA

Another mistake by the Supreme Court of Canada is once again attributable to Mr Marshall's change of position with respect to the 1752 Treaty. In 1752 Nova Scotia did not have a Legislature. It was governed by the British governor, as it had been since Nova Scotia became a British Colony in 1713, when it was ceded to Britain by France through the Treaty of Utrecht. In that period Nova Scotia was, in effect, a dictatorship. There were very few constraints on the power of the governor. His "prerogative" was unconstrained and his rule was law, leading settlers to complain that they were "slaves of Nova Scotia; the Creatures of Military Governors whose will is our law & whose Person is our God."[51] It was, accordingly, unnecessary for the prosecution in the *Marshall (No. 1)* case to discuss constitutional constraints affecting the governor that might be relevant to the interpretation of any treaties the governor concluded with native people. Everyone's focus was on 1752 and there were few constraints on the governor's powers in 1752.

But in 1758 Nova Scotia's House of Assembly began sitting. The presence of that House of Assembly totally changed the constitutional situation in Nova Scotia. Remember, the Glorious Revolution in England a century before had confirmed that Parliament made laws, and that the "prerogative" power of the king was limited. Once a House of Assembly was established in the Colony, the prerogative power of the king's representative in the Colony, the governor, was similarly limited,[52] including his treaty-making powers. Those limitations on his treaty-making powers were relevant to the Halifax Treaties with native bands in 1760–61. But the point was lost in the evidence because, it seems, everyone's attention was originally focused on the 1752 Treaty. When the trial judge wrote his decision in the *Marshall (No. 1)* case, he only touched very briefly on the constitutional position of the governor. He noted that the Legislature began sitting in 1758, but then he said this: "The Governor

retained the authority to negotiate treaties with the aboriginals after 1758 and approval by the Legislature of such treaties was not necessary."[53] In a certain sense, what the trial judge said here was right. The governor *did* have authority to negotiate treaties with native bands even after 1758, and there *were* some things for which legislative approval was not necessary. But in another sense, he was wrong. The law of treaties is more subtle than his statement suggests. There were important limitations on the power of the governor. In fact he had no constitutional ability to bind the British to the treaty that the Supreme Court of Canada would eventually decide that he agreed to. More than that, there was clear evidence of the governor's understanding of and adherence to his constitutional limitations. Unfortunately, the Supreme Court of Canada was not attentive to this.

THE NATIVE "WAY OF LIFE"

Yet another comment of the trial judge deserves mention, both because it influenced the decision of the Supreme Court of Canada and because it is perplexing. In asking himself whether the "truckhouse" clause gave the Mi'kmaq any right to fish or to sell fish, Trial Judge Embree said:

> The Mi'kmaq of the 18th century lived and obtained their food by hunting, fishing and gathering. It is clear that the British in Nova Scotia in 1760 would have understood that. The Mi'kmaq had been trading (primarily furs, but generally whatever their hunting, fishing and gathering produced) with Europeans for approximately 250 years before 1760. The price list negotiated to establish the values of certain skins and feathers that would be traded at the truckhouses illustrates some of the items that, it was anticipated, would be traded for the various commodities in the truckhouses. That was not an exclusive list. All three witnesses who testified concluded that fish might be among the items that the Mi'kmaq would bring to trade at the truckhouses. (That fish might be fresh or dried.)

I accept as inherent in these treaties that the British recognized and accepted the existing Mi'kmaq way of life. Moreover, it's my conclusion that the British would have wanted the Mi'kmaq to continue their hunting, fishing and gathering lifestyle. The British did not want the Mi'kmaq to become a long-term burden on the public treasury although they did seem prepared to tolerate certain losses in their trade with the Mi'kmaq for the purpose of securing and maintaining their friendship and discouraging their future trade with the French. I am satisfied that this trade clause in the 1760–61 Treaties gave the Mi'kmaq the right to bring the products of their hunting, fishing and gathering to a truckhouse to trade.[54]

So, according to the trial judge, the British, in the Halifax Treaties, "recognized and accepted the existing Mi'kmaq way of life," their "hunting, fishing and gathering lifestyle." It seemed to follow from this, according to the trial judge, that the Mi'kmaq had a *treaty* right to "bring the products of their hunting, fishing and gathering to a truckhouse to trade." As I have already described, he went on to say that this right only lasted as long as the truckhouse system, so that when the truckhouse system collapsed later in 1761–62, the native right to bring things to it for trade perished as well. Accordingly, in the view of the trial judge, the Halifax Treaties of 1760–61 contained no treaty right that continued into the present day. They did not give Mr Marshall a right to fish and to sell fish. So he was guilty of fishing eels in breach of federal fisheries regulations.

The trial judge's suggestion that the British must have accepted "as inherent in these treaties" the "existing Mi'kmaq way of life," is a remarkably bold and sweeping statement. It is also very perplexing, as it is unclear precisely what he meant by the comment. He might have meant merely that Mi'kmaq lived in Nova Scotia, that they had a particular way of life, and that this was something the British were aware of and was an assumption underlying the treaties. If this was what the trial judge meant, he was merely stating the obvious. But in saying that "*inherent in these treaties* ..." the British recognized and

accepted the existing Mi'kmaq way of life, the trial judge's comments seem to suggest that the Mi'kmaq "way of life" became a treaty right. If this is what he meant, it is not very plausible. There are ready examples of native practices that would have been unacceptable to the British. To illustrate, consider the point that Nova Scotia made at the Supreme Court of Canada in *Stephen Marshall*. It is well documented that in the eighteenth century the whole of Nova Scotia (including present-day New Brunswick) was a valuable preserve of timber for the Royal Navy. So precious were the pine forests in Nova Scotia that in 1721 and 1729 the British Parliament at Westminister passed legislation prohibiting cutting any pine trees in Nova Scotia.[55] It is also well documented that native peoples commonly burned the forests to promote the growth of the forage preferred by moose, which native people hunted.[56] Burning trees ruined them for timber. The point being that it is simply incorrect to say that the British "accepted" the Mi'kmaq "way of life." The British would not and could not have "accepted" such a practice as burning forests, something that was very much part of the native "way of life." The trial judge was imprudent in so sweepingly suggesting that the British accepted the native way of life. Later, the Supreme Court of Canada was equally imprudent in accepting the point uncritically. It is a remarkable leap of judicial imagination to propose that a treaty clause modestly prohibiting trade except at "truckhouses," encompasses a treaty right to an entire "way of life."

THE EVIDENCE OF MI'KMAQ FISHING AND TRADE IN FISH

While Mr Marshall had fished eels, and had been charged for unlawfully fishing eels, it was evident that the case was a "test" case about a broader native claim to fish commercially. In this context, it is fair to expect that the judges would pay close attention to the evidence of fishing that had been presented at trial and describe that evidence. Unfortunately, the trial judge spoke in generalities. He said, "the Mi'kmaq had been trading (pri-

marily furs, but generally whatever their hunting, fishing and gathering produced) with Europeans for approximately 250 years before 1760."[57]

The evidence was more subtle. There is no doubt that the Mi'kmaq had traded furs with Europeans from earliest contact with Europeans in the early 1500s. There was substantial evidence of the fur trade. But the evidence of fishing and any trade in fish was different. First, the evidence of the species of fish harvested by native peoples was limited. This is what the expert historian who testified for Mr Marshall said in response to the question "what species of marine resources were harvested": "Salmon, bass, eels, herring was another one, alewives,[58] seals. To a limited extent, walruses ... Those are the principal fish resources, at least that I've encountered."[59]

Second, the evidence of native *trade* in fish was extremely limited. The *only* clear example of this trade between natives and non-natives was Reverend Seycombe's purchase of eels in 1761 which, as we have seen, was unlawful. The witnesses described trade in fish as an "occasional" or "incidental" trade[60] between native people and settlers. Dr John Reid, a historian called to testify for Mr Marshall, distinguished between the fur trade at the truckhouses and a smaller scale trade between natives and settlers: "It seems that there were native persons who were selling small amounts of fish ... who came into settlements to do that, and that a certain amount of buying and selling went on of that nature. Q. And what did you mean when you referred to substantial trade ... ? It seems to me this trade that took place on a less formal basis was on a relatively small scale. It's a case of some individuals coming in with a few things to sell, whereas my sense of the more formal trade is that it would be of large volume. There would be ... certainly among the major commodities would be furs and that those would be the distinctions that I would make."[61]

So any trade in fish, according to the evidence, was an occasional and small-scale trade, limited to a few species, which took place between natives and settlers *outside* the truckhouses. It was not clear that the truckhouse trade involved trade in fish.

There was no historical evidence of such a trade. The trial judge said that "fish *might* be among the items that the Mi'kmaq would bring to trade at the truckhouse."[62] In fact, none of the historians referred to any evidence suggesting that fish was *in fact* traded at truckhouses.[63] This is remarkable since the historians who testified for Mr Marshall referred in great detail to the native history in New England and the extensive experience with truckhouses in Massachusetts. It was overwhelmingly clear that natives traded furs at truckhouses. But there was no evidence of a native trade in fish at truckhouses. Dr Reid, as we have seen, distinguished between the fur trade at the truckhouses and the trade of fish to settlers.

But when the case reached the Supreme Court of Canada, Justice Binnie does not appear to have looked at the evidence *behind* the trial judge's comment that for 250 years the Mi'kmaq had traded "whatever their hunting, fishing, and gathering produced." He simply took the trial judge's generalizations, and ran with them, transforming a small-scale, occasional, incidental trade of a few fish species into an apparently wide-open commercial right to fish for a moderate livelihood. Moreover, he interpreted the "truckhouse" clause to encompass a right to harvest and trade fish in the absence of any historical evidence that fish had been traded at truckhouses, and in the *face* of evidence that the trade at truckhouses was of a different character from any native trade in fish. The trade at the truckhouses was a large-scale fur trade, whereas any native trade in fish, according to the evidence, was a small-scale, occasional trade limited to individuals *outside* the truckhouses.

5

The Court of Appeal

The trial judge convicted Mr Marshall of unlawful fishing. Mr
Marshall appealed to the Nova Scotia Court of Appeal. Before
looking at their decision, I need to explain the role of that court,
compared to the role of the trial judge.

Courts of Appeal are courts of error and courts of "principle." Their job is to correct mistakes, particularly legal mistakes, made by the trial courts. By and large, appeal courts are
preoccupied with the application of law, and this points to an
extremely important difference between trial courts and appeal
courts – their approach to evidence. Trial judges are "triers of
fact." They weigh the evidence and decide what the facts are.
Suppose, for example, someone is charged with theft. It is the
trial judge's job to consider all the evidence, assess the credibility
of the witnesses, and make a "finding of fact" as to whether the
accused person took what was said to have been stolen. It is
only very rarely that Courts of Appeal involve themselves in
findings of fact. As one text puts it, "the findings of fact of the
trial judge are almost sacrosanct."[1] Instead, Courts of Appeal
usually deal with questions of law. In our example, if the trial
judge finds that the accused in fact took the thing, it is highly
unlikely that the Court of Appeal would overrule that decision;
the evidence would have to be compelling and clear that the
accused obviously did not take the thing before a Court of
Appeal would overturn the trial judge's decision. But it is a ques-

tion of law whether "taking" is theft. That is something a Court of Appeal would deal with. The Supreme Court of Canada, in this context, is just another Court of Appeal. Its job is not to make findings of fact but to rule on questions of law. These are long-established rules fundamental to the structure of our judicial system, and there is very good practical reason for them. Lower courts have the time – in the case of *Marshall (No. 1)*, forty days spread over nineteen months – to carefully review the evidence and documents, read extensive written submissions, hear detailed oral arguments, and ask questions. In the trial court in *Marshall (No. 1)* there were 4,300 pages of testimony, hundreds of pages of exhibits and written submissions, and three days of argument. In contrast, at the Supreme Court of Canada, written submissions are typically limited to forty pages for each side, and each side can argue for one hour. After all, the courts of appeal are supposed to be occupied with matters of principle, not the minutiae of specific historical fact.

In the Nova Scotia Court of Appeal Mr Marshall raised three arguments of particular interest. First, he argued that the Treaties of 1760–61 incorporated the earlier treaties. The Court of Appeal rejected this argument. It said the trial judge had looked carefully at all the historical evidence and decided that the earlier treaties were not part of the 1760–61 Treaties. This was a finding of fact. The Court of Appeal was not going to interfere with it.[2]

Mr Marshall's second argument in the Court of Appeal, and the court's answer to it, is more interesting. This was Mr Marshall's main argument to the trial judge that *implicit* in the truckhouse clause was a native *right* to catch and sell fish. Remember, the truckhouse clause was a prohibition, "we will not traffic ... but with ... the managers of such truckhouses ..." The Court of Appeal could find no precedent for suggesting that such a negative clause could be said to grant a *right*.[3] They rejected the argument, and they were right in doing so. There is little logic in saying that because an agreement prohibits "X," it entitles the doing of "Y." Doing Y might well be permissible, but our entitlement to do things flows from a long-standing pre-

sumption of British law that anything is lawful unless it is prohibited.[4] A *right* to catch and sell fish could not arise from a
prohibition on trading except at truckhouses. It could arise only
from the presumption of British law that catching and selling
fish was lawful, unless prohibited.[5] And under the Treaties of
1760-61, said the Court of Appeal, the Mi'kmaq "became British subjects and received the benefit of British law."[6] Any rights
Mr Marshall had to fish or trade fish were the rights accorded
to him by British laws, which his forebears had submitted to by
treaty. But nothing in, or implicit in, the treaty could be
described as a special "treaty right" to fish or sell fish. On this
analysis the trial judge was wrong to suggest even that there was
a treaty right to "bring" things to the truckhouse, while the
truckhouse system lasted.

Also, in response to the suggestion that a right to catch and
sell fish should be implied in the truckhouse clause, the Court of
Appeal raised an extremely important point. The Instructions to
Nova Scotia's governor from the British Government in London
said very clearly that he was not to "consent to any law wherein
the natives or inhabitants of the Province of Nova Scotia ... are
put on a more advantageous footing than those of this Kingdom." What is important about this point is that it raises the
issue of the authority of the governor to grant the treaty right
the natives were claiming. The Court of Appeal pointed to this
Instruction and said the governor could not have given natives
"a preferential trading position."[7] This point would give Justice
Binnie trouble at the Supreme Court of Canada. But it would
also distract him from the more fundamental problem of the
governor's authority; one that is fatal to the treaty right he
would go on to describe.

The third argument presented to the Court of Appeal by Mr
Marshall's lawyer, Mr Wildsmith, is not as significant for its
substance as it is for its genesis. Remember the change of position at trial, first relying solely on the 1752 Treaty and then
announcing a wholly new basis for the defence under the Treaties of 1760–61. In the Court of Appeal Mr Marshall once again
advanced a wholly new position. As the court commented, it

had not been "urged upon the trial judge nor raised in his factum," but was only raised "in oral submission before the panel."[8] The point was this: the "truckhouse clause" provided (obviously) for the establishment of truckhouses; but the British had ceased providing truckhouses in the early 1760s, and this, it was argued, was a violation of the treaty. The Court of Appeal said that the end of the truckhouse system meant merely that natives were no longer limited to trading at truckhouses. They could trade with whomever they liked. There was no enduring right to truckhouses or to trade at them. So the Court of Appeal dismissed the new argument. But Mr Marshall would once again change his position in the Supreme Court of Canada – this time with powerful effect. The Supreme Court of Canada would fully accept the new argument. Yet a close analysis of the documents reveals how frail the argument was.

6

The Decision of the Supreme Court of
Canada: *Marshall (No. 1)*

Mr Marshall's appeal had been denied by the Nova Scotia Court of Appeal. Again he appealed, this time to the Supreme Court of Canada. The appeal was argued in November 1998. The attorney general of New Brunswick intervened in the appeal, as did two native groups and a group representing Nova Scotia fishermen. Intervenors are entitled to make arguments on issues raised in the appeal, and can argue in support of one side or another. Nova Scotia did not intervene in the case, even though it was entitled to do so.

Seven judges of the Supreme Court of Canada heard Mr Marshall's appeal: Chief Justice Lamer, Justice L'Heureux Dubé, Justice Gonthier, Justice Cory, Justice Iacobucci, Justice Binnie, and Justice McLachlin. It is worth noting that none of them was from the Maritime Provinces. The court was not unanimous in its decision, splitting 5–2. Justice Binnie wrote the majority decision, finding that Mr Marshall had a treaty right to fish and sell fish, one aspect of a wider treaty right to hunt, fish, gather, and trade for a moderate livelihood. Justice McLachlin[1] wrote a minority opinion, with Justice Gonthier, disagreeing with the majority and arguing that there was no such treaty right.

Decisions of the Supreme Court of Canada are not usually light reading. They are often very difficult for lawyers to read and understand, let alone members of the public untrained in law. This decision was different only in the sense that it is more

difficult to read than many. The analysis is not straightforward. (If you want to read the decision, see the appendix.) The decision is, of course, the only source of the court's analysis and reasons. Judges do not, for example, give interviews to elaborate their decisions. But one other useful source of information is the transcript of the oral argument before the court. The lawyer for each side is given one hour to present its case, and the judges often ask questions of the lawyers. Those questions are typically very pointed and sometimes reveal the judges' thinking respecting the critical issues in the case. The transcript of the oral argument is available from the court, and it is helpful in understanding the *Marshall (No. 1)* decision. What follows is a brief description of Justice Binnie's decision as well as the major points of disagreement raised by Justice McLachlin.

Justice Binnie said the trial judge made mistakes in his decision. He pointed out that the trial judge said that the British "accepted the Mi'kmaq way of life in the treaties" so that they gave the Mi'kmaq the "right to bring the products of their hunting, fishing and gathering to a truckhouse to trade." He also pointed out that the trial judge said the written treaties contained "all the terms and conditions mutually agreed to." He said these two comments were contradictory. They couldn't stand together.[2] The treaty document clearly didn't grant any right to a "way of life," so it made no sense to say in the same breath that the treaty document contained all the agreed terms, and that it encompassed the Mi'kmaq way of life. He went on to say that the trial judge had erred in law by failing to consider the concerns of native people, reflected in the records of the treaty negotiations, in assessing their treaty rights. So the trial judge's analysis was wrong. Justice Binnie went on to substitute his own analysis.

He agreed that the written language of the "truckhouse" clause, considered by itself, did not help Mr Marshall. "The words," he said, "standing in isolation do not support the appellant's [Mr Marshall's] argument."[3] In saying this, Justice Binnie was essentially agreeing with what the Court of Appeal had said. But Justice Binnie said it was necessary to look beyond the words of the treaty: "the question is whether the underlying

negotiations produced a broader agreement between the British and the Mi'kmaq" that the treaty only partly recorded.[4] "The bottom line," said Justice Binnie, was the need to discern the "common intention" of the parties to the treaty.[5] As a matter of principle, this approach cannot be faulted. The truckhouse clause alone clearly contains no right to hunt, fish, or gather. If in fact there was an agreement that wasn't fully recorded, then the agreement should be given effect. But as a practical matter, such an enquiry is fraught with danger. It led Justice Binnie to try to piece together what must have taken place in specific discussions over 250 years ago, with few written records to guide him. And it was in finding an agreement outside the written terms of the treaty that Justice Binnie drove off the rails.

Justice Binnie referred to the record of discussions between the British and chiefs of the Maliseet and Passamaquoddy Indians of the St. John River and Passamaquoddy Bay in present day New Brunswick, in February 1760. These, he said, were the "key negotiations."[6] In particular, Justice Binnie referred to a document dated 11 February 1760, which contains the following passages:

His Excellency then demanded of them, Whether they were directed by their Tribes, to propose any other particulars to be Treated upon at this time. To which they replied that *their Tribes had not directed them to propose any thing further than that there might be a Truckhouse established, for the furnishing them with necessaries*, in Exchange for their Peltry, and that it might, at present, be at Fort Frederick.

Upon which His Excellency acquainted them that in case of their now executing a Treaty in the manner proposed, and its being ratified at the next General Meeting of their Tribes the next Spring, a Truckhouse should be established at Fort Frederick, agreable to their desire, and likewise at other Places if it should be found necessary, for furnishing them with such Commodities as shall be necessary for them, in Exchange for their Peltry & and that great care should be taken, that the Commerce at the said Truckhouses should be

managed by Persons on whose Justice and good Treatment, they might always depend; and that it would be expected that the said Tribes should not Trafic or Barter and Exchange any Commodities at any other Place, nor with any other Persons. Of all which the Chiefs expressed their entire Approbation. [Emphasis added.][7]

The document had been the subject of considerable interest to the Judges in the oral argument at the Supreme Court of Canada. In Justice Binnie's view, the words in this document that I have highlighted showed that the Indians had demanded a truckhouse. And the fact that the Indians had demanded truckhouses was critically important. It showed that they had "pushed a trade agenda."[8] "It cannot be supposed," said Justice Binnie, "that the Mi'kmaq raised the subject of trade concessions [the demand for truckhouses] merely for the purpose of subjecting themselves to a trade restriction" [the requirement that they trade *only* at truckhouses].[9] Instead, according to Justice Binnie, it must have been intended that the natives were to have "continuing access to wildlife to trade."[10] They had, as he put it, a treaty right to "continue to provide for their own sustenance by taking the products of their hunting, fishing and other gathering activities, and trading for what in 1760 was termed "necessaries."[11] In other words, natives had a treaty right to hunt, fish, and gather commercially. Justice Binnie was careful to qualify this commercial right. It was not an open-ended treaty right to accumulate wealth, but a more modest right to a "moderate livelihood" including "such basics as food, clothing and housing, supplemented by a few amenities."[12]

In sharp disagreement with Justice Binnie, Justice McLachlin dissented. She essentially agreed with the trial judge in her dissent. She said that the truckhouse clause of the treaties gave natives the "right to bring goods" to the truckhouses so long as the truckhouses survived. When the truckhouses were done away with, the native right to bring goods to them also died out. There was no native treaty right to trade separate or independ-

ent from the truckhouses.[13] Accordingly, there was no treaty right that survived to the present that could assist Mr Marshall in defence of the charges against him for unlawful fishing.

Justice McLachlin referred to the same 11 February 1760 . document of British-Maliseet discussions that figured so prominently in Justice Binnie's decision. She was not impressed by Justice Binnie's suggestion that the document reflected a native *demand* for truckhouses. Instead she referred to other clauses in the document, and said that the document merely "highlights the concessions" made by both the natives and the British, to achieve peace.[14] The "dominant purpose" of the treaties, she said, was to "prevent the Mi'kmaq from maintaining alliances with the French."[15] The deal, according to Justice McLachlin, was that the Mi'kmaq agreed not to trade with the French, and in return the British provided them with truckhouses where they would have "stable trade at guaranteed and favourable terms."[16]

Justice McLachlin also pointed out that under the treaties, native peoples acknowledged British sovereignty and "automatically acquired all rights enjoyed by other British subjects in the region," including the liberty to trade, except to the extent that the treaty limited that right by confining native trade to truckhouses. It was expected, she said, that native peoples would continue to trade as British subjects, not through any treaty entitlement. While the truckhouse system lasted, their trade was restricted, but when the truckhouse system collapsed, natives were "free to trade with whomever they wished 'under the' general laws of the province."[17]

Justice McLachlin's dissent, then, was based on her agreement with the trial judge's findings, her review of the language of the treaty, and her review of the historical circumstances surrounding the treaty – the treaty's "historical and cultural backdrop."[18] To support her dissent, Justice McLachlin summarized the principles of treaty interpretation that were scattered in various previous decisions of the Court. This summary may prove to be an enduring statement of the interpretive approach to treaties, and it is relevant to set out the principles Justice McLachlin described:

1   Aboriginal treaties constitute a unique type of agreement
    and attract special principles of interpretation ...

2   Treaties should be liberally construed and ambiguities or
    doubtful expressions should be resolved in favour of the
    aboriginal signatories ...

3   The goal of treaty interpretation is to choose from
    among the various possible interpretations of common
    intention the one which best reconciles the interests of
    both parties at the time the treaty was signed ...

4   In searching for the common intention of the parties, the
    integrity and honour of the Crown is presumed ...

5   In determining the signatories' respective understanding
    and intentions, the court must be sensitive to the unique
    cultural and linguistic differences between the parties ...

6   The words of the treaty must be given the sense which
    they would naturally have held for the parties at the
    time ...

7   A technical or contractual interpretation of treaty word-
    ing should be avoided ...

8   While construing the language generously, courts cannot
    alter the terms of the treaty by exceeding what "is possi-
    ble on the language" or realistic ...

9   Treaty rights of aboriginal peoples must not be inter-
    preted in a static or rigid way. They are not frozen at the
    date of signature. The interpreting court must update
    treaty rights to provide for their modern exercise. This
    involves determining what modern practices are reason-
    ably incidental to the core treaty right in its modern con-
    text ...[19]

Justice McLachlin reasoned that because these principles dictated that "each treaty must be considered in its unique historical and cultural context,"[20] it was not proper to make a
distinction suggested by the Nova Scotia Court of Appeal, dif-
ferentiating land cession treaties and peace treaties. It was not,
she said, "useful to slot treaties into different categories, each
with its own rules of interpretation."[21]

While the principle expressed by Justice McLachlin that each treaty must be interpreted in its unique historical context may well make it unnecessary to "pigeon-hole" different treaties with different rules of interpretation, the distinction urged by the Court of Appeal has the merit of acknowledging the unique character of Nova Scotia treaties. Treaties elsewhere in Canada, such as the "Robinson Treaties" in Ontario, the "Douglas Treaties" in British Columbia, and the "Numbered Treaties" in the west were made with native peoples as non-native settlement peacefully advanced. The treaties on the east coast had a different genesis. Uniquely, treaties in this region[22] were made by native peoples who shared defeat in a brutal war. As we will see, failure to acknowledge this fact assisted in the failure of the majority's analysis in *Marshall (No. 1)*.

Most of the cases establishing the principles summarized by Justice McLachlin arose out of the western treaties. That may explain why those principles are incomplete. Two more principles should, in my view, inform native treaty interpretation in our Courts. First, while Justice McLachlin's summary of principles refers to "treaty rights," it does not mention native treaty obligations. The language of native treaty claims in our courts has been the persistent discussion of treaty "rights," ignoring the reality of native treaty obligations. As we will see, the Halifax treaties specify significant native obligations. A principled approach to native treaty obligations is no less imperative than a principled approach to native rights.[23] Second, none of the enumerated principles expressly recognizes the problem of constraints on treaty-making. For example, the British governor in Nova Scotia was limited by law in the treaty terms he could negotiate. Similarly, in some native societies, native laws or customs may have limited native signatories. Either way, an approach that mandates "liberal interpretation" and "reconciling interests" has a particular force and does not acknowledge the possibility of constraints. It was, in part, the failure of the Supreme Court of Canada to recognize relevant constraints on the treaty-making powers of the governor of Nova Scotia that led it astray in *Marshall (No. 1)*.

7

Fire on the Water, and *Marshall (No. 2)*

It is not my purpose to detail the reaction to *Marshall (No. 1)* in communities in the Maritime Provinces.[1] But that reaction cannot be ignored. The uncertainty, antagonism, violence, and rhetoric that followed the decision are, in part, why it demands such close scrutiny.

Almost immediately after the release of the decision, in September 1999, native people asserted that their new-found treaty right entitled them to exploit many of the Maritime region's natural resources, including the lobster fishery. The lobster industry is one of the few remaining viable fisheries sustaining rural coastal communities in the Maritimes. The richest lobster grounds are in southwest Nova Scotia and in the southern Gulf of St Lawrence. Elsewhere the lobster harvest is less lucrative, but everywhere the industry is highly regulated. Everything, including numbers of licencees, numbers of traps, minimum lobster size, and open and closed seasons, is tightly controlled. Native peoples had already been accorded a limited lobster "food-fishery," but *Marshall (No. 1)* spoke of commercial rights. Following the decision, natives from Burnt Church in Miramichi Bay, New Brunswick, set traps in the water, disregarding the closed season in that area, as did natives in southwest Nova Scotia and elsewhere. Lobster fishing in most areas is limited to about two months annually. Non-natives watched in frustration as natives engaged in a fishery that ignored the care-

ful controls of the regulated fishery. In the context of rhetoric
from the native community emphasizing their treaty entitlement
to a "moderate livelihood," and the presence in the water of
unknown numbers of lobster pots, certainly many thousands,
non-natives were anxious, fearing that their investments in
boats and gear, and their incomes, were threatened. As one representative put it, referring to the thousands of native people
apparently capable of asserting "treaty rights," "I don't know
what the court meant by a reasonable livelihood ... but if it's in
the order of $30,000 to $40,000 ... the current industry doesn't
have the capacity. That represents over 30 percent of the entire
landed value of the Nova Scotia fishery."[2] For others, the anxiety took on a more sinister character. "Nobody wants [violence]
but we've all got guns"..."I don't want to see anybody get hurt
... but I'm not going to be a second-class citizen."[3]

For their part, many natives felt that they were merely exercising their legitimate lawful rights. After all, hadn't the
Supreme Court of Canada just decided that they had a treaty
right to fish and sell their catch? Natives variously claimed the
right to fish for scallops and snow-crab; "if some fisherman gets
300,000 pounds of snowcrab, then we expect to get that quota
for every single Mi'kmaq," said one native leader.[4] It was a recipe for disaster. In early October in Miramichi Bay, non-natives
in perhaps 100 or more boats destroyed several thousand native
traps, a scene that was repeated near Yarmouth. A school in
Burnt Church and fish processing plants on the north shore
of New Brunswick were vandalized. Buildings were burned on
the Burnt Church Reserve. Non-native vehicles were torched.
Native "warriors" occupied the wharf at Burnt Church, and the
RCMP reinforced the local detachment. Later that month,
charges were laid against non-natives for their part in these
events. The violence continued into the summer of 2000 when
native fishermen undertook a commercial lobster fishery in St.
Mary's Bay, Nova Scotia, and federal fisheries officials boarded
boats and impounded equipment.

All the while, a torrent of stories in local newspapers, and on
television and the radio reported on developments. Hardly a

day went by without discussion of the *Marshall* case and its implications. Some native leaders issued very broad assertions of native entitlement that the decision of the Supreme Court of Canada appeared to endorse. One native leader said this: "We've never surrendered our land or our resources and that's the question that has to be answered. In our view, the treaty is just an off-shoot of that notion of aboriginal title. And aboriginal title covers all aspects – whether it's hunting, fishing, mining, land or return of our land."[5] Similarly, the federal minister of Indian Affairs suggested that "the treaties were ways of sharing the resources" and that the decision in *Marshall (No. 1)* "will likely not be confined to fish."[6]

Such comments, and native activities "on the water," must be considered in the social and economic context in which they arose. While there are pockets of flourishing economic activity and industrial expansion in the Maritimes, rural New Brunswick and Nova Scotia are highly resource-dependent and economically struggling. For many years the region, and particularly its rural constituency, has experienced out-migration for want of economic opportunity. Natural resources are the economic mainstay, meagre though it may be, for much of the rural Maritime Provinces. And here was a decision from the highest court in the country that appeared to place a significant burden on those resources – a burden that was uncertain in scope and seemed to pose a significant threat to non-native livelihoods.

So intense was the fallout from the Court's decision in *Marshall (No. 1)*, and so great was the confusion, that in mid-October one of the intervenors in the appeal took an unprecedented step. The "West Nova Fishermen's Coalition" applied to the Supreme Court of Canada for a "rehearing" of certain issues, for a new trial, and for a "stay" of the court's decision in *Marshall (No. 1)*. Of particular concern to West Nova was what it perceived as a threat to the very lucrative lobster fishery and the economic interests of its members by an unregulated native fishery in areas and at times closed to non-native fishermen.

This motion was highly unusual. In September the majority of the Supreme Court of Canada had acquitted Mr Marshall of the

charges against him. Justice Binnie said that very thing: "I would therefore allow the appeal and order an acquittal on all charges."[7] Mr Marshall's trial was over. He was a free man. He was not guilty of the charges against him according to the highest court in the land. Accordingly, there was nothing to "stay." There was nothing to "rehear." Mr Marshall could not be "retried." It is a fundamental rule of our judicial system that a person finally tried and acquitted cannot be retried on the same charges. In any ordinary case, the West Nova application would have been dismissed out of hand.

But *Marshall (No. 1)* was no ordinary case. The East Coast was in an uproar, and the Supreme Court of Canada seized upon the West Nova application to comment on their own decision. Any other method of asking the court to revisit its decision would have taken months or years to work its way back up to the Supreme Court of Canada, and in the meantime the uncertainty would remain. West Nova offered a shortcut, albeit through an inappropriate application to the Court. Six[8] of the seven judges who had heard *Marshall (No. 1)* presided in the "rehearing." They rejected the West Nova application, but in doing so they issued several pages of comments on their earlier decision, "clarifying" that decision.

In large part, both the West Nova application and the Court's response to it were prompted by suggestions from native groups that natives could now fish and hunt, and exploit other resources, without regard to licensing regimes, closed seasons, quotas, or other regulations. Tight regulation has long controlled the lobster fishery, which was the main concern of West Nova, and every one of the issues described in the West Nova application, as the basis for a rehearing and stay, referred to the federal government's power to regulate native fishing. While rejecting the West Nova application, the Court confirmed that government could regulate the native fishery and that native peoples were *not* guaranteed an "open season in the fisheries."[9] The focus of the argument in *Marshall (No. 1)* was on whether or not a treaty right existed, not on the extent to which such a right could be regulated. So the Court's comment on this point

was welcome reassurance to non-natives, but was, while unusual, not remarkable. Government regulatory authority over native rights had been discussed in other decisions of the Court, and the Court simply pointed to those decisions.[10] In other respects, however, the Court's comments were quite exceptional. Issues that were simply not addressed by the Court in its original decision were now elaborated. The Court said, for example, that the native treaty right to "gather" meant "the types of the resources traditionally 'gathered' in an aboriginal economy."[11] The comment was no doubt calculated to assuage concerns respecting native assertions of rights to a variety of natural resources, including oil and minerals, and would be the focus of much attention in the *Stephen Marshall* case, which dealt with native claims to log. Particularly exceptional was this passage: "The emphasis ... was in 1760 ... on assuring the Mi'kmaq equitable access to identified resources for the purpose of earning a moderate living."[12]

Nothing in the original *Marshall (No. 1)* decision supports this assertion that the treaty right was only a right to "equitable access," and it represented a significant change in the Court's description of the treaty right. In *Marshall (No. 1)* the right to "hunt, fish and gather" was described as that very thing, a right. On ordinary principles described by earlier decisions of the Supreme Court of Canada, that treaty right could only be abridged where "as little infringement as possible" occurred, and where, if treaty rights were expropriated, fair compensation was available.[13] Now the right was qualified as a right to "equitable access." The treaty right did not need to be "satisfied before non-natives have access to the same resources for recreational or commercial purposes."[14] While the comment was probably intended to mute the exuberance of native demands following *Marshall (No. 1)*, it also increased the confusion surrounding the decision. What is "equitable access"? How is it measured? How were native rights to hunt, to fish, and to gather for a moderate livelihood squared with a right to "equitable access"?

Equally perplexing was the Court's comment that "the exercise of the treaty rights will be limited to the area traditionally used by the local community," meaning the community's "traditional hunting and fishing grounds."[15] Donald Marshall, Jr, was from Membertou, Cape Breton, an Indian Reserve near Sydney. Yet the charges against him in *Marshall (No. 1)* were for fishing in Pomquet Harbour, Antigonish County, near the Afton Indian Reserve. Mr Marshall had been fishing a long way from anywhere that would likely be considered the "traditional" fishing grounds of Cape Breton natives. Nowhere did the trial judge suggest that Mr Marshall had been fishing in his "traditional hunting grounds." As one commentator put it, Mr Marshall had "demonstrated no entitlement to a treaty right in that area."[16] So based on *Marshall (No. 2)*, Mr Marshall should have been convicted in *Marshall (No. 1)*.

The Court's comments in *Marshall (No. 2)* were roundly criticized, and rightly so.[17] In significant respects, the judges added to the confusion that their original decision had caused. They had gone well beyond their proper judicial role, responding to an application that was wholly without merit, not by dismissing it out of hand but by significantly rewriting the decision they had rendered. Judges are meant to decide cases that come before them. Each case is decided by its own facts, and the principles relevant to those facts. Over time, cases build into a body of law that instructs and guides judges, lawyers, governments, and the public. This is the "age-old tradition of the common law."[18] Courts have no business making pronouncements outside the confines of the cases they are called upon to decide. It was that very thing that contributed to the failures in the *Marshall (No. 1)* decision in the first place. Certainly nothing in the West Nova application required the Court to comment as it did in *Marshall (No. 2)*. But of course, the reality was that some East Coast communities were in turmoil. Public sentiment against the court was running high. Criticism of it was scathing. It is hard to characterize the Court's comments in *Marshall (No. 2)* as anything less than a response to public concern – a response that was in a

limited, but very real, sense a political response meant at once to calm fears of excessive native claims in light of *Marshall (No. 1)* and restore confidence in the Supreme Court of Canada. It was then, an exercise of pure judicial power, without foundation in law and falling outside the procedures that properly govern our courts.

Still, the decision in *Marshall (No. 1)* was not overruled. It was merely tempered. It remained a powerful lever for claims by native groups to local resources and, ultimately, for native financial claims against government in exchange for which they would forfeit resource claims. Those claims, as we shall see, have been and are being diligently pursued. A significant question is whether the judicial underpinning of those claims is well founded and that requires a closer look at the decision in *Marshall (No. 1)*.

8

Rewriting Nova Scotia History

Appeal Court judges cannot simply change a trial judge's decision because they don't happen to like it. They must, first, find a legal error in the lower court's reasoning. The majority in *Marshall (No. 1)* suggested that the trial judge had made such an error. This was critical. Without it, the majority could not have overturned the trial judge's decision. But a close look shows that the trial judge made no error at all.

Justice Binnie's analysis, finding that the trial had erred, bears repeating:

> 19. ... The treaty document of March 10, 1760 sets out a restrictive covenant and does not say anything about a positive Mi'kmaq right to trade. In fact, the written document does not set out any Mi'kmaq rights at all, merely Mi'kmaq "promises" and the Governor's acceptance. I cannot reconcile the trial judge's conclusion, at para 116, that the treaties "gave the Mi'kmaq the right to bring the products of their hunting, fishing, and gathering to a truckhouse to trade," with his conclusion at para 112 that:
>
>> The written treaties with the Mi'kmaq in 1760 and 1761 which are before me contain, and fairly represent, all the promises made and all the terms and conditions mutually agreed to.

It was, after all, the aboriginal leaders who asked for truckhouses "for the furnishing them with necessaries, in Exchange for their Peltry" in response to the Governor's inquiry "whether they were directed by their tribes, to propose any other particulars to be Treated upon at this time." It cannot be supposed that the Mi'kmaq raised the subject of trade concessions merely for the purpose of subjecting themselves to a trade restriction. As the Crown acknowledges in its factum, "the restrictive nature of the truckhouse clause was British in origin." The trial judge's view that the treaty obligations are all found within the four corners of the March 10, 1760 document, albeit generously interpreted, erred in law by failing to give adequate weight to the concerns and perspective of the Mi'kmaq people, despite the recorded history of the negotiations, and by giving excessive weight to the concerns and perspective of the British who held the pen.

The first point Justice Binnie made here was that the trial judge's analysis was inconsistent. The trial judge said that the written treaties contained "all the terms and conditions mutually agreed to." He also said that the treaties gave the Mi'kmaq the "right to bring the products of their hunting, fishing, and gathering to a truckhouse to trade." Yet there was no such "right to bring" set out in the written treaties. Justice Binnie said that he could not "reconcile" these two comments and, on their face, they do seem to be contradictory. If the written treaties contained all the terms of the treaties, and if those written terms contained no "right to bring" goods to a truckhouse, it doesn't seem to make sense to say that the treaties contained a "right to bring" things to a truckhouse to trade.

What the trial judge said must be examined in context. As discussed earlier, Mr Marshall advanced a "chain of treaties" argument that the Mi'kmaq treaties must have incorporated earlier treaties, in the same way that the Maliseet-Passamaquoddy treaty did expressly. The trial judge rejected that argument. He said that "the written treaties with the Mi'kmaq ... contain ...

all the promises made and all the terms and conditions mutually agreed to."[1] The trial judge then turned his attention to the truckhouse clause of the Halifax treaties and considered whether that *clause* gave rise to *implicit* rights.[2] He said it did. He said that the clause "gave the Mi'kmaq the right to bring the products of their hunting, fishing, and gathering to a truckhouse to trade."[3] With great respect, nothing the trial judge said was in any way contradictory. He was addressing two entirely different issues and his reasoning on one does not conflict with his reasoning on the other. Put shortly, he said that the Mi'kmaq Halifax treaties did not incorporate earlier treaties. There was no treaty chain. He also said that the truckhouse clause of the Halifax treaties involved an implicit right to bring products of the hunt to a truckhouse to trade. Nothing here is particularly hard to reconcile, and it does not reflect any error of law.

The second point that Justice Binnie made in the passage quoted above was that the trial judge "erred in law" in limiting the treaty terms to the "four corners" of the written treaty and "failing to give adequate weight to the concerns and perspective of the Mi'kmaq people despite the recorded history of the negotiations." The Mi'kmaq "perspective" that Justice Binnie was referring to here was the suggestion that native people had made "demands" in those treaty negotiations. ("It was after all the aboriginal leaders who had asked for truckhouses.") Justice Binnie was right that this perspective had not been given "weight" by the trial judge. He never mentions it in his decision. And here it gets interesting and requires elaboration. The reason the trial judge never mentions it is because this particular perspective was never suggested to the trial judge. It wasn't argued. Justice Binnie admonished the trial judge, said he "erred" in not giving adequate weight to a point that was never put to him.

Central to Justice Binnie's decision in *Marshall (No. 1)* was his assertion that in treaty negotiations, natives had demanded truckhouses from the British. His decision repeatedly emphasized this demand,[4] which he saw revealed in the 11 February 1760 document of the treaty discussions at Halifax between the Maliseet and Passamaquoddy chiefs and the British governor.

"It cannot be supposed," said Justice Binnie, that the natives "raised the subject of trade concessions" – truckhouses where natives would be given superior prices for their furs – "merely for the purpose of subjecting themselves to a trade restriction"[5] – the requirement in the treaty that native trade would be limited to the truckhouses. Justice Binnie surmised that there was more to it than what the treaty or even the record of the discussions said. These records were incomplete. They did not accurately record the treaty. The native demand revealed that they were pursuing a "trade agenda." They must have been "assured ... of continuing access to wildlife to trade." Justice Binnie's view is succinctly summarized in the following passage: "I do not think an interpretation of events that turns a positive Mi'kmaq *trade demand* into a negative Mi'kmaq covenant is consistent with the honour and integrity of the Crown. Nor is it consistent to conclude that the Lieutenant Governor, seeking in good faith to address the *trade demands* of the Mi'kmaq, accepted the Mi'kmaq suggestion of a trading facility while denying any treaty protection to Mi'kmaq access to the things that were to be traded [emphasis mine]."[6]

In the decision of the trial judge in the case, Provincial Court Judge Embree, there is no suggestion of any such native "demand." Quite the contrary: Judge Embree referred in one paragraph in his decision to the 11 February 1760 document on which so much turned at the Supreme Court of Canada, and said that the treaty subsequently entered into between the British and the Maliseet and Passamaquoddy "is in conformance with the earlier discussions between the parties."[7] In other words, the treaty discussions were accurately reflected in the treaty document, and it says nothing about rights of access to "things to be traded."

In contrast, according to Justice Binnie, the treaty was *not* in conformance with the "earlier discussions between the parties." He said, "The British-drafted treaty document does not accord with the British-drafted minutes of the negotiating sessions."[8] That is a flat-out contradiction of Judge Embree, who said just

the opposite, and it is a contradiction of Judge Embree on a finding of fact.

So Justice Binnie's decision hinged on an analysis of historical facts. His assessment of those facts differed from and contradicted the historical facts as described by the trial judge. This is remarkable given that appeal courts, and particularly the Supreme Court of Canada, very rarely interfere with the factual findings of trial judges. It is even more remarkable considering that Mr Marshall never argued at the Supreme Court of Canada that the trial judge had made a factual error. Justice Binnie reversed the trial judge on a question of fact, when that point was never put to the Court. All of this is fundamentally at odds with the proper role of the Supreme Court of Canada, which is a court of principle, not a "trier of fact." Its conduct can be fairly described as incautious judicial activism.

A close look at the trial decision reveals that Judge Embree did not explicitly discuss whether the 11 February 1760 document that was so important to Justice Binnie reflected a native demand in the treaty discussions with the British.[9] Why was that? Nowhere, either in the Trial Court or the Court of Appeal did Mr Marshall ever argue that the 11 February 1760 document reflected a native demand and that important consequences for the treaty flowed from such a demand. The Trial Court heard three full days of oral argument. At no time in those three days did Mr Marshall's lawyer ever refer to the 11 February 1760 document.[10] He did not even cross-examine the Crown's expert witness on the document. The expert historians who testified for Mr Marshall both mentioned the document but did not accord it any prominence. When Dr Wicken summarized the thrust of his evidence to highlight key documents, he made no reference to the document, but he did refer to the Record of the Governor's Farm Ceremony.[11] Never was it suggested that the 11 February 1760 document reflected a native demand. The suggestion that the document was crucial and that it reflected a demand was advanced for the first time at the Supreme Court of Canada.[12] The trial judge did not discuss

whether the 11 February 1760 document reflected native treaty demands, because it was never argued that it did.

So when Mr Marshall's case went to the Supreme Court of Canada, he began arguing for the first time that a historical fact that had never been suggested to, commented on, or accepted by any lower court, and that, indeed, is inconsistent with a more general factual finding of the lower court, was critical to a decision in his favour.[13] As mentioned, the judicial process is governed by strict rules. Courts of appeal cannot overturn lower court decisions unless they are in error. Justice Binnie said that the trial judge erred in law in failing to give adequate weight to the native perspective reflected in the 11 February "demand." How can the trial judge have "erred" in relation to a point that was never argued? Justice Binnie accepted the argument that in their treaty negotiations with the British, natives had made the demand that he said was reflected in the 11 February 1760 document. In short, he made a finding of historical fact, something that was properly the role of the Trial Court.

Do the historical documents that were in evidence in *Marshall (No. 1)* reveal what Justice Binnie said they reveal? Quite the contrary. Far from revealing any native demand of the British, the documents reveal unilateral and unconditional native surrender to British authorities in 1759 and 1760. Justice Binnie's analysis is an unfounded rewriting of the history of the Maritime Provinces, not supported by the evidence.

Recapping the uncontroversial historical background of these treaties, it should be recalled that, in 1759, Britain and France were engaged in the Seven Years War. In Nova Scotia, and in North America generally, things were going well for the British. Soldiers from New England had captured Fort Beausejour from the French in 1755. Soon after, the infamous expulsion of the Acadians would significantly reduce the French presence in mainland Nova Scotia. In 1758 British regular forces captured Fortress Louisbourg. Then, in September of 1759 British forces under General Wolfe stormed the heights around Quebec City, routing French General Montcalm's forces in a pitched battle

outside the city. A few days later, on September 18, 1759, Quebec City capitulated to the British.

The witness who testified for Mr Marshall stated that in this period neither the French nor their native allies were yet defeated, and that the British were not yet conclusively victorious. This view seems to have been adopted by Justice Binnie. This summary of the balance of power closely resembled the evidence given by Dr Wicken, evidence largely rejected by the trial judge. In early 1760, Justice Binnie said, when the first of the Halifax Treaties were signed, "Montreal would continue to be part of New France until it fell in June of 1760." The "Treaty of Paris" ending the war was still three years in the future.[14] The Mi'kmaq, said Justice Binnie, were a "considerable fighting force," but by 1760 both they and the British had a "mutual self-interest" in terminating hostilities and "establishing the basis for a stable peace."[15] The sense one gets from these comments, is that Justice Binnie thought the natives in this region came to the treaty negotiations in a position of some strength. In Justice Binnie's view, this was the larger context for the "demand" he said native people would make at the treaty negotiations.[16] But he made fundamental mistakes in taking this view. First, the trial judge specifically rejected the defendant's evidence respecting the context of the treaties. "The interpretation offered on behalf of the Defendant of the trade clause and the treaties, placed in the historical context which is suggested as the appropriate one, is not one that I accept."[17] Second, it does not in any event appear to have been clear to Justice Binnie that most of the Halifax Treaties, including the Cape Breton Treaty relevant to Mr Marshall, were signed in 1761 and later, long after Montreal had fallen and British victory in North America was secured. Moreover a close look at the evidence of the earlier Halifax Treaties tells a very different story from that described by Justice Binnie.

Among the evidence that was before the Supreme Court of Canada in *Marshall (No. 1)* was a record of the "Executive Council of Nova Scotia" – the forerunner of today's Cabinet –

dated 30 November 1759, two months after the fall of Quebec and two months before the February 1760 record of discussions that figured so prominently in Justice Binnie's reasons. The document says this: "His Excellency ... represented that some of the Chiefs of the St. John's Indians had also arrived at Fort Frederick, and had taken the Oath of Allegiance to His Majesty and promised to live in Peace and Friendship."[18]

Fort Frederick was a British fort at the mouth of the St. John River in present-day New Brunswick. The "St. John's Indians" were also known as the "Maliseet." Recall that Justice Binnie referred to the 11 February 1760 document to suggest that it reflected treaty "negotiations," and that in those negotiations the Maliseet and Passamaquoddy chiefs had made a significant demand. But here we have explicit evidence that sometime before the end of November, Maliseet chiefs had sworn allegiance to the king and promised to live in peace. In other words, they surrendered. Already, Justice Binnie's analysis does not seem to hold water. A "demand" is not consistent with an earlier surrender.

The document continues: "From which Circumstances His Excellency apprehended that some overture for further cultivating a good harmony and understanding with them might be favourably received." So the Maliseet had made their peace. Now the lieutenant-governor was suggesting that "some overture" be made to them for "further cultivating a good harmony." The document then says: "The Council having taken this matter into consideration advised that Colonel Arbuthnot should be directed to give them encouragement to come to Halifax, where they may be sure of having a favourable reception, *and an opportunity of extending their Trade, by the establishment of Truckhouses amongst them*, under such Regulations as shall be agreed upon [emphasis mine]."

This passage is critical. Colonel Arbuthnot was the commander of Fort Frederick. He would have accepted the Maliseet's earlier surrender. He was to ask the Maliseet to come to Halifax. He was to tell them that they would be "favourably

received" and that they would have "an opportunity of extending their trade through the establishment of Truckhouses."

The 11 February 1760 document, which was so important in the *Marshall (No. 1)* decision, is another record of the Nova Scotia Executive Council. It begins with the following passage: "His Excellency the Governor acquainted the Council that Two Indian Chiefs of the Passamaquoddy and St. John's River Tribes were arrived here with Colonel Arbuthnot the Commanding Officer of Fort Frederick to negotiate a Treaty of Peace in behalf of the said Tribes." Apparently, Colonel Arbuthnot did as he had been asked to do by Council in November, arriving in Halifax with two chiefs.

The document goes on to describe the discussions between the governor and the chiefs. The chiefs confirmed that they had come to make a treaty and that they were authorized by their tribes to do so. They confirmed that they would renew their submissions from their earlier Treaties of 1725 and 1749. They agreed not to assist or trade with the French and they agreed that their wives and children would camp by Fort Frederick as hostages to the British to ensure performance of the treaty. Any demands here are all British demands. Nothing yet can be described as a native demand. Then we come to the critical passage that Justice Binnie emphasized: "His Excellency then demanded of them, Whether They were directed by Their Tribes, to propose any other particulars to be Treated upon at this time. To which they replied that Their Tribes had not directed them to propose anything further than that there might be a Truckhouse established, for the furnishing them with necessaries, in Exchange for their peltry, and that it might, at present, be at Fort Frederick."

Now, if this were the only document in evidence, you might say, as Justice Binnie did, that this passage describes a native "demand." The previous passages describe British demands: native submission, hostages, and an embargo on trade with the French. Here, in contrast, the passage says the chiefs "propose ... that there might be truckhouses established."

But remember what the November document says. Already Maliseet chiefs had "taken the oath of Allegiance to His Majesty and promised to live in Peace and Friendship." They had surrendered, and they had made no demands as a condition of their surrender. They had surrendered unconditionally. Moreover, in November, it was Council that proposed truckhouses; "Colonel Arbuthnot should be directed to give them encouragement to come to Halifax where they may be sure of having a favourable reception and an opportunity of extending their trade, by the Establishment of Truckhouses." The British had proposed truckhouses to the natives, through Colonel Arbuthnot. In February, Maliseet and Passamaquoddy chiefs had merely accepted a British offer.

This is extremely important. Justice Binnie said in his decision that the truckhouse clause of the Treaty did not capture the real treaty terms. He said that the demand for truckhouses in the February 11 document showed that the natives "pushed a trade agenda." It showed that they sought "trade concessions." He surmised that they must have sought and been assured "continuing access" to the things that they traded. Justice Binnie built his unwritten treaty term to hunt, fish, gather, and trade for necessaries around a native demand. Yet there was no such thing. The British had proposed truckhouses to native peoples. Natives had already surrendered, and merely accepted the offer. A straightforward reading of the documents shows that there was never a native "demand" upon which to piggyback Justice Binnie's treaty terms.

How did this happen? How is it that the 30 November 1759 document, which reveals Justice Binnie's analysis to have been factually incorrect, is never referenced in his decision? Certainly the document was in evidence before the court. It had only to be read to reveal the error.[19] One problem is that the Crown's historian never testified about the document because his testimony was in response to the representation by Mr Marshall's lawyer that the defence was relying on the Treaty of 1752. Only after he completed his testimony was it made clear that the defence would rely on the Halifax Treaties, and even then there was no suggestion of a native demand. So Dr Patterson's evidence

explaining the document in its historical context was missing. And his evidence of the historical context of the treaties had been accepted by the trial judge. Yet the Supreme Court of Canada was not inhibited by the absence of his evidence.

Another problem also goes all the way back to the trial, and Mr Marshall's original reliance on the Treaty of 1752. The federal Crown responded by saying that the 1752 Treaty was irrelevant; "The operative Treaties for determining Mr Marshall's Treaty rights, in this case, are the Treaties of 1760 and 61." In light of this, the analysis of the treaties, at every level of court, centred on the *written* treaties executed at Halifax in that 1760–61 period and the discussions *at Halifax* relevant to them in that same time period. This may have encouraged a very narrow view of what evidence was relevant to those Halifax Treaties, since at the Supreme Court of Canada only the documents of the discussions *in Halifax* were cited. But too much cannot be made of this. Justice Binnie himself said that the trial judge took too "narrow" a view of what constituted the treaty and that he should have looked not just at the treaty itself, but at the February 11 "minutes of the negotiating sessions."[20] Unfortunately, Justice Binnie does not appear to have recognized that other documents were relevant to the treaty, particularly the 30 November 1759 document. Beyond all of this, Dr Patterson testified that the terms of the Maliseet Treaty were "dictated by the British."[21] So as well as making a historical finding that is contrary to the documents that were before him, Justice Binnie's analysis is contradicted by the evidence of an expert witness. It is true that the experts who testified for the native side testified that the 11 February 1760 document reflected a native "proposal"[22] or request, but they did not explain that characterization of the document in light of the 30 November 1759 document and their evidence was not preferred by the trial judge. In any event, such a divergence of opinion between experts was a matter to be determined by a trial judge, not the Supreme Court of Canada.

Equally troubling is the failure to appreciate the implications of several other documents that are referenced in the majority's reasons. Two are particularly relevant, as they relate to the

conduct of Cape Breton Indians after the fall of Quebec. (As a Cape Breton native, any treaty rights that Mr Marshall could claim must flow from the treaty that the British concluded with the Cape Breton chief.) The first is a letter from the British commander at Louisbourg complaining that he found it necessary to supply natives with goods or else they would be "very troublesome to this Town." Justice Binnie referred to the letter to suggest that concessions had to be made to native people in their treaties, to avoid a recurrence of hostilities, neglecting to note that the letter is dated 14 November 1760, nine months after the treaty discussions that he considered were critical. Moreover, the opening words of the letter say this: "I acquainted you in some of my letters in December [1759] and January [1760] last that the Indians were come in, and that they had agreed to live with us upon a footing of Friendship. Accordingly, several of their Chiefs came in here and articles were agreed on and signed."[23]

The chief of the Cape Breton Mi'kmaq had made peace at Louisbourg, long before any treaties were signed with the governor in Halifax. There is no reference to any native "demands" or any British promises of the sort envisioned by Justice Binnie.

Equally important is the record of the Governor's Farm Ceremony at Halifax on 25 June 1761. It is puzzling that Justice Binnie referred to only one sentence in such a key document.[24] Quite apart from its central relevance to the case, it is the most complete record of the first enduring British-native treaties in what would become Canada. The document contains the lengthy speeches of Lieutenant-Governor Jonathan Belcher and the Cape Breton chief, as well as a description of the ceremony in which they signed a Halifax Treaty. The Cape Breton chief says: "our intentions were to yield ourselves up to you without requiring any terms on our part" ... "dispose of us as you please" ... "receive us into your arms. Into them we cast ourselves."[25] There is no demand here. This is the language of unconditional surrender and is consistent with General Whitmore's description of the peace made by the Cape Breton chief nearly two years before. In the entire document, there is not a

whisper of any native demands or native rights to trade or native rights to resources. Lieutenant-Governor Belcher did not promise any such thing.

Another document in the evidence was a letter from Colonel Frye, British commander at Fort Cumberland (formerly Fort Beausejour), dated early 1760. Colonel Frye says that in late January, two Mi'kmaq chiefs came to the fort with a French priest. "I have received their submissions for themselves and Tribes to His Britannic Majesty, and sent them to Halifax for the terms by Governor Lawrence." He wrote that he hoped he had "no more Treaties to make," but the priest told him many more would come in after the spring hunt, and listed fourteen chiefs by name.[26] Here again, the description is of native submission, surrender. There is no mention of any native demands as a condition of peace.

The pattern is obvious from these few documents. At Fort Frederick, at Fort Cumberland, and at Fortress Louisbourg in the winter of 1759–60, native chiefs across Nova Scotia surrendered unconditionally to British officers. They demanded nothing in return for their surrender.[27] In the *Stephen Marshall* case, Justice Scanlan characterized these surrenders as treaties.[28] Some chiefs later went to Halifax to execute a formal written "Halifax Treaty." But nowhere was there any evidence that any native chiefs made any demands of the British, either to British officers or to officials in Halifax, respecting trade or access to resources. As noted, at trial, Mr Marshall's expert witness characterized this evidence differently. He suggested that native peoples would not have understood that they were surrendering; that these documents do not accurately reflect the native perception of their dealings with the British at this time. The trial judge considered these suggestions carefully, and rejected them. That left Justice Binnie with little choice but to take the documents at their face value. He didn't. As a result, Justice Binnie got his facts wrong and in doing so rewrote the history of the Maritime Provinces.

All of this also casts a revealing light on a relevant passage from Justice Binnie's reasons, which I will repeat here:

36 The courts have attracted a certain amount of criticism
from professional historians for what these historians see as
an occasional tendency on the part of judges to assemble a
"cut and paste" version of history ...

37 While the tone of some of this criticism strikes the
non-professional historian as intemperate, the basic objection, as I understand it, is that the judicial selection of facts
and quotations is not always up to the standard demanded
of the professional historian, which is said to be more
nuanced. Experts, it is argued, are trained to read the various historical records together with the benefit of a protracted study of the period, and an appreciation of the
frailties of the various sources. The law sees a finality of
interpretation of historical events where finality, according
to the professional historian, is not possible. The reality, of
course, is that the courts are handed disputes that require
for their resolution the finding of certain historical facts. The
litigating parties cannot await the possibility of a stable academic consensus. The judicial process must do as best it can.
In this particular case, however, there was an unusual level
of agreement amongst all of the professional historians who
testified about the underlying expectations of the participants regarding the treaty obligations entered into by the
Crown with the Mi'kmaq ...[29]

Someone unfamiliar with the background discussed above
would find this a persuasive passage. Historians could not agree
on certain historical points. So, the Court has resolved those
uncertainties in favour of native peoples. It is not fair to wait for
historians to reach a consensus. Courts have to make a decision
now. The suggestion may appear reasonable, but it is without
foundation. The comment that the law cannot await a "stable
academic consensus" suggests that there was a vigorous academic debate in the Trial Court on the central historical point
that governed Justice Binnie's decision. There was none. The
Crown's expert was never asked about the document that was
central to the decision of the Supreme Court of Canada. The

experts who testified for Mr Marshall mentioned the document only in passing. Justice Binnie was right in saying that "the courts are handed disputes that require for their resolution the finding of certain historical facts." But the Supreme Court of Canada is not a fact-finding court. That is not its job. With very great respect, Justice Binnie was wrong to make his own historical finding absent a proper basis for it in the historical evidence.

Justice Binnie's further suggestion that there was, at trial, an "unusual level of agreement amongst all of the professional historians about the underlying expectations of the participants regarding the treaty obligations entered into by the Crown," is hard to fathom. Quite the contrary, the expert testimony was fundamentally at odds on the point. Dr Wicken testified, as noted, that no real meaning could be given to the treaty language. But Dr Patterson's competing analysis of the treaties was the one accepted by the trial judge, who said that the essential ingredients of the treaties were in the written language of the treaties. The gulf between the historians could hardly have been wider.

One further important point to be made arises from the documents discussed above. Historical records can sometimes be frustratingly incomplete, leaving important questions unanswered or partly unanswered. This, perhaps, is what Justice Binnie was driving at in discussing the difficulty of achieving historical finality. But the treaty documents of 1759 and 1760 are surprisingly rich in detail, specifically identifying many of the historic predecessors of modern bands. For example, in his letter written at Fort Cumberland in the early winter of 1760, Colonel Frye wrote that two chiefs had come in with a French priest and he had "received their submissions." One of the two was Augustine Michael, "Chief of a Tribe at Richibouctou." To this day, a native band remains at Richibouctou, New Brunswick, known as Big Cove First Nation. The French priest listed fourteen other chiefs who would be "here upon the like business, as soon as their spring Hunting was over." Each of the chiefs is mentioned by name, and by band.[30] For example, he named Louis Francis "Chief of Merimichi," Etienne Alchaba "Chief of Pohomoosh," and Jeanot Pigaluet "Chief of Cape

Breton." At the Governor's Farm Ceremony a year and a half later, in June 1761, the Mi'kmaq chiefs who attended and signed treaties included: "The Chiefs of the Tribes of the Mickmack Indians, called Merimichi, Jediack, Pogmouch and Cape Breton Tribes, on behalf of themselves and their people." To this day, there are Mi'Kmaq bands on the Miramichi (Burnt Church and Red Bank), at Pokemouche (near Shippagan, NB), and in Cape Breton. In 1761 the Cape Breton chief spoke "in the name of the rest." He said, as I have already described, "our intentions were to yield ourselves up to you without requiring any terms on our part." "As long as the Sun and Moon shall endure ... I will be your friend and ally, submitting myself to the Laws of your government." The chiefs of these bands surrendered like the rest. They made no demands of the sort suggested by Justice Binnie, but agreed to be British subjects and live under British law. They have no more treaty right to "hunt, fish and gather" than their neighbours of Scottish, Irish, Acadian, and other European descent.

9

Judicial Levitation: The Hovering Treaty Right

Donald Marshall, Jr, was a Cape Breton Mi'kmaq. We know definitively that the chief of the Cape Breton Mi'kmaq surrendered at Louisbourg in 1759 and signed a treaty at a ceremony in Halifax in June of 1761. But Justice Binnie said that the "key negotiations" revealing the unwritten treaty right to "hunt, fish and gather and trade for necessaries" were between the Maliseet and Passamaquoddy and the British in Halifax on 11 February 1760. How did the unwritten treaty term get from those Maliseet and Passamaquoddy discussions into the Cape Breton treaty eighteen months later? The answer is found in a tortured tangle of legal argument and historical analysis.

In the trial court, Mr Marshall, through his lawyer, initially relied on the Treaty of 1752. Then they dropped that stance and said they would be relying on the Treaties of 1760–61. But in adopting that position, they made their "chain of treaties" argument. They argued strenuously that the Treaties of 1760–61 were part of a chain of treaties that incorporated all the terms of all of the previous treaties (remember that the treaties of 1726 and 1752 contain terms that they considered advantageous to their argument). The Maliseet Halifax Treaty of 1760 and the Mi'kmaq Halifax Treaties of 1760–61 are different in an interesting way. The Maliseet Halifax Treaty expressly incorporates parts of the earlier Maliseet Treaties of 1749 and 1726. In contrast, the Mi'kmaq Halifax Treaties make no mention of any

earlier treaties with the Mi'kmaq. What Mr Marshall argued was that even though the Mi'kmaq Halifax Treaties of 1760–61 make no reference to earlier treaties, it must have been understood that the Mi'kmaq treaties incorporated the earlier treaties.

Accordingly, the trial judge had to answer the question posed by Mr Marshall. As the trial judge put it, "Did the Mi'kmaq consider that previous treaties were renewed by and combined with the 1760–61 Treaties?"[1] In answering this question, the judge carefully reviewed the historical evidence leading up to the signing of the Halifax Treaties, including the evidence respecting the Maliseet and Passamaquoddy Treaty. Ultimately, the trial judge said very firmly that "the 1760–61 Mi'kmaq Treaties did not renew earlier treaties."[2] But the important thing is that in all of this discussion the *only* reason the trial judge referred to the Maliseet and Passamaquoddy Treaty discussions was by way of assessing Mr Marshall's argument that the Mi'kmaq treaties must have incorporated earlier treaties, even though they did not expressly say so.

As mentioned, Mr Marshall's argument changed at the Supreme Court of Canada. For the first time he argued that the treaty right his client claimed flowed from the "demand" supposedly evidenced by the 11 February 1760 record of the Maliseet and Passamaquoddy treaty discussions. In accepting this argument, Justice Binnie said this: "The trial judge considered that the *key negotiations* took place not with the Mi'kmaq people directly, but with the St. John River Indians."[3]

Respectfully, the trial judge said nothing of the kind. He only ever mentions the 11 February 1760 discussions on one occasion and in passing. He certainly never characterizes those discussions as the "key negotiations." The only conclusion he draws from them is that the record of those discussions conforms with the written terms of the Maliseet treaty. This is what the trial judge said in the only paragraph in which he mentions the 11 February 1760 document: "Governor Lawrence and the Council met with representatives of the Maliseet and Passamaquoddy at Halifax on February 11, 1760, twelve days before the treaty with them was signed. Likewise Paul Laurent and Michel

Augustine met with the Governor and Council on February 29, 1760 and then signed their treaties on March 10th. Minutes of both those Council meetings were before me in evidence. The treaty entered into between the British and the Maliseet and Passamaquoddy is in conformance with the earlier discussions between the parties."[4]

To suggest from that passage that the trial judge was of the view that the Maliseet negotiations were "key" to the Mi'kmaq treaties is not consistent with what the trial judge said and what he was responding to in saying it. He was, after all, simply responding to Mr Marshall's argument that the Mi'kmaq treaties incorporated earlier treaties in the same way that the Maliseet Treaty incorporated earlier treaties. Justice Binnie elevated the 11 February 1760 discussion, giving it a critically important character, when it had never been more than barely relevant in the lower courts. In fact, in his submission to the trial judge, Mr Marshall never emphasized the 11 February 1760 document. Neither did he emphasize it in his written submissions in the Court of Appeal.[5]

But how did the treaty right Justice Binnie would say that document reflected move out of the British-Maliseet context, and into a Mi'kmaq treaty? After all, the 11 February 1760 discussions were between the Maliseet and the British, while the accused, Mr Marshall, was a Mi'kmaq. Once again, Justice Binnie referred to what the trial judge had said: "The trial judge found as a fact at para. 108 that the relevant Mi'kmaq treaty 'did make peace upon the same conditions as the Maliseet and Passamaquoddy'."[6] For Justice Binnie, it was as simple as that. The "oral treaty term" of the Maliseet and Passamaquoddy discussions was transferred to the Mi'kmaq treaties because the trial judge said they had made peace on the same conditions. But here again, the analysis is mistaken. In reaching the conclusion that Justice Binnie pointed to here, the trial judge had merely been comparing the *written* language of the Maliseet Halifax Treaty with the *written* language of the Mi'kmaq Treaties. Again, in doing so, he was responding to Mr Marshall's argument that the Mi'kmaq Treaties, like the Maliseet Treaty,

incorporated earlier treaties. Judge Embree noted that, unlike the Maliseet Treaty, the Mi'kmaq treaty did not renew submissions in earlier treaties, but "beyond that, the contents of these treaties are essentially the same," the "thrust is the same."[7]

The trial judge was very clearly saying simply that the written language of the treaties was essentially alike. He was not addressing an "oral term" arising from the Maliseet negotiations, which Justice Binnie would later purport to discover. The trial judge's comments cannot reasonably be taken to suggest that any oral term of Maliseet negotiations had been incorporated into treaties with various Mi'kmaq bands. Remember, Justice Binnie found, by reference to the 11 February 1760 document, a term of the *Maliseet* Treaty that had never been written down; an *unwritten* treaty term. When the trial judge said the Mi'kmaq and Maliseet Treaties contained "the same conditions," he was talking about the *written* terms. How did the Mi'kmaq get the advantage of the *unwritten* term? Justice Binnie never pointed to anything in the Mi'kmaq record that could be construed as a native "demand." It seems the supposed oral term of the Maliseet discussions just floated up in the air, and eighteen months later landed in the treaty at the governor's farm. That was the ceremony, remember, where the Cape Breton chief said his intention was to "yield ourselves up to you without requiring any terms on our part."

A closer look reveals just how unsatisfactory Justice Binnie's conclusion is. The treaty right to "hunt, fish and gather," that Justice Binnie discovered in the Maliseet and Passamaquoddy negotiations, was "oral." It was "recorded incompletely in the truckhouse clause." The natives, Justice Binnie surmised, were "assured ... of continuing access, implicitly or explicitly, to wildlife to trade." But the British, who "held the pen," had not accurately recorded what had been agreed.

But in June 1761 at the Governor's Farm Ceremony the Cape Breton chief said: "We come here to assure you, in the name of all those of whom we are chiefs, that the propositions which you have been pleased to cause to be sent to us in writing have been very acceptable to me and my Brethren and that our inten-

tions were to yield ourselves up to you without requiring any terms on our part."[8]

The "written propositions" that are referred to in this paragraph do not seem to have been preserved. But there is no suggestion in the chief's speech that the standard form of the written Halifax Treaty that we know he signed that day varied from those "written propositions." It is clear, therefore, that no other term was included in the treaties signed at the governor's farm.[9] Moreover, there is no basis for saying that an oral treaty right to "hunt, fish and gather" somehow made its way out of the Maliseet and Passamaquoddy discussions with the British in February 1760, and into the Cape Breton Halifax Treaty in June 1761. The Cape Breton chief, after all, was satisfied with "written propositions."

This makes sense from another perspective. Assume for a moment that there really was a treaty right of the nature suggested by Justice Binnie. If we consider Justice Binnie's suggestion that the British failed to write down the "real" agreement with the Maliseet and Passamaquoddy, then that failure was either advertent or inadvertent. In other words, the British either *intentionally* refrained from writing down the supposed agreement with the Maliseet and Passamaquoddy, or they *unintentionally* failed to write the supposed agreement down. If the first, they lied – they did not have the "true" treaty right to "hunt, fish and gather" recorded in the Maliseet and Passamaquoddy Halifax Treaty. With respect to the Cape Breton Treaty, the Governor's Farm Ceremony records that "written propositions" – the written treaty terms – were sent to the natives by the British. It is absurd to think that either those "propositions" or anything said to the Cape Breton chief would have included a term that the British previously *intentionally* refused to include in writing in the Maliseet and Passamaquoddy Treaty.

The other alternative is that the "promise" that Justice Binnie said had been made to the Maliseet and Passamaquoddy was unintentionally not recorded. In other words, the British were careless and because they were careless they did not accurately record the treaty. If this was the case, it is still irrational to

suppose that a promise to the Maliseet and Passamaquoddy made its way into the Cape Breton Treaty. It makes no sense at all to suppose that the British included in the "written propositions" they sent to the Cape Breton chief before the Governor's Farm Ceremony oral terms that many months before they had carelessly failed to include in a treaty with entirely different tribes.

So not only was Justice Binnie mistaken in his analysis that the Maliseet-Passamaquoddy negotiations were "key" and reflected a "demand" and consequent treaty right to "hunt, fish and gather," his reasoning in suggesting that any such treaty right attached to the Cape Breton Halifax Treaty (or any other Halifax Treaty) is inadequate. He took the trial judge's comments about the written terms of the treaties being the same out of context and he never addressed the fundamental problem of how to attribute an "oral term" of the Maliseet-Passamaquoddy Treaty to the other Halifax Treaties.

How did this happen? Inattentiveness may have been a factor. Several times in his judgment Justice Binnie discusses the 11 February 1760 document as if it describes a Mi'kmaq rather than a Maliseet-Passamaquoddy demand. For example, and there are several, he said this at one point in his reasons. "I do not think an interpretation of events that turns a positive *Mi'kmaq* trade demand into a negative Mi'kmaq covenant is consistent with the honour and integrity of the Crown. Nor is it consistent to conclude that the Lieutenant-Governor, seeking in good faith to address the *trade demands of the Mi'kmaq,* accepted the *Mi'kmaq suggestion* of a trading facility while denying any treaty protection to Mi'kmaq access to the things that were to be traded" [emphasis mine].[10]

This is obviously a reference to the Maliseet-Passamaquoddy discussions in the 11 February 1760 document, but Justice Binnie here mistakenly refers to them as Mi'kmaq discussions. It is possible to see how that mistake would have hidden the need to analyze the "transfer" of an oral treaty term from the Maliseet-Passamaquoddy to the Mi'kmaq. After all, if you thought the Mi'kmaq made the "demand," there is less reason to wonder how the treaty term made its way into the Mi'kmaq

Halifax Treaties. But such inattentiveness cannot excuse the ultimate decision. And that decision does seem to reflect the underlying problem: an inclination to rule in favour of a native claim, rather than carefully review evidence and apply reasoned analysis based upon that evidence.

It would, however, be wrong to fault Justice Binnie entirely on this issue. Part of the problem seems to have arisen because the trial judge chose not to fashion his decision by reference to the Cape Breton Halifax Treaty of 1761 – the only treaty that was properly before him. He chose instead to make sweeping statements to the effect that all Mi'kmaq had Halifax Treaties, and that they were all similar. That issue was simply not before him and he should not have made such sweeping statements. They encouraged Justice Binnie's analysis by leading him to think he could describe all treaty rights in the Maritimes by reference to the discussions with one tribe. Still, Justice Binnie should have seen the error in this. After all, the Supreme Court of Canada has said emphatically that the rights of aboriginal peoples are "not general," but depend on the history of each aboriginal community.[11]

10

Trade, Treaties, and the Constitution

The Supreme Court of Canada ignored fundamental doctrines of constitutional law in *Marshall (No. 1)*. Put shortly, the majority decision is constitutionally unsound.

For many years after the British won possession of mainland Nova Scotia in 1710, Nova Scotia was governed by a governor and Council. As I have noted, it was, in effect, a dictatorship. In the 1750s there was considerable pressure to have an elected assembly. British settlers at Halifax, which had been established in 1749, demanded their rights as Englishmen, as did New England Planters, who would flood into Nova Scotia in the late 1750s to take up lands vacated by the Acadian expulsion. They were accustomed to the elected assemblies of the American colonies. Nova Scotia's House of Assembly began sitting in 1758.

The presence of a House of Assembly in Nova Scotia was a watershed event. Recall that at the conclusion of the English constitutional struggles less than a century before, it was finally settled that Parliament – elected legislatures – made law. The King's assent to laws was necessary. Parliament could not make law without him. But neither could the King make law without Parliament. There were some "prerogative" powers that the King could exercise without Parliament, but those prerogative powers were relatively limited. These are fundamental constitutional principles. They survive to the present day. Setting aside questions of the "Constitution Act, 1867" and the "Charter,"

any attempt to regulate or prohibit what a person does must have as its source a law enacted by our elected representatives in Parliament or in the provincial legislature. So prior to the establishment of Nova Scotia's House of Assembly, Crown officers appointed to govern Nova Scotia did so "absolutely." That all changed in 1758. Now laws had to be passed by the House of Assembly.

How does this apply to treaties? It has always been the authority or "prerogative" of the king to make treaties. Historically, for example, the king could decide to go to war or make peace, without asking permission from Parliament. In fact, the king could make Treaties of Peace or treaties of pretty much any sort, without Parliament's permission. But it is one thing to make a treaty, and it is quite another to give it effect.[1] It has been the law for hundreds of years that rights, privileges, or prohibitions in a treaty are of no effect – they are not law – without legislation. This only makes sense. If it were not the law, then governments could make laws through treaties, and Parliament and Legislatures would be neutered. So, for example, in 1728 Britain's attorney general said that a treaty prohibition on trade "could not have had its effect with respect to His Majesty's subjects, unless the said articles had been confirmed either by the Act of Parliament of Great Britain, or by acts of assembly within the respective plantations."[2]

There was a very good example of this in the evidence at trial in *Marshall (No. 1)*. Dr John Reid, who was called to testify by Mr Marshall, is an expert on the history of New England. He described treaty discussions in 1713 between Governor Dudley of Massachusetts and Abenaki chiefs from present-day Maine. In those discussions, Governor Dudley told the chiefs that "the places of trade and the regulating of the same"[3] would be dealt with by the Massachusetts House of Representatives. Dudley was very anxious that the Indian trade should be regulated, to avoid the abuses of unregulated trade: "A trade managed by private persons will be liable to be corrupted by extorted prices and selling them drink, which will procure quarrels."[4] Dudley wanted a system in which natives could trade only with salaried

managers of truckhouses. But the House of Representatives saw things differently. They refused to "insist upon their [the Indians] being confined or restrained from visiting the towns or trading with any Her Majesty's [sic] good subjects."[5] They would not countenance an exclusive truckhouse system.

All of this illustrates the underlying constitutional principle. Governor Dudley could conclude a treaty with native peoples. But the regulation of trade was not something he could accomplish by treaty because the regulation of trade required laws. Only the Massachusetts House of Representatives could regulate the Indian trade by passing the necessary laws. Unfortunately, this point was never drawn out of the material. Dr Reid referred to this evidence to make an entirely different point, and Dr Patterson had already testified, so he was unable to make the point in evidence.

Again, the historical documents help explain the point as it relates to the Halifax Treaties of 1760–61 and Justice Binnie's decision in *Marshall (No. 1)*. The best place to start is with the by-now-familiar 11 February 1760 meeting. At that meeting the British met with the Maliseet and Passamaquoddy chiefs and discussed the terms of their treaty, including the establishment of truckhouses to which native trade would be restricted; they would not trade "at any other Place, nor with any other Persons."

One week later, on 18 February 1760, Governor Lawrence wrote to the "Gentlemen of the House of Assembly" that he was "upon the conclusion of a Treaty of Submission and Amity with the Indians of St. John's River and Passsamaquodie." He went on to say: "you may rightly conceive from the Treaty itself the necessity of a law to prevent such pernicious practices from a private Commerce with these people, as have too often interrupted that Harmony and good understanding between them and the neighbouring colonies."[6]

The speaker of the House of Assembly replied to the governor the very next day. "And as we are sensible of the necessity of having a Law to prevent pernicious practices from private commerce, with the savages, your Excellency may depend on our joint Endeavours with His Majesty's Council, to concert proper

measures for that purpose, as soon as the Treaties now on foot, and other matters relative thereto, are laid before us."[7]

The treaty with the St. John's and Passamaquoddy was signed by those chiefs the following week, on 23 February 1760. It contains a "truckhouse clause," part of which I will repeat here for convenience: "and that, for the more effectually preventing any such Correspondence and Commerce with any of His Majesty's Enemies the said Tribes shall at all times hereafter Trafic and barter and exchange commodities with the Managers of such Truckhouses as shall be established for that purpose by his Majesty's Governors of this Province at Fort Frederick or elsewhere within the said Province and at no other place without permission from His Majesty's Government."[8]

On 11 February 1760, then, the Maliseet and Passamaquoddy chiefs accepted the British offer of truckhouses and the British requirement that they would trade nowhere else and with no one else. The Treaty of February 23 reflects that very thing. But it was not enough. *Nova Scotia's Governor could not make law by a treaty.* To prohibit non-natives trading with natives, the House of Assembly had to pass a law to that effect. The correspondence between Governor Lawrence and the House of Assembly shows that everybody was well aware that it would be necessary to make a law. And, in due course, one month later, the House of Assembly enacted a statute, "An Act to prevent any private Trade or Commerce with the Indians." This is the statute that Reverend Seycombe violated when he bought eels from two Indian women a year or so later. It says, very simply, that none other than truckmasters or licencees may "buy, sell, truck, Barter ... any kind of Provisions ... to or from any of the aforesaid Indians."

"So what?" you might rightly ask. What relevance has this to Justice Binnie's decision in *Marshall (No. 1)*? A treaty is an agreement. The "oral" treaty term that Justice Binnie discovered was, he said, the "common intention"[9] of both the British and the Maliseet-Passamaquoddy. The treaty term that he described was the right to hunt, fish, gather, and trade. In fact, Justice Binnie said it was a *legal* right.[10] The treaty term Justice

Binnie described was also a *restricted* right: "it is not a right to trade generally for economic gain, but rather a right to trade for necessaries."[11]

The problem is that in Nova Scotia, in 1760, the British governor had no *legal* authority with respect to a treaty term *entitling* native people to hunt, fish, and gather for trade. It was the authority of the House of Assembly to establish legal rights, through laws. The regulation of trade was the authority of the House of Assembly, not the governor. By the same token, *Governor Lawrence could not, through a treaty, have limited native trade to "necessaries."* Only the Legislature could have done that. This is not to say that the governor could not have signed a treaty containing those terms. He could have done so. But without a law enacted by the Legislature a treaty right to hunt, fish, and gather for trade was irrelevant. It had no *legal* effect. A court could not enforce it. So the treaty term Justice Binnie described is constitutionally unsound.

Moreover, Governor Lawrence's correspondence with the House of Assembly shows that he was well aware of his constitutional limitations. Indeed these constitutional limitations were well-established in the British Colonies and illustrated by the example involving Governor Dudley and the Massachusetts House of Representatives in 1713. Governor Lawrence knew that to limit native trade to truckhouses as the treaty was to provide, he needed a law. He asked the Legislature for that law. He knew what his constitutional limitations were, and acted in conformity with them. It is absurd to think in this context that the governor disregarded his constitutional limitations by agreeing to the treaty term described by Justice Binnie. He would be conforming to, and disregarding, his constitutional authority, in the very same breath. Governor Lawrence cannot be supposed to have agreed to a treaty term that was beyond his constitutional authority, when the evidence explicitly shows that he carefully conformed to his constitutional role. If it really had been intended British "strategy," as Justice Binnie surmised,[12] that natives would have a treaty right to hunt, fish, and gather for trade, limited to necessaries, Governor Lawrence would have

asked the House of Assembly to pass a law. He didn't. That is
compelling evidence that the treaty term Justice Binnie found
after it went missing for 250 years, never existed to begin with.

Unfortunately, failure to refer to this point reflects a decision
rendered despite evidence and doctrine to the contrary. All of
the documents referred to above were before the Court. It is fair
to say that the historians who testified at trial did not elaborate
this constitutional principle,[13] but the federal Crown raised the
point, in one sentence, in their written argument to the Court.[14]
In response the judges simply avoided the issue, making no reference to it in their decision. While one can legitimately criticize
the federal Crown for not sufficiently emphasizing a significant
argument, the fact remains that the point was made and the
Court was not mindful of it. This omission is particularly
remarkable given that the major criticism of judicial activism is
that activist courts lack respect for the role of parliament. In
Marshall (No. 1) the supremacy of Parliament, a doctrine of law
fatal to the Court's reasoning, was ignored.

Fundamental Laws: The Rights of British Subjects and a "Promenade Down Barrington Street"

The majority in *Marshall (No. 1)* never referred to the fundamental constitutional doctrine discussed in chapter 10. A further examination of that doctrine reveals serious inadequacies in the court's reasoning.

The minority reasons of Justice McLachlin are in sharp disagreement with Justice Binnie. Justice McLachlin pointed out that it was important to distinguish between two things: first, a right to trade under the law applicable to all citizens, and second, a treaty right to trade. Every British subject in Nova Scotia in 1760–61 had a right to trade. When the Mi'kmaq signed treaties "they automatically inherited this general right."[1] Remember that in the speeches at the Governor's Farm Ceremony in June 1761, the lieutenant governor said that the natives would be "under the Same Laws and for the same Rights and Liberties," while the Cape Breton chief said they were "submitting to the laws of your Government."

So, in Justice McLachlin's view, Mi'kmaq rights to trade were the same rights everybody else enjoyed under the "laws of the land." Beyond this, like the trial judge, she thought that a limited right to "bring" goods to the truckhouses to trade was implicit in the treaties. She reasoned that since the treaties obliged the British to provide truckhouses for Mi"kmaq trade, this obligation "gave rise to a limited Mi'kmaq 'right to bring' goods to trade at these outlets."[2] This was something less than the general treaty right to

trade envisaged by Justice Binnie. The same constitutional defect that is fatal to Justice Binnie's treaty right is fatal to the one Justice McLachlin described, since only a legislature could establish a meaningful right to bring goods to a truckhouse. Still, it was a significant objection that Justice Binnie had to grapple with, since it followed that the treaty right ended when the truckhouse system collapsed. Justice Binnie accepted that Justice McLachlin was right to distinguish between rights applicable to everyone and treaty rights, but he characterized the distinction somewhat differently. He said that the distinction was between "a *liberty* enjoyed by all citizens and a *right conferred by a specific legal authority, such as a treaty,* to participate in the same activity."[3] He went on to illustrate his point with this example: "A treaty could, to take a fanciful example, provide for a right of the Mi'kmaq to promenade down Barrington Street, Halifax, on each anniversary of the treaty. Barrington Street is a common thoroughfare enjoyed by all. There would be nothing "special" about the Mi'kmaq use of a common right of way. The point is that the treaty rights-holder not only has the right or liberty "enjoyed by other British subjects" but may enjoy special treaty protection against interference with its exercise. So it was with the trading arrangement."[4]

According to Justice Binnie, then, native peoples did not have merely a right to trade common to all other citizens. They had a treaty right. And Justice Binnie differentiated the two by describing the treaty right as "legal authority." The treaty right, he said, "enjoyed special treaty protection against interference with its exercise."

This is simply wrong. As mentioned in chapter 10, treaties do not create rights or liabilities. A treaty right to "promenade down Barrington Street" did not, in 1760 or 1761, "enjoy special treaty protection." In a colony like Nova Scotia, which had a Legislature, such a treaty right would have had *no protection whatever, absent a law.* No court could have enforced it.

Justice Binnie went on to say that after 1982 changes to Canada's Constitution gave constitutional protection to treaty rights. But he failed to note the very basic constitutional point that the

treaty right he discovered in 1999 by reference to discussions in 1760 could have had no legal effect in the intervening 239 years. That alone should have given him pause. It is really not very plausible that the British agreed in 1760 to give native peoples a treaty right that was neither legal nor enforceable.

How is it that the judges of our highest court could have been mistaken on such a fundamental point? It seems their attention was diverted in grappling with a less important point that had troubled the Court of Appeal. That point involved the governor's Royal Instructions, which prevented him from agreeing to any law putting persons in Nova Scotia in a preferential trading position over other British subjects. The Court of Appeal referred to this as an objection to the right claimed by Mr Marshall. Justice Binnie's response was to say that the treaty did not need to give native people "preferential trading rights." All the treaty needed to do was give "treaty rights," which now, with the changes to our Constitution in 1982, had constitutional protection.[5]

But this discussion, whether the right claimed by Mr Marshall was "preferential" or not, diverted Justice Binnie from the bigger problem: the lack of legal force of the treaty right he espoused. Without ever describing *why* or *how* the treaty right he discovered was a legal or protected right, he just said it was. But it could not have been.

In deciding that there was a native treaty right to "hunt, fish and gather for trade," Justice Binnie buttressed his finding by referring to the evidence of Dr Patterson. The passage of his testimony that Justice Binnie emphasized is set out in full here. It is a part of his evidence on cross-examination. It should be noted, once again, that this evidence was given before there was any suggestion from the defence that they were relying upon the Treaties of 1760–61 and not the Treaty of 1752.

Q. I guess it's fair to say that the British would have understood that the Micmac lived and survived by hunting and fishing and gathering activities.
A. Yes, of course.

Q. And that in this time period, 1760 and '61, fish would be amongst the items they would have to trade. And they would have the right under this treaty to bring fish and feathers and furs into a truckhouse in exchange for commodities that were available.

A. Well, it's not mentioned but it's not excluded. So I think it's fair to assume that it was permissible.

Q. Okay. It's fair to say that it's an assumption on which the trade truckhouse clause is based.

A. That the truckhouse clause is based on the assumption that natives will have a variety of things to trade, some of which are mentioned and some not. Yes, I think that's fair.

Q. Yes. And wouldn't be out of line to call that a right to fish and a right to bring the fish or furs or feathers or fowl or venison or whatever they might have, into the truckhouses to trade.

A. Ah, a right. I think the implication here is that there is a right to trade under a certain form of regulation –

Q. Yes.

A. – that's laid down. And if you're saying right to fish, I've assumed that in recognizing the Micmac by treaty, the British were recognizing them as the people they were. They understood how they lived and that that meant that those people had a right to live in Nova Scotia in their traditional ways. And, to me, that implies that the British were accepting that the Micmac would continue to be a hunting and gathering people, that they would fish, that they would hunt to support themselves. I don't see any problem with that. It seems to me that that's implicit in the thing. Even though it doesn't say it, and I know that there seems to, in the 20th century, be some reluctance to see the value of the 1760 and 1761 treaties because they're not so explicit on these matters, but I personally don't see the hang-up. Because it strikes me that there is a recognition that the Micmac are a people and they have the right to exist. And that has ... carries

certain implications with it. More than this, the very fact that there is a truckhouse and that the truckhouse does list some of the things that natives are expected to trade, implies that the British are condoning or recognizing that this is the way that natives live. They do live by hunting and, therefore, this is the produce of their hunting. They have the right to trade it.[6]

Dr Patterson, said Justice Binnie, was of the view that the treaty gave native people a treaty right to fish and trade for fish. After all, said Justice Binnie, he used the word "right." This is what Justice Binnie said: "He initially uses the words 'permissible' and 'assumption,' but when asked specifically by counsel about a 'right' to fish and to trade fish, he says, 'Ah, a right' (emphasis added), then, weighing his words carefully, he addresses a 'right to fish' and concludes that 'by treaty' the British did recognize that the Mi'kmaq 'had a right to live in Nova Scotia in their traditional ways.'"[7]

Justice Binnie's reliance upon this passage of Dr Patterson's testimony became very controversial. The question of the rights contained in a treaty is a question of law and the responsibility of courts, not witnesses. Dr Patterson stated publicly that his words had been taken out of context.[8] Justice Binnie's characterization of the passage is, in my view, an unfair reading of Dr Patterson's testimony. Even if this passage is examined in complete isolation from the rest of Dr Patterson's testimony, it is at best, ambiguous. He does indeed use the word "right," so that might be taken as a suggestion that Dr Patterson's view was that the treaty included a specific treaty right to fish and trade. But the passage also includes broader comments. Dr Patterson talked about "a right to trade under a certain form of regulation," and said that the British were "recognizing the Micmac by treaty" so they "had a right to live in Nova Scotia in their traditional ways." These statements are consistent with the point made repeatedly by Dr Patterson that by virtue of the treaties, the Mi'kmaq would now live as other British subjects with

the same rights as other British subjects ,including the right to fish and the right to trade.

One does not have to read very far into Dr Patterson's testimony to understand the point he was making. He made it repeatedly and consistently in his evidence. He said, for example, referring to the speeches at the Governor's Farm Ceremony of June 1761, that under the treaties "the laws of Nova Scotia will protect the Mi'kmaq, and they will be protected in the same fashion as any other of His Majesty's subjects."[9] He referred to the situation in seventeenth-century Massachusetts where natives were brought under Massachusetts law and were made subjects of the king "to regulate their activities in the way they would regulate the activities of other persons" and said natives in Nova Scotia were brought within that "framework."[10] He spoke of native peoples becoming subjects of the Crown under the Treaties,[11] and spoke of native trade "on the same terms as any other British subject" after the demise of the truckhouses.[12] He spoke of subjects of the British Crown having "the rights of Englishmen" meaning "freedom within a framework of law."[13]

In short, in the context of the whole of his evidence, Dr Patterson simply cannot be taken as saying that native peoples were given any specific treaty right to trade under the Halifax Treaties. He was saying, rather, that the rights accruing to native peoples under those treaties were the rights of subjects under British law. Those rights were the consequence of the native submission. As subjects of the king they would be entitled to "live in Nova Scotia in their traditional ways." But that does not mean native peoples had "treaty rights" to follow their traditional ways. The suggestion involves the absurdly broad proposition that all native ways – even those contrary to British law and policy (burning forests is one of the examples, already discussed) – were encompassed as treaty rights. That logic should have caused the majority to reconsider how such rights could be imposed by treaty. In Nova Scotia in 1760, meaningful treaty rights to "promenade down Barrington Street" or rights to trade fish required legislation.

The Court's failure to comment on, or even acknowledge, the thrust of Dr Patterson's evidence is remarkable. It is no small thing that native people agreed, in the words of the 1761 Governor's Farm Ceremony record, that thereafter they would "live under the same laws and for the same rights and liberties" as their "fellow" British "subjects." One might think that worth mentioning. One might also think that such a foundation for future relations between natives and non-natives would leave little room for the extraordinary treaty rights the majority would describe.

THE MAGNA CARTA

Above all else, fish drew Europeans to present-day Atlantic Canada. Cod were abundant on the banks off Newfoundland and Nova Scotia. Already in the sixteenth century, hundreds of ships crossed the Atlantic for the annual fishery. Canso, Nova Scotia, became a major fishing station for British and New England fishermen. Fishing was, in short, a vital economic activity in both Britain and Nova Scotia. Not surprisingly, British law made special provision for fishing, and it was found in the Magna Carta, a great bedrock of British Constitutional law. It is another reason why the treaty right discovered by Justice Binnie is unsound.[14]

The Magna Carta originated in a crisis between King John and his Barons in 1215. They met at Runnymede, outside London, and negotiated a deal – the Magna Carta – that restricted the king's powers and for a short time averted war. Interestingly, the original Magna Carta was only law for about nine weeks.[15] But in succeeding years it was changed and reissued, reaching its final form in 1225. It was confirmed as English statute in 1297. The Magna Carta is most remembered today for the clause that prohibited the imprisonment of freemen "except by the lawful judgment of his peers," the root of our trial by jury, and for clauses that have been linked to *habeas corpus*. Another less known clause is important to our story, translated here from the original Latin: "All forests ... shall forthwith be disafforested;

and a similar course shall be followed with regard to river-banks
that have been placed 'in defence' by us in our time."

In King John's time, falconry or "fowling" was a favourite
sport. The king claimed to be able to place rivers "in defence,"
prohibiting others from fowling where he would go. This was
resented, and the Magna Carta prohibited the practice. Over
time, the language and the interpretation of the clause changed.
What is important for the decision in *Marshall (No. 1)* is that
from sometime in the thirteenth century, and ever since, this
clause of the Magna Carta was taken to refer not to "fowling"
but to *fishing*.[16] As a British statute, the Magna Carta applied to
colonies such as Nova Scotia, and its effect was to prevent the
Crown from interfering with the public right to fish.[17] The
Crown had no prerogative power to interfere with that right:
"the title of the public to fish in tidal waters ... had ... been made
unalterable except by a legislature possessing competent authority since Magna Carta."[18]

Justice Binnie described the treaty right as a right to fish (and
hunt and gather) and trade those fish, but "not a right to trade
generally for economic gain ... rather a right to trade for necessaries." The fishing rights of British subjects in Nova Scotia in
1760 were protected by the Magna Carta. *The Crown could
not unilaterally limit those fishing rights in any way.* Only a
statute passed either by the Nova Scotia House of Assembly or
the British Parliament could limit the Magna Carta and restrict
the public right to fish. Indeed the Crown had no power whatever over fisheries.[19]

As subjects of the Crown under the treaties, natives in this
region had equal benefit of British law, including the Magna
Carta. No British official could limit their right to fish, by treaty
or otherwise, to "necessaries" or in any other way. As subjects
of the Crown in 1760 native peoples were entitled to catch as
much fish as they possibly could. Their rights in this respect
were no different from the rights of the most rapacious British
fisherman. Only a duly enacted law could limit the fishing
of either native or non-native. Accordingly, the treaty right
described by Justice Binnie was constitutionally flawed. He said,

moreover, that the treaty right he discovered must have been the "common intention" of the British and natives in 1760. But once again, his reasoning would have the British governor intending something that he was not constitutionally able to do. We have already seen that Governor Lawrence was well aware of the constitutional restrictions placed upon his power. What is very unfortunate is that none of this fundamental constitutional law was considered by the judges of the Supreme Court of Canada who signed the majority decision in *Marshall (No. 1)*. It does not appear to have been brought to their attention by any party. This reflects, in my respectful view, a wider failure to acknowledge historic constraints, including legal constraints, on broad assertions of native treaty rights.

12

After the *Marshall* Decisions: Legal Uncertainty and Government Response

In the months after the release of the Supreme Court of Canada decisions in *Marshall (No. 1)* and *Marshall (No. 2)* in the fall of 1999, little was known and less said about the mistakes in these decisions. Only Dr Patterson spoke up to point out some of the historical errors the court had made.[1] In the meantime, throughout the Maritime Provinces, native bands demanded settlement of their "*Marshall (No. 1)* fishing rights." After all, while the Supreme Court of Canada had toned down its language in *Marshall (No. 2)*, *Marshall (No. 1)* had not been overruled. On the contrary, the court had reaffirmed native treaty entitlement in the fishery. It has been suggested that native peoples in the Maritime Provinces "came away from the Supreme Court in *Marshall (No. 1)* with ... more than any Aboriginal group in any other case in the history of the Court."[2] The response of the federal government was to appoint James MacKenzie, the chief federal negotiator for Labrador land claims, to negotiate fishing agreements with native bands in the region. By early 2004 agreements were reached with twenty-nine of the thirty-four bands. Under the agreements, native communities received benefits such as fishing vessels, licences, gear, and training. The cost to the Canadian taxpayer was "over half a billion dollars."[3] For example, the band at Burnt Church, New Brunswick, agreed to a $20 million package of benefits. But the Shubenacadie Band in Nova Scotia refused a similar $20 million agreement in the

spring of 2004. Their chief said that the proposal was "an insult
to us ... our rights are worth more than that."[4] The licences
granted to native bands included scallop, lobster, snow crab,
tuna, groundfish, and shrimp licences. To illustrate the value of
these licences, in Burnt Church the band was given seventeen
fishing licences worth $400,000 each (including boats and gear)
by 2002.[5]

The licences provided to native peoples under these agreements have caused controversy. For example, to maintain catch
levels and prevent overfishing and consequent pressure on
stock, while integrating aboriginals into the lobster fishery, federal government strategy has been to "buy out" the licences of
retiring fishermen and transfer those licences to native bands.
The cost of licences has, accordingly, escalated so that "the cost
is now well beyond the reach of the next generation of non-
Aboriginals who aspire to fish lobster."[6] A reallocation of the
snow crab quota in the spring of 2003 led to riots in Shippegan, New Brunswick, destruction of native traps and boats, and
arson at a processing plant.[7] By 2006 most remaining native
bands in the Maritime region had entered into a fishing agreement with the federal government. All agreements expired in
2006, when the federal Department of Fisheries and Oceans
undertook negotiation of longer-term agreements. Presumably,
the cost to the Canadian taxpayer will be more than the half billion dollars already spent. And the entire basis for these agreements and the expenditure of federal monies that they mandate
is said to be the decision of the Supreme Court of Canada in
Marshall (No. 1).

The effect of the *Marshall* decisions at the provincial level has
been no less dramatic. Nova Scotia came under intense pressure
after the *Marshall (No. 1)* decision was released. At about that
time, there was a great deal of activity in Nova Scotia's offshore
gas fields. Commercial production began, and construction
started on a pipeline to carry natural gas to markets in New
England. "Lateral" pipelines were built to carry gas to Halifax
and to Point Tupper, Nova Scotia. Native groups began legal
proceedings over each of these pipelines, asserting various rights

including *Marshall* treaty rights, and demanding a halt to the
pipelines pending resolution of their claims. In light of *Marshall*
(*No. 1*) this was a potent threat to a valuable economic opportunity for Nova Scotia. At the same time, in both New Brunswick and Nova Scotia, native groups had initiated "test" cases
in the courts, asserting "*Marshall* (*No. 1*) treaty rights" to log
on Crown land and claiming aboriginal title to – in other words,
ownership of – all or most of both provinces. These claims were
bold and breathtaking in their scope and implications. In
another era they would have been rejected outright. But after
Marshall (*No. 1*), even with the cautionary comments of *Marshall* (*No. 2*), they appeared to present a substantial threat, with
extraordinary economic implications for non-native individuals
and governments in Nova Scotia and New Brunswick. The grav-
ity of these claims was borne out in New Brunswick when the
majority of the Court of Appeal of that province announced its
decision in the *Bernard* case in the fall of 2003. They said that in
the same way the Supreme Court of Canada found the Halifax
Treaties gave native peoples a right to fish commercially, the
treaties gave native peoples the right to log commercially on
Crown land. Not only that, but the Chief Justice of New Brunswick, Joe Daigle, said that the Mirimachi Mi'kmaq owned the
northwest Mirimachi watershed, an enormous area of the province. In the same case, another judge of the Court of Appeal said
he agreed with Chief Justice Daigle, but that it was unnecessary
to decide the point. So, a majority of the Court of Appeal of
New Brunswick was essentially saying that most of the province was owned by native peoples. Even *privately* owned land
appeared to be encompassed in Judge Daigle's ruling.

The majority opinion of the New Brunswick Court of Appeal
that most of New Brunswick was native-owned did not follow
directly from the majority of the Supreme Court of Canada in
Marshall (*No. 1*). But it is hard to imagine that the activist
approach to the decision in *Marshall* (*No. 1*) was not influential
in encouraging the New Brunswick court in its sweeping statements. In Nova Scotia, the *Stephen Marshall* native logging test
case, nearly identical to that in New Brunswick, was making its

way through the courts at the same time. The Native claim was rejected in the lower courts, but in the Nova Scotia Court of Appeal it was received more sympathetically. While the court did not go as far as the New Brunswick Court of Appeal, it said that a more expansive approach should be taken both to native claims of aboriginal title and to native claims to log under the Halifax Treaties than had been taken in the lower courts. The native claims were not endorsed, but they were not rejected either. The Nova Scotia Court of Appeal said there should be a new trial. These appeal court decisions created enormous legal uncertainty in the Maritime Provinces. Until they were reversed at the Supreme Court of Canada, Chief Justice Daigle's comments in New Brunswick threw into doubt the ownership of billions of dollars worth of privately held real estate. Treaty rights to commercial logging on Crown lands jeopardized the employment or income of non-native loggers in New Brunswick.

Shortly after the *Marshall (No. 1)* decision was rendered, the Province of Nova Scotia established an entirely new department of government, the Office of Aboriginal Affairs, to deal with native matters. In July 2002, the Nova Scotia government, through the Office of Aboriginal Affairs, and the federal government agreed with Nova Scotia's Mi'kmaq community to enter negotiations on a wide range of native matters and thereby resolve existing uncertainties by agreement. It is anticipated that these negotiations could last for a decade or longer. Prominent among those things that are to be the subject of negotiations are "treaty rights." The preamble to the document that initiates these negotiations specifically refers to the case of *R. v. Marshall (No. 1)*. When, in February 2007, the federal and provincial governments and Mi'kmaq representatives signed a Framework Agreement for their negotiations, *Marshall (No. 1)* was cited prominently as justification for the negotiations. "The Courts are what got us here," said the lawyer for the Mi'kmaq, referencing the decision in *Marshall (No. 1)*.[8] It is no exaggeration to say that the creation of a whole new level of provincial bureaucracy and the province's decision to undertake long-term negoti-

ations with native people in Nova Scotia were almost entirely the result of the decision in *Marshall (No. 1)*.[9]

Dramatic shifts in the policies of both provincial and federal governments followed the decision. Those shifts in policy have entailed the expenditure of enormous sums of taxpayer's money, money that might otherwise be allocated to the many other pressing needs that affect native and non-native peoples alike. Underlying all of this are the fundamental historical and legal errors of *Marshall (No. 1)*.

13

Stephen Marshall/Bernard

The issues raised in *Stephen Marshall/Bernard* have been described above in some detail. They are a very important part of this story because, when these cases reached the Supreme Court of Canada in 2005, they presented that Court with its first opportunity to revisit its decisions in *Marshall (No. 1)* and *Marshall (No. 2)*. The Court's view of those cases would govern the outcome in the *Stephen Marshall/Bernard* cases. In the end, the Supreme Court of Canada significantly restricted the *Marshall (No. 1)* treaty right and rejected the claims to aboriginal title. But there is a good deal to tell about these cases before they ever reached that Court.

In the *Bernard* case in New Brunswick, native people cut logs on Crown lands near the Little Sevogle River, one of the tributaries of the Northwest Miramichi River, about 60 km from Miramichi City. Mr Bernard drove the tractor-trailer hauling spruce logs and was charged with unlawful possession of timber from Crown lands under New Brunswick's Crown Lands and Forests Act. As noted, he argued that he was authorized by treaty to harvest these logs. He also claimed that aboriginal title to the lands from which they were cut meant that the logs were native-owned. The trial was not concluded when the Supreme Court of Canada rendered its decision in *Marshall (No. 1)*.

In the *Stephen Marshall* case in Nova Scotia, the facts were a little more complex. Over a period of several months in 1998 and

1999, thirty-five Mi'kmaq in fourteen locations scattered over Mainland Nova Scotia and Cape Breton entered Crown lands and cut timber without permission. They were charged with violating Nova Scotia's Crown Lands Act. They claimed "*Marshall (No. 1)* treaty rights" to log on Crown land. They also claimed aboriginal title to, in effect, the whole of Nova Scotia.

In Nova Scotia, the trial judge convicted the native loggers, and they appealed to the Nova Scotia Supreme Court.[1] This appeal presented Nova Scotia with the first opportunity to challenge one of the fundamental mistakes in the *Marshall (No. 1)* case. While *Marshall (No. 1)* involved one native person from Cape Breton, the trial court in the case and the Supreme Court of Canada dealt with *Marshall (No. 1)* as if it involved all native bands in the Atlantic region of Canada. This was clearly improper. In *Stephen Marshall* so many natives from so many different parts of Nova Scotia were involved that the prosecution was able to question whether they could all claim *Marshall (No. 1)* treaty rights under a Halifax Treaty of 1760–61. If a native person could not legitimately claim to be a beneficiary of a band that signed a Halifax Treaty, they were obviously ineligible to claim "*Marshall (No. 1)* treaty rights." Justice Scanlan agreed. He said, "it is not clear that all bands had in fact signed treaties"[2] and pointed to evidence that perhaps only half of the bands signed a Halifax Treaty in 1760–61.[3] Despite these comments, the federal government determined to procure "fishing agreements" with every one of the thirty-four native bands in the Atlantic Region, all the while suggesting that these agreements are necessary to acquit "*Marshall (No. 1)* treaty rights." For example, the federal program pursuant to which fisheries agreements with native bands have been negotiated, and the quota reduced for non-native fishers to allow native commercial access, was named the "*Marshall* Response Initiative."[4] The suggestion that these agreements were constitutionally required to vindicate native treaty rights precludes any real public debate about them. Any objection can be met with the response that the Constitution must be complied with. Quite apart from the constitutional and historical flaws in *Marshall (No. 1)*, the fact is

that agreements with *all* native bands were *not* constitutionally required.[5] Taxpayers are entitled to more frank disclosure from their government. These fishing agreements were social policy initiatives whose constitutional basis was highly questionable. As noted earlier, this is not a book about policy. It may well be that as a matter of policy it is a good thing to widen native participation in various fisheries. That may be the appropriate approach to assist native communities if, in the past, they have been unfairly hindered from participating in the fishery, or as an economic development initiative for native bands. But policy should not be characterized as constitutional obligation.

As the *Stephen Marshall* and *Bernard* cases worked their way up the judicial appeal process, one simple point was very troubling. In *Marshall (No. 1)* very limited evidence of a native trade in fish had been transformed by the Supreme Court of Canada into a substantial treaty entitlement to fish commercially. There had been no evidence that fish were traded at truckhouses, while the only evidence of a trade in fish was of a trade that was occasional or incidental. In the *Stephen Marshall* and *Bernard* cases evidence suggested that native people had occasionally traded wooden items such as snowshoes and canoes to non-natives. There was very little evidence of this, but there was some. So why would the Supreme Court of Canada not simply say that, as with fish, there was also a treaty right to harvest and sell timber? This, after all, is what the New Brunswick Court of Appeal had said.

The critical document in an appeal to the Supreme Court of Canada is the written argument, known as the "factum." Nova Scotia's factum in the *Stephen Marshall* case (which was to be heard together with the *Bernard* case) was due to be filed in the early fall of 2004. About two weeks before the factum was due to be filed, it suddenly dawned on us that somewhere there was a reference to an old British law that dealt with timber in the British colonies. But where? There were about 10,000 pages of trial testimony and thousands of pages of documentary exhibits in the *Stephen Marshall* case and nearly that much again in the *Bernard* case. An exhaustive search located the document, and

it led to a whole chapter, obscure but important, of the colonial history of Nova Scotia.

In the 1700s Britain had run out of ship timber and masts for the Royal Navy. The British viewed Nova Scotia as a great store of valuable naval timber. By statute in 1721 and 1729 the British Parliament had specifically reserved pine timber in Nova Scotia for the Navy.[6] Moreover, the Instructions to the British governors in Nova Scotia directed them to safeguard the province's timber resources for the Navy. The importance of this was in relation to the analysis of the Supreme Court of Canada in *Marshall (No. 1)*. Justice Binnie had said the treaty benefits were the "common intention" of the British and natives. Now it could be shown very clearly that the British *could not* have intended to grant timber rights to native people under the Halifax Treaties. The British governor who negotiated the treaties could not have intended to violate British law and his own Instructions by granting away timber rights. The point was neat, simple, soundly grounded in law and history, and difficult to assail. As the filing date for the factum approached, there was good reason to be very confident that this argument alone could be decisive against the treaty claim to log on Crown lands. At the same time, it was necessary to advance the arguments challenging the decision in *Marshall (No. 1)*. There was significant uncertainty as to how government should respond by way of policy to *Marshall (No. 1)*, and the answer to these points would provide much-needed guidance. But next came a crisis and a very near miss.

As the *Bernard* and *Stephen Marshall* cases made their way along, Nova Scotia developed a strong relationship with the prosecutors for New Brunswick who were arguing the *Bernard* case. The week before factums were due to be filed at the Supreme Court of Canada, there was a small reason to telephone a colleague in New Brunswick. In the course of that chat, the colleague mentioned a concession that New Brunswick was making in their factum. What he said was disturbing. New Brunswick would be conceding that natives in the province had a treaty right, under the Halifax Treaties, to be consulted and

accommodated in respect of New Brunswick's natural resources. This concession had been endorsed by the attorney general of New Brunswick himself. There was no basis whatever for this concession in the evidence. Moreover *Stephen Marshall* and *Bernard* dealt only with logs. New Brunswick's intended concession dealt with all New Brunswick's natural resources – hydroelectric power at Mactaquak, coal at Minto, potash at Sussex – quite apart from logs. Any decision with respect to any natural resources of the province would have to be discussed with native people. Not only that, but "accommodation" meant that native people would have a financial claim on those resources.[7] New Brunswick was giving away the farm. Time was now of the essence. New Brunswick's factum was scheduled to be filed at the first of the week, and it was now nearly the weekend. Could they be convinced to drop their argument before their filing deadline? The telephones hummed. How the ultimate decision was made is not entirely clear. Apparently, political and industry heavyweights were involved and, ultimately, Premier Bernard Lord ordered that the concession be dropped. What seems clear is that much of the impetus for the concession came from the *Marshall (No. 1)* decision. It did not, of course, say anything like what New Brunswick intended to concede. But the thrust and tone of the decision seem to have led responsible people to think that the Court's mind on other matters was made up, and nothing was left but to acquiesce. Such is the power of the Supreme Court of Canada. But for a chance phone call to a New Brunswick colleague to chat about small unrelated matters, that province would have committed itself to a treaty interpretation that would have cost New Brunswick hundreds of millions of dollars. The concession itself would have caused tangled legal confusion. Would it have been binding for all time? Could New Brunswick ever have resiled from it? What effect would it have had on Nova Scotia? What effect would it have had on the Supreme Court of Canada's analysis of the *Stephen Marshall/ Bernard* cases? Fortunately, those problems never arose.

Before turning to the Court's decision in *Stephen Marshall/ Bernard*, a small point is worth mentioning. A factum for the

Supreme Court of Canada is limited in length to forty pages. That is not a lot of space to argue the weighty issues that were to be dealt with in *Stephen Marshall/Bernard*: whether there was a treaty right to log on Crown lands and the legal framework for analyzing issues of aboriginal title in Nova Scotia and New Brunswick. In addition, it was decided to argue that *Marshall (No. 1)* was wrongly decided. Forty pages could not possibly do all of this justice, and in August 2004 an application to the Court was made for permission to file a longer factum, explaining why the extra space was necessary. This was the first inkling the other side had that the question of whether *Marshall (No. 1)* was wrong would be put forcefully to the Court.[8] It triggered an interesting response. Native chiefs in Nova Scotia petitioned the provincial Minister of Justice, asking him to order that the argument not be made. The irony is that because of the Report of the Marshall Inquiry into the wrongful imprisonment of Mr Marshall, the Nova Scotia Public Prosecution Service is effectively independent of the political arena. As a result, the chiefs' petition went nowhere. The challenge to the decision in *Marshall (No. 1)* would proceed.

So when Nova Scotia filed its factum, it argued specifically and unambiguously that the decision of the majority of the Supreme Court of Canada *in Marshall (No. 1)* was wrongly decided. Nova Scotia argued "there is no right to hunt, fish and gather and trade for necessaries under the Halifax Treaties,"[9] and went on to raise several of the points that have been set out in earlier chapters of this book.[10] In oral argument the point was elaborated, "the Governor could not have intended to agree to a treaty term as described by this court in *Marshall (No. 1)*."

This is how Chief Justice McLachlin, writing for the majority, characterized Nova Scotia's position: "The appellant Crown takes a narrower view of the import of the truckhouse clause. *It accepts Marshall 1 and 2*, but argues that the respondents misread them."[11] Nova Scotia did not "accept *Marshall 1 and 2*." Nova Scotia argued that *Marshall (No. 1)* was wrongly decided. There can have been no misunderstanding here. Nova Scotia's position was expressed clearly and directly. But, rather than deal

with the merits of the arguments, the Supreme Court of Canada avoided them and in doing so misrepresented Nova Scotia's position. This was not a case that was decided with dispatch, where inattentiveness could be blamed. Logging is critical to the economy of the Maritime Provinces, and the Court was well aware of that. Nova Scotia's submissions challenged a case that had caused divisiveness, including violence, on the East Coast and was for that reason without precedent. Much was riding on the decision in *Stephen Marshall/Bernard* and the Court deliberated for six months before rendering its decision.

It is difficult to characterize the Court's comments as other than reflecting a disinclination to consider its earlier decision in error. This is, in my opinion, a political choice about legal decision-making. It may be that judicial decisions of the highest court in the land should ordinarily be considered final. But, in other areas of the law, the Supreme Court of Canada has reversed itself.[12] *Marshall (No. 1)* led to antagonism, violence, instability, and uncertainty. It shattered long-standing legal and regulatory regimes. And it is full of mistakes. It is perplexing that in these circumstances the Supreme Court of Canada would not address the arguments that are fatal to an earlier decision and, in avoiding those arguments, misrepresent Nova Scotia's position. There is merit in the wisdom of the Supreme Court of the United States, which has not infrequently reversed itself. "The Court has a special responsibility where questions of constitutional law are involved to review its decisions from time to time and where compelling reasons present themselves to refuse to follow erroneous precedent; otherwise, its mistakes in interpreting the Constitution are extremely difficult to alleviate."[13]

When representatives of the attorney general of a province state unequivocally that a previous decision of the Court is wrongly decided, the point should not to be ignored. Governments look to the Court to express the law that will guide policy-making. When the law is not clarified, governments are left uncertain of their obligations. This is especially problematic in the field of aboriginal law, where the Courts have repeatedly exhorted governments and natives to negotiate.[14] When test

cases present questions whose answers will guide those negotiations, courts are remiss when they avoid answering. They
plunge the negotiations into uncertainty and provide a recipe
for failure of the very negotiations the courts have promoted.
Apologists for judicial activism often describe activist judicial
decisions as merely part of a "dialogue" between the courts and
the legislature. A dialogue contemplates diligent attention to the
hard points of the conversation.

Turning to the substance of the decision of the Supreme Court
of Canada in *Stephen Marshall/Bernard*, the Court rejected
both the native claim of a treaty right to log and the native
assertions of aboriginal title. Moreover, the Court substantially
restricted its earlier decision in *Marshall (No. 1)*. The majority
decision, written by Chief Justice McLachlin, said that the
"truckhouse clause" in the Halifax Treaties was concerned with
"continued trade in the products the Mi'kmaq had *traditionally
traded* with Europeans."[15] Since logging was "not a traditional
Mi'kmaq activity,"[16] native peoples had no treaty right to log or
sell logs. The Halifax Treaties, said Chief Justice McLachlin,
grant only "the right to practice a traditional 1760 trading
activity."[17] This severely limits what natives can now claim is
their treaty entitlement. What native peoples had traditionally
traded in this region were furs and feathers, possibly some wild
fruits and berries, and occasionally perhaps items like baskets,
canoes, and snowshoes. Chief Justice McLachlin reiterated that
the majority in *Marshall (No. 1)* said the Mi'kmaq had historically traded fish. But the Court insisted that the treaty right
encompassed only traditionally *traded* products,[18] and not merely
natural resources traditionally *used* by native people.[19] On this
analysis, it is very difficult to see how native people have any
treaty right to commercially harvest such things as snow crab,
scallops, lobster, or shrimp, licences for all of which have been
provided by the federal government under the fishing agreements concluded with East Coast bands. It is highly unlikely
that any of these things were traditionally traded by native
people on the East Coast given that the harvest of these species,
particularly deepwater species like snow crab, shrimp, and

scallops, would have involved technology historically unknown to native peoples.[20]

So the result of the *Stephen Marshall/Bernard* decision was to severely restrict native claims under *Marshall (No. 1)* in relation to the fishery, the forests, and other natural resources in the Maritime Provinces. But while tattered and clipped, *Marshall (No. 1)* was not overruled. It was upheld and read down. And precisely how this was accomplished is not very convincing.

The majority in *Stephen Marshall/Bernard* confirmed that the "truckhouse clause" of the Halifax Treaties "granted the Mi'kmaq the right to continue to trade in items traded in 1760–61."[21] They made three points in so concluding. None of their points is compelling. Their first point was that the clause was "concerned with *what* could be traded," and "thus ... was concerned with traditionally traded products."[22] This really is a highly implausible reading of the clause. The clause prohibits trade with the French or anyone else except persons licensed by the government. So it is concerned with *who* could trade with natives. It prohibits trade "but with such persons or the managers of such Truckhouses as shall be appointed ..." So it could be said to be concerned with *where* trade would take place. But the clause says absolutely nothing about *what* would be traded or what could be harvested to trade. Moreover, if the truckhouse clause was "concerned with traditionally traded products," it must have been concerned with what was traditionally traded *at truckhouses*. But remember, there was no evidence in *Marshall (No. 1)* of any trade in fish at truckhouses. So the Court's analysis in *Stephen Marshall/Bernard* is not consistent with *Marshall (No. 1)*. If the truckhouse clause was concerned with what was traditionally traded at truckhouses (*Stephen Marshall*) and if fish were not traditionally traded at truckhouses, it is hard to see how there is any treaty right to fish. On the analysis in *Stephen Marshall/Bernard* Mr Marshall should have been convicted in *Marshall (No. 1)*.

Even more perplexing, the whole thrust of reasoning in *Marshall (No. 1)* envisaged the right to "hunt, fish and gather" as a term of the treaty *outside* the truckhouse clause. The Court said

that if the language of the truckhouse clause *alone* was considered Mr Marshall would have failed. Justice Binnie had found in the "underlying negotiations a "broader agreement" than was recorded in the treaty document.[23] But now in *Stephen Marshall/Bernard* the Court was suggesting that a right to hunt, fish, gather, and trade flowed from the truckhouse clause itself. In *Marshall (No. 1)* even Justice Binnie had agreed that the truckhouse clause "standing in isolation" did not support Mr Marshall.[24] The reasoning in *Marshall (No. 1)* and *Stephen Marshall/Bernard* is wholly contradictory.

The second point the majority in *Stephen Marshall/Bernard* made, in suggesting that the treaty granted a right to trade traditionally traded items, was to point to the language of the truckhouse clause. They said that "Nothing" in the clause "comports a general right to harvest or gather all natural resources then used."[25] No one could quarrel with that. But this just confirms what the clause *does not* say or mean. It does not say how the clause *confers rights* to traditionally traded resources.

For that, and this was their third point, they simply relied on *Marshall (No. 1)*. They mentioned vaguely the "historic records" referred to in that decision, quoted some of the Court's comments in *Marshall (No. 1)* and *Marshall (No. 2)* and left it at that.[26] The fact that the majority in *Marshall (No. 1)* had badly misread the "historic records" and the fact that the treaty right described in that case was constitutionally unsound, were simply ignored.

What are we to make of all of this? I think it reflects a particular species of judicial choice, rather than constitutional law. Having decided *Marshall (No. 1)* as they had, the Supreme Court of Canada felt it could not overrule itself – not because its decision was the proper decision having regard to the evidence and applicable law but, rather, because the Court felt it would be inappropriate to overturn a decision that meant so much to native people on the East Coast. It seems that they were concerned that the Court not "lose face." Instead of overturning it, they gave it a very limited reach. In my view, that decision can be fairly characterized as political, made not by reference to law and evidence

but to policy and expediency.[27] We are left with the sinking suspicion that other difficult decisions will be based not primarily on law and evidence, but on political expediency. The result is not the rule of law. It is the rule of power without law.

14

The Failure of Judicial Activism

There is no pleasure in the criticism advanced here of the decision of the Supreme Court of Canada in *Marshall (No. 1)*. *Marshall (No. 1)* has come to represent, among native peoples in the Maritime provinces, something of a vindication of native grievances. Whether those grievances are justified and, if so, how they should be addressed, are matters of policy for the public, governments, and native communities to debate and discuss. That topic is far beyond the scope of this book and no opinion on it is expressed here. But the Supreme Court of Canada decision in *Marshall (No. 1)* intrudes as a powerful constitutionalized statement in that discussion, notwithstanding that it has been clipped by subsequent decisions and despite the unfortunate failure of Nova Scotia to participate in the case. The extraordinary impact of the decision on the people of the Maritime provinces demands that it be scrutinized closely, however much that scrutiny reveals it to be a false beacon to native peoples.

Neither is there pleasure in criticizing the authors of *Marshall (No. 1)* for the decision they rendered. Judges of the Supreme Court carry enormous responsibility. They are overwhelmed with work. They are inundated with submissions and arguments. They are still breaking sod with a relatively new Constitution, and they are ultimately charged to do "justice," a most difficult and elusive ideal. So the comments in this book are expressed with utmost respect. At the same time, it is precisely

because of the great power of our judges that their decisions must be examined closely and flaws revealed.

There is little doubt that mistakes were made in the trial court that contributed to the failure at the Supreme Court of Canada. *Marshall* (*No. 1*) dealt with *one* native person from Cape Breton, but the trial judge went well beyond his proper role to make rulings as to whether or not all other native peoples in the Maritime Provinces were subject to Halifax Treaties. This mistake drew no reproach from the Supreme Court of Canada. More than this, the federal Crown was thrown off as to the defence that Mr Marshall would rely on. They were told at the beginning of trial that the defence would be the Treaty of 1752. Not until after Dr Patterson had testified was it made clear that the defence would be entirely different. In my view, the federal Crown's position was so prejudiced that the trial ought to have been aborted and a new trial begun. Put shortly, the legal and historical basis necessary to fully rebut the defence based on the Halifax Treaties of 1760–61 was not elaborated. This would become crystal clear at the Supreme Court of Canada where Mr Marshall would claim that the 11 February 1760 document was central to his defence, yet the Crown's expert historian had never been asked about the document either by the Crown's lawyer or on cross-examination by Mr Wildsmith. This is a patent failure of the judicial process. In a case governed entirely by the historical record, it is unsatisfactory that the case should turn against a party on the characterization of a historical document that the party's expert historian has been precluded from discussing in his testimony. Yet this drew no comment from the Supreme Court of Canada. The majority adopted an analysis of the document that had not been advanced in or scrutinized by any lower court: historical analysis that is not persuasive and was rebutted by other documents and other evidence.

Another weakness in the trial judge's decision was in his summary of the evidence of native "fishing" and "trading." He said that for 250 years before the Halifax Treaties of 1760 the Mi'kmaq had traded "whatever their hunting, fishing and gathering produced" with Europeans. But the whole point of the

case was to discern what, if any, rights to trade fish were encompassed by the truckhouse clause of the treaties. He should have mentioned that there was no evidence of any trade of fish at truckhouses, that any trade in fish was small scale, occasional, and limited to individuals outside truckhouses and that in contrast the "truckhouse" trade was large-volume commercial trade in furs and feathers. But the Supreme Court of Canada equally ignored these subtleties, going on to conclude – in the absence of any evidence that fish were historically traded at truckhouses – that the truckhouse clause contemplated a commercial fishery.

Yet again, the trial judge's comment that the British accepted as "inherent in the treaties" the "existing Mi'kmaq way of life" was a sweeping and incautious statement that was embraced by the Supreme Court of Canada. It is something of a leap of judicial imagination to propose that a treaty clause modestly prohibiting trade outside truckhouses should be taken, rather, as a treaty right to an entire "way of life."

None of these shortcomings in the trial judge's decision was the subject of adverse comment by the Supreme Court of Canada. Indeed, the Court drew from them in support of its ultimate decision to find a treaty right and acquit Mr Marshall. At the same time, elsewhere in its decision, the Court's approach to law and evidence was incautious.

From the outset the Court's decision is doubtful. It describes a treaty right that was unheard of for 250 years, one that is not described in any historical document, and one that is a product of judicial conjecture as to what must have taken place in discussions long ago. All of that would seem to warrant that the decision be solidly supported, yet the analysis is unconvincing.

The finding that the trial judge had made an "irreconcilable" error is not borne out on a close examination of the trial judge's reasoning. More than that, the majority analysis of the treaty discussions flatly contradicted the facts found by the trial judge, and the majority went on to conclude that the trial judge had erred in not giving "adequate weight" to an argument that had never been suggested at trial.

Probably the most remarkable of the Court's mistakes was the approach it took to the 11 February 1760 document. That document was characterized by Justice Binnie as reflecting a Mi'kmaq demand, and that demand was the foundation for the treaty right he would go on to describe. But such a characterization of the document was inconsistent with a host of other evidence, including documents and expert opinion, showing that native peoples had surrendered without making any demands of the British. Moreover, the suggestion of a native demand and the treaty right said to flow from it was inconsistent with the trial judge's findings on questions of fact to which Justice Binnie was obliged to defer. It is difficult to understand how a review of the evidence and the trial judge's rulings could lead to the characterization of the document adopted by the majority. Moreover, it should have been apparent that Justice Binnie was dabbling in matters of fact not open to him. The trial judge had said that the treaty resulting from the discussions recorded in the 11 February 1760 document was "in conformance" with those discussions. That being the case, there could be no treaty right as described by Justice Binnie. Everyone agreed that the treaty document contained no such treaty right, and the trial judge said that the treaty conformed with the earlier discussions. Remember too that the document was never emphasized in argument in the courts below and Dr Patterson was never asked about it. So, at the stage of the case when the significant historical facts which would set the stage for legal argument were being established, the document was never considered significant. That alone should have served as notice to the majority that their interpretation of the document was historically novel. But Justice Binnie was not heedful of these warnings, choosing instead to fashion a history of native-British relations in Nova Scotia that had no basis in the record before the Court.

Beyond this, the "migration" of the treaty right out of the British Maliseet discussions and into Mi'kmaq treaties, some of which were signed many months later after native chiefs submitted unconditionally to the British, is not compelling. In this endeavour, Justice Binnie's reasoning is dubious – first, suggest-

ing the trial judge saw the 11 February discussions as "key" when that was not the case and, second, suggesting that because the *written* terms of all the treaties were alike, "oral" terms that he fashioned from the 11 February discussions must be common to them all.

What lies behind all of these mistakes is the Court's dabbling in matters of historical fact, the theatre of the trial judge, rather than in matters of law and principle, the proper role of the Supreme Court of Canada. In doing this, the majority relied on evidence that the trial judge had rejected, while relying on Dr Patterson's evidence for a proposition it does not fairly support. Quite simply, the majority decision lacks sufficient attention to the historical evidence.

It is little different in the Court's approach to law. The treaty right described by the Court is constitutionally unsound by reference to the constitutional framework of 1760s Nova Scotia. The governor of Nova Scotia could not, by treaty or otherwise, unilaterally confer upon native peoples legal rights of the sort described by Justice Binnie. Only the Legislature could do that. Yet the evidence revealing explicitly that both the governor and the House of Assembly were aware of and complied with their constitutional constraints was overlooked. Nor could the governor restrict rights unilaterally, as Justice Binnie suggested the treaty rights were restricted, to "necessaries." With respect to fishing, the *Magna Carta* prevented that very thing.

When the mistakes in *Marshall* (*No. 1*) are assembled, they show compellingly, in my opinion, that the decision is deeply in error. Native people in the Maritime Provinces do not have treaty rights anything like those described by Justice Binnie in *Marshall* (*No. 1*). The ruling that they do is unfounded, pure and simple. But beneath the mistakes a more insidious problem appears to lie. The problem is uninhibited judicial activism. In the earlier s. 35 cases of *Sparrow*, *Van der Peet*, and *Delgamuukw*, and later in *Haida*, we saw judicial activism manifested in an incautious approach to the language of the Constitution and an unwarranted departure from long-standing common-law rules. *Marshall (No. 1)* went still further in its disregard of

evidence, its unwarranted forays into "fact finding," its disregard for procedural impropriety, its inattention to the rulings of the trial judge, and its failure to reference fundamental constitutional principle. What *Marshall (No. 1)* appears to reflect is a judicial attitude that inclines to a result, and a lack of caution that too quickly overlooks inconsistent evidence, law, and procedural impropriety.[1]

Marshall (No. 2) and *Stephen Marshall/Bernard* are similarly flawed. *Marshall (No. 2)* was an exercise in judicial damage control – purely an exercise in judicial power calculated to appease public opinion and restore public confidence. In a "political" sense, perhaps, it was necessary, given the trespasses of *Marshall (No. 1)*. But when public opinion is the dominant concern of our judges in rendering their judgments, then the rule of law is sorely wounded. *Stephen Marshall/Bernard* contains a misrepresentation to avoid grappling with the errors of *Marshall (No. 1)*. Its analysis of the supposed *Marshall (No. 1)* treaty rights is so flawed as to be wholly inconsistent with *Marshall (No. 1)* itself. The decision seems as calculated as was *Marshall (No. 2)* – an effort to reduce the impact of *Marshall (No. 1)* and thereby cater to non-native anxiety, without wholly overturning the case, a result which would obviously have been excoriated by native opinion. Here again, the approach of the Court is to exercise power regardless of law, evidence, and argument, and apparently with careful regard to public sentiment. In a constitutional democracy, courts of law fail us *unless* their decisions are governed by law and evidence.

Beyond this, the discussion of federal native policy in the public forum should not be taking place under the guise of constitutional requirement. Yet this is precisely what has happened in the Maritime Provinces. Hundreds of millions of dollars of taxpayers' money, which could be used for the many pressing demands of the general public, have been diverted to acquit *Marshall (No. 1)* "treaty rights." These, the public are told, are constitutional obligations. There is no choice but to satisfy them. An entire policy of the federal Department of Fisheries and Oceans, it is said, including distribution of various fishing

licences, training programs, and equipment purchases, has been calculated to meet this constitutional requirement. Even setting aside the fundamental historical and constitutional objections to the decision in *Marshall (No. 1)*, it is clear that not all native bands in the Maritime Provinces can claim the treaty rights described in that case and, based on the evidence in that case, it is difficult to discern an entitlement to fish species such as lobster, snow crab, shrimp, or scallops. The public has been led to believe quite the contrary. Federal policy is an exercise of federal power. It is not an exercise of law or constitutional obligation, yet it is proclaimed as that very thing. Provincial policies have also been affected by by *Marshall (No. 1)*. The Province of Nova Scotia has created an entire new department of government and, with the federal Crown, has embarked on an entire generation of "treaty negotiations," all as a consequence of the Court's decision.

When Prime Minister Trudeau engineered changes to our Constitution in 1982, vesting unprecedented powers in our judges, he left us vulnerable. We do not have the tools to respond when judicial power is improperly exercised. Our only appeal is to the judges themselves. *Stephen Marshall/Bernard* illustrates just how inadequate that resort is. I will leave it for others to discuss what controls or mechanisms should be invoked. My purpose is more narrow: to illustrate the problem of judges exceeding their proper powers and to suggest that the problem demands an effective remedy. It may be that a mechanical or structural repair is not the best response. It may be that the best solution is to caution the judiciary that "activism" as it appears to have manifested itself in *Marshall (No. 1)* is unacceptable and that courts must insist that their decisions are governed by law and evidence, even if that means that sometimes they must reverse themselves.

We should not be so naive as to think that our judges or our judicial system are perfect. Mere mistakes should not worry us unduly as long as they are acknowledged and corrected. Neither should we expect that judges will be wholly lacking in predisposition. Human nature and experiences incline us to opinions and

points of view, and judges are no different. But what we must expect from our judges is diligent attention to law and rigorous attentiveness to evidence. The rule of law, which we pride ourselves is the foundation of our Western democratic system, can be reduced to those two simple demands. The majority decision in *Marshall (No. 1)*, in my view, fails on both counts. It is an exercise in judicial power hardly constrained by law or evidence – power without law – and it should not be followed.

Earlier I mentioned comments made by two judges of the Supreme Court of Canada, Justice L'Heureux-Dube (now retired) and Chief Justice McLachlin. Their comments identified the controls inherent in judicial reasoning that could serve to limit judicial excess. For example, judges should "stick to the issue raised by the case" and justify results "in accordance with the principles of legal reasoning." These guiding principles were not honoured in *Marshall (No. 1)*. Had they been, the Supreme Court of Canada would not have strayed so badly. It is my hope that revealing the excesses of *Marshall (No. 1)* will lead other courts to be careful not to repeat the same mistakes. Whether this is enough to control determined judicial activists is not certain. Institutional, structural, or procedural reform may be necessary. Whatever the answer, there is little doubt that a correction is required when judges exercise powers absent the proper constraints on judicial authority. Today we call it "judicial activism." There is a beguiling innocence in that term. The words suggest that judges are doing merely what judges have always done, but with some greater imagination or panache. But when judges decide cases without due regard to procedure, law, evidence, or argument, their misdeeds cannot be denied by beguiling terminology. They have exercised power without law. That is a violation of our Constitution and the rule of law, and it is the legacy of *Marshall (No. 1)*.

Another legacy of the decision is the court's profoundly unfortunate failure to grasp – or even mention – the inspiring words of the 1761 Governor's Farm Treaty Ceremony. In a brutal age, during a brutal war, in a time when Acadians were ripped from their homes and transported and other races were

dehumanized to justify enslavement, native chiefs and British officials in Nova Scotia agreed that ever after they would be "under the same laws and for the same rights and liberties." That noble ideal resonates still, after 250 years. Truly it is a treaty term worthy of recognition and affirmation under section 35 of our modern Constitution.

R. v. Marshall

Donald John Marshall, Jr. v. Her Majesty The Queen and The Attorney General for New Brunswick, the West Nova Fishermen's Coalition, the Native Council of Nova Scotia and the Union of New Brunswick Indians

The judgment of Lamer C.J. and L'Heureux-Dubé, Cory, Iacobucci and Binnie JJ. was delivered by

1 BINNIE J. – On an August morning six years ago the appellant and a companion, both Mi'kmaq Indians, slipped their small outboard motorboat into the coastal waters of Pomquet Harbour, Antigonish County, Nova Scotia to fish for eels. They landed 463 pounds, which they sold for $787.10, and for which the appellant was arrested and prosecuted.

2 On an earlier August morning, some 235 years previously, the Reverend John Seycombe of Chester, Nova Scotia, a missionary and sometime dining companion of the Governor, noted with satisfaction in his diary, "Two Indian squaws brought seal skins and eels to sell". That transaction was apparently completed without arrest or other incident. The thread of continuity between these events, it seems, is that the Mi'kmaq people have sustained themselves in part by harvesting and trading fish (including eels) since Europeans first visited the coasts of what is now Nova Scotia in the 16th century. The appellant says that they are entitled to continue to do so now by virtue of a treaty right agreed

to by the British Crown in 1760. As noted by my colleague, Justice McLachlin, the appellant is guilty as charged unless his activities were protected by an existing aboriginal or treaty right. No reliance was placed on any aboriginal right; the appellant chooses to rest his case entirely on the Mi'kmaq treaties of 1760–61.

3 The trial judge ([1996] N.S.J. No. 246 (QL) (Prov. Ct.)) accepted as applicable the terms of a Treaty of Peace and Friendship signed on March 10, 1760 at Halifax. The parties disagree about the existence of alleged oral terms, as well as the implications of the "trade clause" written into that document. From this distance, across more than two centuries, events are necessarily seen as "through a glass, darkly". The parties were negotiating in March 1760 in the shadow of the great military and political turmoil following the fall of the French fortresses at Louisbourg, Cape Breton (June 1758) and Quebec (September 1759). The Mi'kmaq signatories had been allies of the French King, and Montreal would continue to be part of New France until it subsequently fell in June 1760. The British had almost completed the process of expelling the Acadians from southern Nova Scotia. Both the Treaty of Paris, ending hostilities, and the Royal Proclamation of 1763 were still three years in the future. Only six years prior to the signing of the treaties, the British Governor of Nova Scotia had issued a Proclamation (May 14, 1756) offering rewards for the killing and capturing of Mi'kmaq throughout Nova Scotia, which then included New Brunswick. The treaties were entered into in a period where the British were attempting to expand and secure their control over their northern possessions. The subtext of the Mi'kmaq treaties was reconciliation and mutual advantage.

4 I would allow this appeal because nothing less would uphold the honour and integrity of the Crown in its dealings with the Mi'kmaq people to secure their peace and friendship, as best the content of those treaty promises can now be ascertained. In reaching this conclusion, I recognize that if the present dispute had arisen out of a modern commercial transaction between two parties of relatively equal bargaining power, or if, as held by

the courts below, the short document prepared at Halifax under the direction of Governor Charles Lawrence on March 10, 1760 was to be taken as being the "entire agreement" between the parties, it would have to be concluded that the Mi'kmaq had inadequately protected their interests. However, the courts have not applied strict rules of interpretation to treaty relationships. In *R. v. Denny* (1990), 55 C.C.C. (3d) 322, and earlier decisions cited therein, the Nova Scotia Court of Appeal has affirmed the Mi'kmaq aboriginal right to fish for food. The appellant says the treaty allows him to fish for trade. In my view, the 1760 treaty does affirm the right of the Mi'kmaq people to continue to provide for their own sustenance by taking the products of their hunting, fishing and other gathering activities, and trading for what in 1760 was termed "necessaries". This right was always subject to regulation. The Crown does not suggest that the regulations in question accommodate the treaty right. The Crown's case is that no such treaty right exists. Further, no argument was made that the treaty right was extinguished prior to 1982, and no justification was offered by the Crown for the several prohibitions at issue in this case. Accordingly, in my view, the appellant is entitled to an acquittal.

ANALYSIS

5 The starting point for the analysis of the alleged treaty right must be an examination of the specific words used in any written memorandum of its terms. In this case, the task is complicated by the fact the British signed a series of agreements with individual Mi'kmaq communities in 1760 and 1761 intending to have them consolidated into a comprehensive Mi'kmaq treaty that was never in fact brought into existence. The trial judge, Embree Prov. Ct. J., found that by the end of 1761 all of the Mi'kmaq villages in Nova Scotia had entered into separate but similar treaties. Some of these documents are missing. Despite some variations among some of the documents, Embree Prov. Ct. J. was satisfied that the written terms applicable to this dispute were contained in a Treaty of Peace and Friendship entered

into by Governor Charles Lawrence on March 10, 1760, which in its entirety provides as follows:

Treaty of Peace and Friendship concluded by [His Excellency Charles Lawrence] Esq. Govr and Comr. in Chief in and over his Majesty's Province of Nova Scotia or Accadia with Paul Laurent chief of the LaHave tribe of Indians at Halifax in the Province of N.S. or Acadia.

I, Paul Laurent do for myself and the tribe of LaHave Indians of which I am Chief do acknowledge the jurisdiction and Dominion of His Majesty George the Second over the Territories of Nova Scotia or Accadia and we do make submission to His Majesty in the most perfect, ample and solemn manner.

And I do promise for myself and my tribe that I nor they shall not molest any of His Majesty's subjects or their dependents, in their settlements already made or to be hereafter made or in carrying on their Commerce or in any thing whatever within the Province of His said Majesty or elsewhere and if any insult, robbery or outrage shall happen to be committed by any of my tribe satisfaction and restitution shall be made to the person or persons injured.

That neither I nor any of my tribe shall in any manner entice any of his said Majesty's troops or soldiers to desert, nor in any manner assist in conveying them away but on the contrary will do our utmost endeavours to bring them back to the Company, Regiment, Fort or Garrison to which they shall belong.

That if any Quarrel or Misunderstanding shall happen between myself and the English or between them and any of my tribe, neither I, nor they shall take any private satisfaction or Revenge, but we will apply for redress according to the Laws established in His said Majesty's Dominions.

That all English prisoners made by myself or my tribe shall be sett at Liberty and that we will use our utmost endeavours to prevail on the other tribes to do the same, if any prisoners shall happen to be in their hands.

And I do further promise for myself and my tribe that we will not either directly nor indirectly assist any of the enemies of His most sacred Majesty King George the Second, his heirs or Successors, nor hold any manner of Commerce traffick nor intercourse with them, but on the contrary will as much as may be in our power discover and make known to His Majesty's Governor, any ill designs which may be formed or contrived against His Majesty's subjects. <u>And I do further engage that we will not traffick, barter or Exchange any Commodities in any manner but with such persons or the managers of such Truck houses as shall be appointed or Established by His Majesty's Governor at Lunenbourg or Elsewhere in Nova Scotia or Accadia.</u>

And for the more effectual security of the due performance of this Treaty and every part thereof I do promise and Engage that a certain number of persons of my tribe which shall not be less in number than two prisoners shall on or before September next reside as Hostages at Lunenburg or at such other place or places in this Province of Nova Scotia or Accadia as shall be appointed for that purpose by His Majesty's Governor of said Province which Hostages shall be exchanged for a like number of my tribe when requested.

And all these foregoing articles and every one of them made with His Excellency C. L., His Majesty's Governor I do promise for myself and on of sd part — behalf of my tribe that we will most strictly keep and observe in the most solemn manner.

In witness whereof I have hereunto putt my mark and seal at Halifax in Nova Scotia this day of March one thousand
Paul Laurent

I do accept and agree to all the articles of the forgoing treaty in Faith and Testimony whereof I have signed these present I have caused my seal to be hereunto affixed this day of march in the 33 year of His Majesty's Reign and in the year of Our lord – 1760
Chas Lawrence [Emphasis added.]

6 The underlined portion of the document, the so-called "trade clause", is framed in negative terms as a restraint on the ability of the Mi'kmaq to trade with non-government individuals. A "truckhouse" was a type of trading post. The evidence showed that the promised government truckhouses disappeared from Nova Scotia within a few years and by 1780 a replacement regime of government licensed traders had also fallen into disuse while the British Crown was attending to the American Revolution. The trial judge, Embree Prov. Ct. J., rejected the Crown's argument that the trade clause amounted to nothing more than a negative covenant. He found, at para. 116, that it reflected a grant to the Mi'kmaq of the positive right to "bring the products of their hunting, fishing and gathering to a truckhouse to trade". The Court of Appeal ((1997), 159 N.S.R. (2d) 186) found that the trial judge misspoke when he used the word "right". It held that the trade clause does not grant the Mi'kmaq any rights. Instead, the trade clause represented a "mechanism imposed upon them to help ensure that the peace was a lasting one, by obviating their need to trade with enemies of the British" (p. 208). When the truckhouses disappeared, said the court, so did any vestiges of the restriction or entitlement, and that was the end of it.

7 The appellant's position is that the truckhouse provision not only incorporated the alleged right to trade, but also the right to pursue traditional hunting, fishing and gathering activities in support of that trade. It seems clear that the words of the March 10, 1760 document, standing in isolation, do not support the appellant's argument. The question is whether the underlying negotiations produced a broader agreement between the British and the Mi'kmaq, memorialized only in part by the Treaty of Peace and Friendship, that would protect the appellant's activities that are the subject of the prosecution. I should say at the outset that the appellant overstates his case. In my view, the treaty rights are limited to securing "necessaries" (which I construe in the modern context, as equivalent to a moderate livelihood), and do not extend to the open-ended accumulation of

wealth. The rights thus construed, however, are, in my opinion, treaty rights within the meaning of s. 35 of the *Constitution Act, 1982*, and are subject to regulations that can be justified under the *Badger* test (*R. v. Badger*, [1996] 1 S.C.R 771).

8 Although the agreed statement of facts does not state explicitly that the appellant was exercising his rights for the purpose of necessaries, the Court was advised in the course of oral argument that the appellant "was engaged in a small-scale commercial activity to help subsidize or support himself and his common-law spouse". The Crown did not dispute this characterization and it is consistent with the scale of the operation, the amount of money involved, and the other surrounding facts. If at some point the appellant's trade and related fishing activities were to extend beyond what is reasonably required for necessaries, as hereinafter defined, he would be outside treaty protection, and can expect to be dealt with accordingly.

EVIDENTIARY SOURCES

9 The Court of Appeal took a strict approach to the use of extrinsic evidence when interpreting the Treaties of 1760–61. Roscoe and Bateman JJ.A. stated at p. 194: "While treaties must be interpreted in their historical context, extrinsic evidence cannot be used as an aid to interpretation, in the absence of ambiguity". I think this approach should be rejected for at least three reasons.

10 Firstly, even in a modern commercial context, extrinsic evidence is available to show that a written document does not include all of the terms of an agreement. Rules of interpretation in contract law are in general more strict than those applicable to treaties, yet Professor Waddams states in *The Law of Contracts* (3rd ed. 1993), at para. 316:

> The parol evidence rule does not purport to exclude evidence designed to show whether or not the agreement has been "reduced to writing", or whether it was, or was not, the intention of the parties that it should be the exclusive

record of their agreement. Proof of this question is a pre-condition to the operation of the rule, and all relevant evidence is admissible on it. This is the view taken by Corbin and other writers, and followed in the Second Restatement.

See also <u>International Casualty Co. v. Thomson</u> (1913), 48 S.C.R. 167, per Idington J., at p. 191, and G. H. Treitel, *The Law of Contract* (9th ed. 1995), at p. 177. For an example of a treaty only partly reduced to writing, see *R. v. Taylor and Williams* (1981), 62 C.C.C. (2d) 227 (Ont. C.A.) (leave to appeal dismissed, [1981] 2 S.C.R. xi).

11 Secondly, even in the context of a treaty document that purports to contain all of the terms, this Court has made clear in recent cases that extrinsic evidence of the historical and cultural context of a treaty may be received even absent any ambiguity on the face of the treaty. MacKinnon A.C.J.O. laid down the principle in *Taylor and Williams*, supra, at p. 236:

... if there is evidence by conduct or otherwise as to how the parties understood the terms of the treaty, then such understanding and practice is of assistance in giving content to the term or terms.

The proposition is cited with approval in *Delgamuukw v. British Columbia*, [1997] 3 S.C.R. 1010 , at para. 87, *and R. v. Sioui*, [1990] 1 S.C.R. 1025 , at p. 1045.

12 Thirdly, where a treaty was concluded verbally and afterwards written up by representatives of the Crown, it would be unconscionable for the Crown to ignore the oral terms while relying on the written terms, per Dickson J. (as he then was) in *Guerin v. The Queen*, [1984] 2 S.C.R. 335. Dickson J. stated for the majority, at p. 388:

Nonetheless, the Crown, in my view, was not empowered by the surrender document to ignore the oral terms which the Band understood would be embodied in the lease. The oral representations form the backdrop against which the

Crown's conduct in discharging its fiduciary obligation must be measured. They inform and confine the field of discretion within which the Crown was free to act. After the Crown's agents had induced the Band to surrender its land on the understanding that the land would be leased on certain terms, it would be unconscionable to permit the Crown simply to ignore those terms.

The *Guerin* case is a strong authority in this respect because the surrender there could only be accepted by the Governor in Council, who was not made aware of any oral terms. The surrender could not have been accepted by the departmental officials who were present when the Musqueam made known their conditions. Nevertheless, the Governor in Council was held bound by the oral terms which "the Band understood would be embodied in the lease" (p. 388). In this case, unlike *Guerin,* the Governor did have authority to bind the Crown and was present when the aboriginal leaders made known their terms.

13 The narrow approach applied by the Court of Appeal to the use of extrinsic evidence apparently derives from the comments of Estey J. in *R. v. Horse*, [1988] 1 S.C.R. 187 , where, at p. 201, he expressed some reservations about the use of extrinsic materials, such as the transcript of negotiations surrounding the signing of Treaty No. 6, except in the case of ambiguity. (Estey J. went on to consider the extrinsic evidence anyway, at p. 203.) Lamer J., as he then was, mentioned this aspect of *Horse* in *Sioui,* supra, at p. 1049, but advocated a more flexible approach when determining the existence of treaties. Lamer J. stated, at p. 1068, that "[t]he historical context, which has been used to demonstrate the existence of the treaty, may equally assist us in interpreting the extent of the rights contained in it".

14 Subsequent cases have distanced themselves from a "strict" rule of treaty interpretation, as more recently discussed by Cory J., in *Badger,* supra, at para. 52:

... when considering a treaty, a court must take into account the context in which the treaties were negotiated, concluded

and committed to writing. The treaties, as written documents, recorded an agreement that had already been reached
orally and they did not always record the full extent of the
oral agreement: see Alexander Morris, *The Treaties of
Canada with the Indians of Manitoba and the North-West
Territories* (1880), at pp. 338–42; *Sioui*, supra, at p. 1068;
Report of the Aboriginal Justice Inquiry of Manitoba
(1991); Jean Friesen, *Grant me Wherewith to Make my
Living* (1985). The treaties were drafted in English by representatives of the Canadian government who, it should be
assumed, were familiar with common law doctrines. Yet, the
treaties were not translated in written form into the lan-
guages (here Cree and Dene) of the various Indian nations
who were signatories. Even if they had been, it is unlikely
that the Indians, who had a history of communicating only
orally, would have understood them any differently. As a
result, it is well settled that the words in the treaty must not
be interpreted in their strict technical sense nor subjected to
rigid modern rules of construction. [Emphasis added.]

"Generous" rules of interpretation should not be confused with
a vague sense of after-the-fact largesse. The special rules are dictated by the special difficulties of ascertaining what in fact was
agreed to. The Indian parties did not, for all practical purposes,
have the opportunity to create their own written record of the
negotiations. Certain assumptions are therefore made about the
Crown's approach to treaty making (honourable) which the
Court acts upon in its approach to treaty interpretation (flexible) as to the existence of a treaty (Sioui, supra, at p. 1049), the
completeness of any written record (the use, e.g., of context and
implied terms to make honourable sense of the treaty arrangement: *Simon v. The Queen*, [1985] 2 S.C.R. 387 , and *R. v. Sundown*, [1999] 1 S.C.R. 393), and the interpretation of treaty
terms once found to exist (Badger). The bottom line is the
Court's obligation is to "choose from among the various possible interpretations of the common intention [at the time the
treaty was made] the one which best reconciles" the Mi'kmaq

interests and those of the British Crown (Sioui, per Lamer J., at p. 1069 (emphasis added)). In *Taylor and Williams*, supra, the Crown conceded that points of oral agreement recorded in contemporaneous minutes were included in the treaty (p. 230) and the court concluded that their effect was to "preserve the historic right of these Indians to hunt and fish on Crown lands" (p. 236). The historical record in the present case is admittedly less clear-cut, and there is no parallel concession by the Crown.

THE 1752 MI'KMAQ TREATY

15 In 1749, following one of the continuing wars between Britain and France, the British Governor at Halifax had issued what was apparently the first of the Proclamations "authorizing the military and all British subjects to kill or capture any Mi'kmaq found, and offering a reward". This prompted what the Crown's expert witness at trial referred to as a "British-Mi'kmaq war". By 1751 relations had eased to the point where the 1749 Proclamation was revoked, and in November 1752 the Shubenacadie Mi'kmaq entered into the 1752 Treaty which was the subject of this Court's decision in *Simon*. This treaty stated in Article 4 that:

> It is agreed that the said Tribe of Indians shall not be hindered from, but have free liberty of Hunting and Fishing as usual and that if they shall think a Truckhouse needful at the River Chibenaccadie or any other place of their resort, they shall have the same built and proper Merchandize lodged therein, to be exchanged for what the Indians shall have to dispose of, and that in the mean time the said Indians shall have free liberty to bring for Sale to Halifax or any other Settlement within this Province, Skins, feathers, fowl, fish or any other thing they shall have to sell, where they shall have liberty to dispose thereof to the best Advantage. [Emphasis added.]

16 It will be noted that unlike the March 10, 1760 document, the earlier 1752 Treaty contains both a treaty right to hunt and

fish "as usual" as well as a more elaborate trade clause. The appellant here initially relied on the 1752 Treaty as the source of his treaty entitlement. In Simon, Dickson C.J., at p. 404, concluded that on the basis of the evidence adduced in that case, "[t]he Crown has failed to prove that the Treaty of 1752 was terminated by subsequent hostilities" and left the termination issue open (at pp. 406–7). The Crown led more detailed evidence of hostilities in this case. It appears that while the British had hoped that by entering the 1752 Treaty other Mi'kmaq communities would come forward to make peace, skirmishing commenced again in 1753 with the Mi'kmaq. France and Britain themselves went to war in 1754 in North America. In 1756, as stated, another Proclamation was issued by the British authorizing the killing and capturing of Mi'kmaq throughout Nova Scotia. According to the trial judge, at para. 63, during the 1750s the "French were relying on Mi'kmaq assistance in almost every aspect of their military plans including scouting and reconnaissance, and guarding the Cape Breton coast line". This evidence apparently persuaded the appellant at trial to abandon his reliance on the 1752 Peace and Friendship Treaty. The Court is thus not called upon to consider the 1752 Treaty in the present appeal.

17 It should be pointed out that the Mi'kmaq were a considerable fighting force in the 18th century. Not only were their raiding parties effective on land, Mi'kmaq were accomplished sailors. Dr. William Wicken, for the defence, spoke of "the Maritime coastal adaptation of the Micmac":

There are fishing people who live along the coastline who encounter countless fishermen, traders, on a regular basis off their coastline.

The Mi'kmaq, according to the evidence, had seized in the order of 100 European sailing vessels in the years prior to 1760. There are recorded Mi'kmaq sailings in the 18th century between Nova Scotia, St. Pierre and Miquelon and Newfoundland. They were not people to be trifled with. However, by 1760, the British

and Mi'kmaq had a mutual self-interest in terminating hostilities and establishing the basis for a stable peace.

FINDINGS OF FACT BY THE TRIAL JUDGE

18 The appellant admitted that he did what he was alleged to have done on August 24, 1993. The only contentious issues arose on the historical record and with respect to the conclusions and inferences drawn by Embree Prov. Ct. J. from the documents, as explained by the expert witnesses. The permissible scope of appellate review in these circumstances was outlined by Lamer C.J. in *R. v. Van der Peet*, [1996] 2 S.C.R. 507 , at para. 82:

> In the case at bar, Scarlett Prov. Ct. J., the trial judge, made findings of fact based on the testimony and evidence before him, and then proceeded to make a determination as to whether those findings of fact supported the appellant's claim to the existence of an aboriginal right. The second stage of Scarlett Prov. Ct. J.'s analysis — his determination of the scope of the appellant's aboriginal rights on the basis of the facts as he found them — is a determination of a question of law which, as such, mandates no deference from this Court. The first stage of Scarlett Prov. Ct. J.'s analysis, however — the findings of fact from which that legal inference was drawn — do mandate such deference and should not be overturned unless made on the basis of a "palpable and overriding error".

19 In the present case, the trial judge, after a careful and detailed review of the evidence, concluded at para. 116:

> I accept as inherent in these treaties that the British recognized and accepted the existing Mi'kmaq way of life. Moreover, it's my conclusion that the British would have wanted the Mi'kmaq to continue their hunting, fishing and gathering lifestyle. The British did not want the Mi'kmaq to become a long-term burden on the public treasury although

they did seem prepared to tolerate certain losses in their
trade with the Mi'kmaq for the purpose of securing and
maintaining their friendship and discouraging their future
trade with the French. <u>I am satisfied that this trade clause in
the 1760–61 Treaties gave the Mi'kmaq the right to bring
the products of their hunting, fishing and gathering to a
truckhouse to trade</u>. [Emphasis added.]

The treaty document of March 10, 1760 sets out a restrictive covenant and does not say anything about a positive Mi'kmaq right
to trade. In fact, the written document does not set out any
Mi'kmaq rights at all, merely Mi'kmaq "promises" and the Governor's acceptance. I cannot reconcile the trial judge's conclusion,
at para. 116, that the treaties "gave the Mi'kmaq the right
to bring the products of their hunting, fishing and gathering to a
truckhouse to trade", with his conclusion at para. 112 that:

> The written treaties with the Mi'kmaq in 1760 and 1761
> which are before me contain, and fairly represent, all the
> promises made and all the terms and conditions mutually
> agreed to.

It was, after all, the aboriginal leaders who asked for truckhouses "for the furnishing them with necessaries, in Exchange
for their Peltry" in response to the Governor's inquiry "Whether
they were directed by their Tribes, to propose any other particulars to be Treated upon at this Time". It cannot be supposed
that the Mi'kmaq raised the subject of trade concessions merely
for the purpose of subjecting themselves to a trade restriction.
As the Crown acknowledges in its factum, "The restrictive
nature of the truckhouse clause was British in origin". The trial
judge's view that the treaty obligations are all found within the
four corners of the March 10, 1760 document, albeit generously
interpreted, erred in law by failing to give adequate weight to
the concerns and perspective of the Mi'kmaq people, despite the
recorded history of the negotiations, and by giving excessive
weight to the concerns and perspective of the British, who held

the pen. (See *Badger*, at para. 41, and Sioui, at p. 1036.) The need to give balanced weight to the aboriginal perspective is equally applied in aboriginal rights cases: *Van der Peet*, at paras. 49–50; *Delgamuukw*, at para. 81.

20 While the trial judge drew positive implications from the negative trade clause (reversed on this point by the Court of Appeal), such limited relief is inadequate where the British-drafted treaty document does not accord with the British-drafted minutes of the negotiating sessions and more favourable terms are evident from the other documents and evidence the trial judge regarded as reliable. Such an overly deferential attitude to the March 10, 1760 document was inconsistent with a proper recognition of the difficulties of proof confronted by aboriginal people, a principle emphasized in the treaty context by *Simon*, at p. 408, and *Badger*, at para. 4, and in the aboriginal rights context in *Van der Peet*, at para. 68, and *Delgamuukw*, at paras. 80–82. The trial judge interrogated himself on the scope of the March 10, 1760 text. He thus asked himself the wrong question. His narrow view of what constituted "the treaty" led to the equally narrow legal conclusion that the Mi'kmaq trading entitlement, such as it was, terminated in the 1780s. Had the trial judge not given undue weight to the March 10, 1760 document, his conclusions might have been very different.

21 The Court of Appeal, with respect, compounded the errors of law. It not only read the Mi'kmaq "right", such as it was, out of the trial judgment, it also took the view, at p. 204, that the principles of interpretation of Indian treaties developed in connection with land cessions are of "limited specific assistance" to treaties of peace and friendship where "the significant 'commodity' exchanged was mutual promises of peace". While it is true that there is no applicable land cession treaty in Nova Scotia, it is also true that the Mi'kmaq were largely dispossessed of their lands in any event, and (as elsewhere) assigned to reserves to accommodate the wave of European settlement which the Treaty of 1760 was designed to facilitate. It seems harsh to put aboriginal people in a worse legal position where land has been taken without their formal cession than where they have agreed

to terms of cession. A deal is a deal. The same rules of interpretation should apply. If, as I believe, the courts below erred as a matter of law in these respects, it is open to an appellate court to correct the errors in an appeal under s. 830 of the *Criminal Code*, R.S.C., 1985, c. C–46.

THE 1760 NEGOTIATIONS

22 I propose to review briefly the documentary record to emphasize and amplify certain aspects of the trial judge's findings. He accepted in general the evidence of the Crown's only expert witness, Dr. Stephen Patterson, a Professor of History at the University of New Brunswick, who testified at length about what the trial judge referred to (at para. 116) as British encouragement of the Mi'kmaq "hunting, fishing and gathering lifestyle". That evidence puts the trade clause in context, and answers the question whether there was something more to the treaty entitlement than merely the right to bring fish and wildlife to truckhouses.

(i) The Documentary Record

23 I take the following points from the matters particularly emphasized by the trial judge at para. 90 following his thorough review of the historical background:

1 The 1760–61 treaties were the culmination of more than a decade of intermittent hostilities between the British and the Mi'kmaq. Hostilities with the French were also prevalent in Nova Scotia throughout the 1750's, and the Mi'kmaq were constantly allied with the French against the British.
2 The use of firearms for hunting had an important impact on Mi'kmaq society. The Mi'kmaq remained dependant on others for gun powder and the primary sources of that were the French, Acadians and the British.
3 The French frequently supplied the Mi'kmaq with food and European trade goods. By the mid–18th century, the Mi'kmaq were accustomed to, and in some cases relied on,

receiving various European trade goods [including shot, gun powder, metal tools, clothing cloth, blankets and many other things].

6 The British wanted peace and a safe environment for their current and future settlers. Despite their recent victories, they did not feel completely secure in Nova Scotia.

24 Shortly after the fall of Louisbourg in June 1758, the British commander sent emissaries to the Mi'kmaq, through the French missionary, Father Maillard (who served as translator at the subsequent negotiations), holding out an offer of the enjoyment of peace, liberty, property, possessions and religion:

> ... my Reverend Father, It is necessary that I make known to you that your Capital Quebec has fallen to the arms of the King, my master, your armies are in flight, thus if you and your people are so reckless to continue [this war] without justification, it is certain that you will perish by starvation since you have no other assistance.
>
> So you, My Reverend Father, would do well to accept the olive branches that I send to you and to put me in possession of the vessels that your people took from me and return them all to me, I am commanded to assure you by His Majesty that you will enjoy all your possessions, your liberty, property with the free exercise of your religion as you can see by the declaration that I have the honour of sending you. [Emphasis added.]

25 In the harsh winter of 1759–1760, so many Mi'kmaq turned up at Louisbourg seeking sustenance that the British Commander expressed concern that unless their demand for necessaries was met, they would become "very Troublesome" and "entirely putt a Stop to any Settling or fishing all along the Coast" or indeed "the Settlement of Nova Scotia" generally. This is stated in the dispatch from the Governor at Louisbourg, Brigadier-General Edward Whitmore to General Jeffrey Amherst, based in New York, who commanded the British forces in North America:

I acquainted you in some of my Letters in December [1759]
and January [1760] last that the Indians were Come in, and
that they had agreed to live with us upon a footing of
Friendship. Accordingly Several of their Chiefs came in here
and articles were agreed on and Signed by Them and Me in
Form. On which Occassion as They pleaded they were
Naked and Starving I Cloathed Them and gave Them Some
Presents of Provisions etc. Afterwards Several Others came
in to whom I was Obliged to do the like. And at this time
the Chief of the Island is here who beside some Cloathing
makes a demand of Powder, Shott, and Arms for four men,
which if I would Remain in Peace with Them I find I must
Comply with. They Say the French always Supplyed Them
with these Things and They expect that we will do the Same.
I can fore See that this will be a Constant annual Expence,
and therefore I should be glad to have Your Directions both
for my own Satisfaction and as a Rule to whoever may be
left to Command here when I am Called away. Its Certain
unless They are keep'd Quiet They might be very Troublesome to this Town with only a Small Garrison in it, and
would entirely putt a Stop to any Settling or fishing all along
the Coast, and which is yet of greater Consequence might
much disturb and hinder the Settlement of Nova Scotia as
They are so near to the back Settlements of that Province.
(Dispatch dated November 14, 1760.)

It is apparent that the British saw the Mi'kmaq trade issue in
terms of peace, as the Crown expert Dr. Stephen Patterson testified, "people who trade together do not fight, that was the the-
ory". Peace was bound up with the ability of the Mi'kmaq
people to sustain themselves economically. Starvation breeds
discontent. The British certainly did not want the Mi'kmaq to
become an unnecessary drain on the public purse of the colony
of Nova Scotia or of the Imperial purse in London, as the trial
judge found. To avoid such a result, it became necessary to protect the traditional Mi'kmaq economy, including hunting, gathering and fishing. A comparable policy was pursued at a later

date on the west coast where, as Dickson J. commented in *Jack v. The Queen*, [1980] 1 S.C.R. 294, at p. 311:
What is plain from the pre-Confederation period is that the Indian fishermen were encouraged to engage in their occupation and to do so for both food and barter purposes.
The same strategy of economic aboriginal self-sufficiency was pursued across the prairies in terms of hunting: see *R. v. Horseman*, [1990] 1 S.C.R. 901 , per Wilson J., at p. 919, and Cory J., at p. 928.

26 The trial judge concluded that in 1760 the British Crown entered into a series of negotiations with communities of first nations spread across what is now Nova Scotia and New Brunswick. These treaties were essentially "adhesions" by different Mi'kmaq communities to identical terms because, as stated, it was contemplated that they would be consolidated in a more comprehensive and all-inclusive document at a later date, which never happened. The trial judge considered that the key negotiations took place not with the Mi'kmaq people directly, but with the St. John River Indians, part of the Maliseet First Nation, and the Passamaquody First Nation, who lived in present-day New Brunswick.

27 The trial judge found as a fact, at para. 108, that the relevant Mi'kmaq treaty did "make peace upon the same conditions" (emphasis added) as the Maliseet and Passamaquody. Meetings took place between the Crown and the Maliseet and the Passamaquody on February 11, 1760, twelve days before these bands signed their treaty with the British and eighteen days prior to the meeting between the Governor and the Mi'kmaq representatives, Paul Laurent of LaHave and Michel Augustine of the Richibucto region, where the terms of the Maliseet and Passamaquody treaties were "communicated" and accepted.

28 The trial judge found (at para. 101) that on February 29, 1760, at a meeting between the Governor in Council and the Mi'kmaq chiefs, the following exchange occurred:

His Excellency then Ordered the Several Articles of the Treaty made with the Indians of St. John's River and

Passamaquody to be Communicated to the said Paul
Laurent and Michel Augustine who expressed their satisfaction therewith, and declar'd that all the Tribe of Mickmacks
would be glad to make peace upon the same Conditions.
[Emphasis added.]

Governor Lawrence afterwards confirmed, in his May 11, 1760
report to the Board of Trade, that he had treated with the
Mi'kmaq Indians on "the same terms".
29 The genesis of the Mi'kmaq trade clause is therefore found
in the Governor's earlier negotiations with the Maliseet and
Passamaquody First Nations. In that regard, the appellant
places great reliance on a meeting between the Governor and
their chiefs on February 11, 1760 for the purpose of reviewing
various aspects of the proposed treaty. The following exchange
is recorded in contemporaneous minutes of the meeting prepared by the British Governor's Secretary:

His Excellency then demanded of them, Whether they were
directed by their Tribes, to propose any other particulars to
be Treated upon at this time. To which they replied that
their Tribes had not directed them to propose any thing further than that there might be a Truckhouse established, for
the furnishing them with necessaries, in Exchange for their
Peltry, and that it might, at present, be at Fort Frederick.
   Upon which His Excellency acquainted them that in case
of their now executing a Treaty in the manner proposed, and
its being ratified at the next General Meeting of their Tribes
the next Spring, a Truckhouse should be established at Fort
Frederick, agreable to their desire, and likewise at other
Places if it should be found necessary, for furnishing them
with such Commodities as shall be necessary for them, in
Exchange for their Peltry & and that great care should be
taken, that the Commerce at the said Truckhouses should be
managed by Persons on whose Justice and good Treatment,
they might always depend; and that it would be expected
that the said Tribes should not Trafic or Barter and

Exchange any Commodities at any other Place, nor with any
other Persons. Of all which the Chiefs expressed their entire
Approbation. [Emphasis added.]

30 It is true, as my colleague points out at para. 97, that the
British made it clear from the outset that the Mi'kmaq were not
to have any commerce with "any of His Majesty's Enemies". A
Treaty of Peace and Friendship could not be otherwise. The subject of trading with the British government as distinguished
from British settlers, however, did not arise until after the Indians had first requested truckhouses. The limitation to government trade came as a response to the request for truckhouses,
not the other way around.

31 At a meeting of the Governor's Council on February 16,
1760 (less than a week later), the Council and the representatives of the Indians proceeded to settle the prices of various articles of merchandise including beaver, marten, otter, mink, fox,
moose, deer, ermine and bird feathers, etc. Prices of "necessaries" for purchase at the truckhouse were also agreed, e.g.,
one pound of spring beaver could purchase 30 pounds of flour
or 14 pounds of pork. The British took a liberal view of "necessaries". Two gallons of rum cost one pound of spring beaver
pelts. The oral agreement on a price list was reflected in an
Order in Council dated February 23, 1760, which provided
"[t]hat the Prizes of all other kinds of Merchandize not
mention'd herein be Regulated according to the Rates of the
Foregoing articles". At trial the Crown expert and the defence
experts agreed that fish could be among the items that the
Mi'kmaq would trade.

32 In furtherance of this trade arrangement, the British established six truckhouses following the signing of the treaties in
1760 and 1761, including Chignecto, Lunenburg, St. John,
Windsor, Annapolis and "the Eastern Battery" along the coast
from Halifax. The existence of advantageous terms at the
truckhouses was part of an imperial peace strategy. As Governor
Lawrence wrote to the Board of Trade on May 11, 1760, "the
greatest advantage from this [trade] Article ... is the friendship of

these Indians". The British were concerned that matters might again become "troublesome" if the Mi'kmaq were subjected to the "pernicious practices" of "unscrupulous traders". The cost to the public purse of Nova Scotia of supporting Mi'kmaq trade was an investment in peace and the promotion of ongoing colonial settlement. The strategy would be effective only if the Mi'kmaq had access both to trade and to the fish and wildlife resources necessary to provide them with something to trade.

33 Accordingly, on March 21, 1760, the Nova Scotia House of Assembly passed *An Act to prevent any private Trade or Commerce with the Indians,* 34 Geo. II, c. 11. In July 1761, however, the "Lords of Trade and Plantation" (the Board of Trade) in London objected and the King disallowed the Act as a restraint on trade that disadvantaged British merchants. This coincided with exposure of venality by the local truckhouse merchants. As Dr. Patterson testified:

> ... the first Indian commissary, Halifax merchant, Benjamin Garrish, managed the system so that it was the Government which lost money while he profited usuriously.

34 By 1762, Garrish was removed and the number of truckhouses was reduced to three. By 1764, the system itself was replaced by the impartial licensing of private traders approved by the London Board of Trade's "Plan for the Future Management of Indian Affairs", but that eventually died out as well, as mentioned earlier.

35 In my view, all of this evidence, reflected in the trial judgment, demonstrates the inadequacy and incompleteness of the written memorial of the treaty terms by selectively isolating the restrictive trade covenant. Indeed, the truckhouse system offered such advantageous terms that it hardly seems likely that Mi'kmaq traders had to be compelled to buy at lower prices and sell at higher prices. At a later date, they objected when truckhouses were abandoned. The trade clause would not have advanced British objectives (peaceful relations with a self-sufficient Mi'kmaq people) or Mi'kmaq objectives (access to the

European "necessaries" on which they had come to rely) unless
the Mi'kmaq were assured at the same time of continuing access,
implicitly or explicitly, to wildlife to trade. This was confirmed
by the expert historian called by the Crown, as set out below.

(ii) The Expert Evidence
36 The courts have attracted a certain amount of criticism from
professional historians for what these historians see as an occasional tendency on the part of judges to assemble a "cut and
paste" version of history: G. M. Dickinson and R. D. Gidney,
"History and Advocacy: Some Reflections on the Historian's
Role in Litigation", *Canadian Historical Review*, LXVIII (1987),
576; D. J. Bourgeois, "The Role of the Historian in the Litigation Process", *Canadian Historical Review*, LXVII (1986), 195;
R. Fisher, "Judging History: Reflections on the Reasons for
Judgment in Delgamuukw v. B.C.", *B.C. Studies*, XCV (1992),
43; A. J. Ray, "Creating the Image of the Savage in Defence of
the Crown: The Ethnohistorian in Court", *Native Studies
Review*, VI (1990), 13.
37 While the tone of some of this criticism strikes the non-professional historian as intemperate, the basic objection, as I
understand it, is that the judicial selection of facts and quotations is not always up to the standard demanded of the professional historian, which is said to be more nuanced. Experts, it
is argued, are trained to read the various historical records
together with the benefit of a protracted study of the period,
and an appreciation of the frailties of the various sources. The
law sees a finality of interpretation of historical events where
finality, according to the professional historian, is not possible.
The reality, of course, is that the courts are handed disputes that
require for their resolution the finding of certain historical facts.
The litigating parties cannot await the possibility of a stable
academic consensus. The judicial process must do as best it can.
In this particular case, however, there was an unusual level of
agreement amongst all of the professional historians who testified about the underlying expectations of the participants
regarding the treaty obligations entered into by the Crown with

the Mi'kmaq. I set out, in particular, the evidence of the Crown's expert, Dr. Stephen Patterson, who spent many days of testimony reviewing the minutiae of the historical record. While he generally supported the Crown's narrow approach to the interpretation of the Treaty, which I have rejected on points of law, he did make a number of important concessions to the defence in a relatively lengthy and reflective statement which should be set out in full:

Q. I guess it's fair to say that the British would have understood that the Micmac lived and survived by hunting and fishing and gathering activities.

A. Yes, of course.

Q. And that in this time period, 1760 and '61, fish would be amongst the items they would have to trade. And they would have the right under this treaty to bring fish and feathers and furs into a truckhouse in exchange for commodities that were available.

A. Well, it's not mentioned but it's not excluded. So I think it's fair to assume that it was permissible.

Q. Okay. It's fair to say that it's an assumption on which the trade truckhouse clause is based.

A. That the truckhouse clause is based on the assumption that natives will have a variety of things to trade, some of which are mentioned and some not. Yes, I think that's fair.

Q. Yes. And wouldn't be out of line to call that a right to fish and a right to bring the fish or furs or feathers or fowl or venison or whatever they might have, into the truckhouses to trade.

A. Ah, a right. I think the implication here is that there is a right to trade under a certain form of regulation –

Q. Yes.

A. — that's laid down. And if you're saying <u>right to fish,</u> I've assumed that in recognizing the Micmac by treaty, the British were recognizing them as the people they were. They understood how they lived and that that

meant that <u>those people had a right to live in Nova Scotia in their traditional ways.</u> And, to me, that implies
that the British were accepting that the Micmac would
continue to be a hunting and gathering people, that they
would fish, that they would hunt to support themselves.
I don't see any problem with that.

It seems to me that <u>that's implicit</u> in the thing. Even
though it doesn't say it, and I know that there seems to,
in the 20th century, be some reluctance to see the value
of the 1760 and 1761 treaties because they're not so
explicit on these matters, but I personally don't see the
hang-up. Because it strikes me that there is a recognition
that the Micmac are a people and they have the right
to exist. And that has — carries certain implications
with it.

More than this, the very fact that there is a truckhouse
and that the truckhouse does list some of the things that
natives are expected to trade, implies that the British are
condoning or recognizing that this is the way that
natives live. <u>They do live by hunting and, therefore, this
is the produce of their hunting. They have the right to
trade it.</u>

Q. And you have, in fact, said that in your May 17th, 1994
   draft article.

A. That's correct.

Q. Yeah. And you testified to that effect in the *Pelletier*
   case, as well.

A. Well, my understanding of this issue, Mr. Wildsmith, has
   developed and grown with my close reading of the material. <u>It's the position that I come to accept as being a reasonable interpretation of what is here in these
   documents.</u> [Emphasis added.]

38 The trial judge gave effect to this evidence in finding a right
to bring fish to the truckhouse to trade, but he declined to find a
treaty right to fish and hunt to obtain the wherewithal to trade,
and concluded that the right to trade expired along with the

truckhouses and subsequent special arrangements. The Court of Appeal concluded, at p. 207, that Dr. Patterson used the word "right" interchangeably with the word "permissible", and that the trade clause gave rise to no "rights" at all. I think the view taken by the courts below rather underestimates Dr. Patterson. No reason is given for doubting that Dr. Patterson meant what he said about the common understanding of the parties that he considered at least implicit in this particular treaty arrangement. He initially uses the words "permissible" and "assumption", but when asked specifically by counsel about a "right" to fish and to trade fish, he says, "Ah, a right" (emphasis added), then, weighing his words carefully, he addresses a "right to fish" and concludes that "by treaty" the British did recognize that the Mi'kmaq "had a right to live in Nova Scotia in their traditional ways" (emphasis added) which included hunting and fishing and trading their catch for necessaries. (Trading was traditional. The trial judge found, at para. 93, that the Mi'kmaq had already been trading with Europeans, including French and Portugese fishermen, for about 250 years prior to the making of this treaty.) Dr. Patterson said his opinion was based on the historic documents produced in evidence. He said that this was "the position that I come to accept as being a reasonable interpretation of what is here in these documents" (emphasis added). Dr. Patterson went on to emphasize that the understanding of the Mi'kmaq would have been that these treaty rights were subject to regulation, which I accept.

39 Dr. Patterson's evidence regarding the assumptions underlying and "implicit" in the treaty were generally agreed with by the defence experts, Dr. John Reid and Dr. William Wicken. While the trial judge was not bound to accept the whole or any particular part of Dr. Patterson's evidence, even if supported by the other experts, I do not think there was any basis in the evidence for the trial judge to find (at para. 129) that the appellant's claim, to the extent it tracked Dr. Patterson's evidence, was "not even among the 'various possible interpretations of the common intention'" of the parties when they entered into the 1760 Treaty. Lamer J. in *Sioui*, supra, at p. 1069, it will be

recalled, said it was the Court's duty to search amongst such reasonable interpretations for the one that best accommodates the interests of the parties at the time the treaty was signed. The trial judge erred, I think, because he thought he was boxed in by the March 10, 1760 document.

40 In my view, the Nova Scotia judgments erred in concluding that the only enforceable treaty obligations were those set out in the written document of March 10, 1760, whether construed flexibly (as did the trial judge) or narrowly (as did the Nova Scotia Court of Appeal). The findings of fact made by the trial judge taken as a whole demonstrate that the concept of a disappearing treaty right does justice neither to the honour of the Crown nor to the reasonable expectations of the Mi'kmaq people. It is their common intention in 1760 — not just the terms of the March 10, 1760 document —to which effect must be given.

ASCERTAINING THE TERMS OF THE TREATY

41 Having concluded that the written text is incomplete, it is necessary to ascertain the treaty terms not only by reference to the fragmentary historical record, as interpreted by the expert historians, but also in light of the stated objectives of the British and Mi'kmaq in 1760 and the political and economic context in which those objectives were reconciled.

42 I mentioned earlier that the Nova Scotia Court of Appeal has held on several occasions that the "peace and friendship" treaties with the Mi'kmaq did not extinguish aboriginal hunting and fishing rights in Nova Scotia: *R. v. Isaac* (1975), 13 N.S.R. (2d) 460, *R. v. Cope* (1981), 132 D.L.R. (3d) 36, *Denny*, supra. We are not here concerned with the exercise of such a right. The appellant asserts the right of Mi'kmaq people to catch fish and wildlife in support of trade as an <u>alternative</u> or supplementary method of obtaining necessaries. The right to fish is not mentioned in the March 10, 1760 document, nor is it expressly noted elsewhere in the records of the negotiation put in evidence. This is not surprising. As Dickson J. mentioned with reference to the west coast in Jack, supra, at p. 311, in colonial

times the perception of the fishery resource was one of "limitless proportions".

43 The law has long recognized that parties make assumptions when they enter into agreements about certain things that give their arrangements efficacy. Courts will imply a contractual term on the basis of presumed intentions of the parties where it is necessary to assure the efficacy of the contract, e.g., where it meets the "officious bystander test": *M.J.B. Enterprises Ltd. v. Defence Construction (1951) Ltd.*, [1999] 1 S.C.R. 619 , at para. 30. (See also: The "*Moorcock*" (1889), 14 P.D. 64; *Canadian Pacific Hotels Ltd. v. Bank of Montreal*, [1987] 1 S.C.R. 711 ; and see generally: Waddams, supra, at para. 490; Treitel, supra, at pp. 190–94.) Here, if the ubiquitous officious bystander had said, "This talk about truckhouses is all very well, but if the Mi'kmaq are to make these promises, will they have the right to hunt and fish to catch something to trade at the truckhouses?", the answer would have to be, having regard to the honour of the Crown, "of course". If the law is prepared to supply the deficiencies of written contracts prepared by sophisticated parties and their legal advisors in order to produce a sensible result that accords with the intent of both parties, though unexpressed, the law cannot ask less of the honour and dignity of the Crown in its dealings with First Nations. The honour of the Crown was, in fact, specifically invoked by courts in the early 17th century to ensure that a Crown grant was effective to accomplish its intended purpose: *The Case of The Churchwardens of St. Saviour in Southwark* (1613), 10 Co. Rep. 66b, 77 E.R. 1025, at p. 67b and p. 1026, and *Roger Earl of Rutland's Case* (1608), 8 Co. Rep. 55a, 77 E.R. 555, at p. 56b and pp. 557–58.

44 An example of the Court's recognition of the necessity of supplying the deficiencies of aboriginal treaties is Sioui, supra, where Lamer J. considered a treaty document that stated simply (at p. 1031) that the Huron tribe "are received upon the same terms with the Canadians, being allowed the free Exercise of their Religion, their Customs, and Liberty of trading with the English". Lamer J. found that, in order to give real value and

meaning to these words, it was necessary that a territorial component be supplied, as follows, at p. 1067:

> The treaty gives the Hurons the freedom to carry on their customs and their religion. No mention is made in the treaty itself of the territory over which these rights may be exercised. There is also no indication that the territory of what is now Jacques-Cartier park was contemplated. However, for a freedom to have real value and meaning, it must be possible to exercise it somewhere. [Emphasis added.]

Similarly, in *Sundown*, supra, the Court found that the express right to hunt included the implied right to build shelters required to carry out the hunt. See also Simon, supra, where the Court recognized an implied right to carry a gun and ammunition on the way to exercise the right to hunt. These cases employed the concept of implied rights to support the meaningful exercise of express rights granted to the first nations in circumstances where no such implication might necessarily have been made absent the sui generis nature of the Crown's relationship to aboriginal people. While I do not believe that in ordinary commercial situations a right to trade implies any right of access to things to trade, I think the honour of the Crown requires nothing less in attempting to make sense of the result of these 1760 negotiations.

RIGHTS OF THE OTHER INHABITANTS

45 My colleague, McLachlin J., takes the view that, subject to the negative restriction in the treaty, the Mi'kmaq possessed only the liberty to hunt, fish, gather and trade "enjoyed by other British subjects in the region" (para. 103). The Mi'kmaq were, in effect, "citizens minus" with no greater liberties but with greater restrictions. I accept that in terms of the content of the hunting, fishing and gathering activities, this may be true. There is of course a distinction to be made between a liberty enjoyed by all citizens and a right conferred by a specific legal authority,

such as a treaty, to participate in the same activity. Even if this distinction is ignored, it is still true that a general right enjoyed by all citizens can nevertheless be made the subject of an enforceable treaty promise. In *Taylor and Williams,* supra, at p. 235, the treaty was found to include a term that "[t]he Rivers are open to all & you have an <u>equal right</u> to fish & hunt on them", and yet, despite the reference to equal rather than preferential rights, "the historic right of these Indians to hunt and fish" was found to be incorporated in the treaty, per MacKinnon A.C.J.O., at p. 236.

46 Similarly, in *Sioui,* at p. 1031, as mentioned above, the treaty provided that the Hurons would be "received upon the same terms with the Canadians" (emphasis added), yet their religious freedom, which in terms of content was no greater than that of the non-aboriginal inhabitants in 1760, was in 1990 accorded treaty protection.

47 The Crown objects strongly to any suggestion that the treaty conferred "preferential trading rights". I do not think the appellant needs to show preferential trading rights. He only has to show treaty trading rights. The settlers and the military undoubtedly hunted and fished for sport or necessaries as well, and traded goods with each other. The issue here is not so much the content of the rights or liberties as the level of legal protection thrown around them. A treaty could, to take a fanciful example, provide for a right of the Mi'kmaq to promenade down Barrington Street, Halifax, on each anniversary of the treaty. Barrington Street is a common thoroughfare enjoyed by all. There would be nothing "special" about the Mi'kmaq use of a common right of way. The point is that the treaty rights-holder not only has the right or liberty "enjoyed by other British subjects" but may enjoy special treaty protection against interference with its exercise. So it is with the trading arrangement. On June 25, 1761, following the signing of the Treaties of 1760–61 by the last group of Mi'kmaq villages, a ceremony was held at the farm of Lieutenant Governor Jonathan Belcher, the first Chief Justice of Nova Scotia, who was acting in the place of Governor Charles Lawrence, who had recently been drowned

on his way to Boston. In reference to the treaties, including the trade clause, Lieutenant Governor Belcher proclaimed:

> The Laws will be like a great Hedge about your Rights and properties, if any break this Hedge to hurt and injure you, the heavy weight of the Laws will fall upon them and punish their Disobedience.

48 Until enactment of the Constitution Act, 1982, the treaty rights of aboriginal peoples could be overridden by competent legislation as easily as could the rights and liberties of other inhabitants. The hedge offered no special protection, as the aboriginal people learned in earlier hunting cases such as *Sikyea v. The Queen*, [1964] S.C.R. 642, and *R. v. George*, [1966] S.C.R. 267. On April 17, 1982, however, this particular type of "hedge" was converted by s. 35(1) into sterner stuff that could only be broken down when justified according to the test laid down in *R. v. Sparrow*, [1990] 1 S.C.R. 1075 , at pp. 1112 et seq., as adapted to apply to treaties in *Badger*, supra, per Cory J., at paras. 75 et seq. See also *R. v. Bombay*, [1993] 1 C.N.L.R. 92 (Ont. C.A.). The fact the content of Mi'kmaq rights under the treaty to hunt and fish and trade was no greater than those enjoyed by other inhabitants does not, unless those rights were extinguished prior to April 17, 1982, detract from the higher protection they presently offer to the Mi'kmaq people.

THE HONOUR OF THE CROWN

49 This appeal puts to the test the principle, emphasized by this Court on several occasions, that the honour of the Crown is always at stake in its dealings with aboriginal people. This is one of the principles of interpretation set forth in *Badger*, supra, by Cory J., at para. 41:

> ... the honour of the Crown is always at stake in its dealings with Indian people. Interpretations of treaties and statutory provisions which have an impact upon treaty or aboriginal

rights must be approached in a manner which maintains the integrity of the Crown. It is always assumed that the Crown intends to fulfil its promises. No appearance of "sharp dealing" will be sanctioned.

50 This principle that the Crown's honour is at stake when the Crown enters into treaties with first nations dates back at least to this Court's decision in 1895, *Province of Ontario v. Dominion of Canada and Province of Quebec; In re Indian Claims* (1895), 25 S.C.R. 434. In that decision, Gwynne J. (dissenting) stated, at pp. 511–12:

> ... what is contended for and must not be lost sight of, is that the British sovereigns, ever since the acquisition of Canada, have been pleased to adopt the rule or practice of entering into agreements with the Indian nations or tribes in their province of Canada, for the cession or surrender by them of what such sovereigns have been pleased to designate the Indian title, by instruments similar to these now under consideration to which they have been pleased to give the designation of "treaties" with the Indians in possession of and claiming title to the lands expressed to be surrendered by the instruments, and further that the <u>terms and conditions expressed in those instruments as to be performed by or on behalf of the Crown, have always been regarded as involving a trust graciously assumed by the Crown to the fulfilment of which with the Indians the faith and honour of the Crown is pledged,</u> and which trust has always been most faithfully fulfilled as a treaty obligation of the Crown. [Emphasis added.]

See also *Ontario Mining Co. v. Seybold* (1901), 32 S.C.R. 1, at p. 2.

51 In more recent times, as mentioned, the principle that the honour of the Crown is always at stake was asserted by the Ontario Court of Appeal in *Taylor and Williams*, supra. In that case, as here, the issue was to determine the actual terms of a

treaty, whose terms were partly oral and partly written. MacKinnon A.C.J.O. said for the court, at pp. 235–36:

> The principles to be applied to the interpretation of Indian treaties have been much canvassed over the years. In approaching the terms of a treaty quite apart from the other considerations already noted, the honour of the Crown is always involved and no appearance of "sharp dealing" should be sanctioned. Mr. Justice Cartwright emphasized this in his dissenting reasons in *R. v. George*, ... [1966] S.C.R. 267 at p. 279, where he said:
>
> We should, I think, endeavour to construe the treaty of 1827 and those Acts of Parliament which bear upon the question before us in such a manner that the honour of the Sovereign may be upheld and Parliament not made subject to the reproach of having taken away by unilateral action and without consideration the rights solemnly assured to the Indians and their posterity by treaty.
>
> Further, if there is any ambiguity in the words or phrases used, not only should the words be interpreted as against the framers or drafters of such treaties, but such language should not be interpreted or construed to the prejudice of the Indians if another construction is reasonably possible: *R. v. White and Bob* (1964), 50 D.L.R. (2d) 613 at p. 652 ... (B.C.C.A.); affirmed ... [1965] S.C.R. vi...

This statement by MacKinnon A.C.J.O. (who had acted as counsel for the native person convicted of hunting offences in George, supra) has been adopted subsequently in numerous cases, including decisions of this Court in *Badger*, supra, para. 41, and *Sparrow*, supra, at pp. 1107–8.

52 I do not think an interpretation of events that turns a positive Mi'kmaq trade demand into a negative Mi'kmaq covenant is consistent with the honour and integrity of the Crown. Nor is it consistent to conclude that the Lieutenant Governor, seeking in good faith to address the trade demands of the Mi'kmaq,

accepted the Mi'kmaq suggestion of a trading facility while denying any treaty protection to Mi'kmaq access to the things that were to be traded, even though these things were identified and priced in the treaty negotiations. This was not a commercial contract. The trade arrangement must be interpreted in a manner which gives meaning and substance to the promises made by the Crown. In my view, with respect, the interpretation adopted by the courts below left the Mi'kmaq with an empty shell of a treaty promise.

CONTRADICTORY INTERPRETATIONS OF THE TRUCKHOUSE CLAUSE

53 The appellant argues that the Crown has been in breach of the treaty since 1762, when the truckhouses were terminated, or at least since the 1780s when the replacement system of licensed traders was abandoned. This argument suffers from the same quality of unreasonableness as does the Crown's argument that the treaty left the Mi'kmaq with nothing more than a negative covenant. It was established in *Simon*, supra, at p. 402, that treaty provisions should be interpreted "in a flexible way that is sensitive to the evolution of changes in normal" practice, and *Sundown*, supra, at para. 32, confirms that courts should not use a "frozen-in-time" approach to treaty rights. The appellant cannot, with any show of logic, claim to exercise his treaty rights using an outboard motor while at the same time insist on restoration of the peculiar 18th century institution known as truckhouses.

54 The Crown, on the other hand, argues that the truckhouse was a time-limited response to a temporary problem. As my colleague McLachlin J. sets out at para. 96, the "core" of the treaty was said to be that "[t]he Mi'kmaq agreed to forgo their trading autonomy and the general trading rights they possessed as British subjects, and to abide by the treaty trade regime. The British, in exchange, undertook to provide the Mi'kmaq with stable trading outlets where European goods were provided at favour-

able terms while the exclusive trade regime existed". My disagreement with that view, with respect, is that the aboriginal
people, as found by the trial judge, relied on European powder,
shot and other goods and pushed a trade agenda with the British
because their alternative sources of supply had dried up; the real
inhibition on trade with the French was not the treaty but the
absence of the French, whose military had retreated up the St.
Lawrence and whose settlers had been expelled; there is no suggestion in the negotiating records that the truckhouse system
was a sort of transitional arrangement expected to be temporary, it only became temporary because the King unexpectedly
disallowed the enabling legislation passed by the Nova Scotia
House of Assembly; and the notion that the truckhouse was
merely a response to a trade restriction overlooks the fact the
truckhouse system offered very considerable financial benefits
to the Mi'kmaq which they would have wanted to exploit,
restriction or no restriction. The promise of access to "necessaries" through trade in wildlife was the key point, and where a
right has been granted, there must be more than a mere disap-
pearance of the mechanism created to facilitate the exercise of
the right to warrant the conclusion that the right itself is spent
or extinguished.

55 The Crown further argues that the treaty rights, if they
exist at all, were "subject to regulation, *ab initio*". The effect,
it is argued, is that no *Badger* justification would be required.
The Crown's attempt to distinguish *Badger* is not persuasive.
Badger dealt with treaty rights which were specifically
expressed in the treaty (at para. 31) to be "subject to such regulations as may from time to time be made by the Government
of the country". Yet the Court concluded that a *Sparrow*-type
justification was required.

56 My view is that the surviving substance of the treaty is not
the literal promise of a truckhouse, but a treaty right to continue
to obtain necessaries through hunting and fishing by trading the
products of those traditional activities subject to restrictions
that can be justified under the *Badger* test.

THE LIMITED SCOPE OF THE TREATY RIGHT

57 The Crown expresses the concern that recognition of the existence of a constitutionally entrenched right with, as here, a trading aspect, would open the floodgates to uncontrollable and excessive exploitation of the natural resources. Whereas hunting and fishing for food naturally restricts quantities to the needs and appetites of those entitled to share in the harvest, it is argued that there is no comparable, built-in restriction associated with a trading right, short of the paramount need to conserve the resource. The Court has already addressed this issue in *R. v. Gladstone,* [1996] 2 S.C.R. 723 , per Lamer C.J., at paras. 57–63, L'Heureux-Dubé J., at para. 137, and McLachlin J., at para. 164; *Van der Peet,* supra, per L'Heureux-Dubé J., at para. 192, and per McLachlin J., at para. 279; *R. v. N.T.C. Smokehouse Ltd.,* [1996] 2 S.C.R. 672 , per L'Heureux-Dubé J., at para. 47; and *Horseman,* supra, per Wilson J., at p. 908, and Cory J., at pp. 928–29. The ultimate fear is that the appellant, who in this case fished for eels from a small boat using a fyke net, could lever the treaty right into a factory trawler in Pomquet Harbour gathering the available harvest in preference to all non-aboriginal commercial or recreational fishermen. (This is indeed the position advanced by the intervener the Union of New Brunswick Indians.) This fear (or hope) is based on a misunderstanding of the narrow ambit and extent of the treaty right.

58 The recorded note of February 11, 1760 was that "there might be a Truckhouse established, for the furnishing them with <u>necessaries</u>" (emphasis added). What is contemplated therefore is not a right to trade generally for economic gain, but rather a right to trade for necessaries. The treaty right is a regulated right and can be contained by regulation within its proper limits.

59 The concept of "necessaries" is today equivalent to the concept of what Lambert J.A., in *R. v. Van der Peet* (1993), 80 B.C.L.R. (2d) 75, at p. 126, described as a "moderate livelihood". Bare subsistence has thankfully receded over the last

couple of centuries as an appropriate standard of life for aboriginals and non-aboriginals alike. A moderate livelihood includes such basics as "food, clothing and housing, supplemented by a few amenities", but not the accumulation of wealth (*Gladstone*, supra, at para. 165). It addresses day-to-day needs. This was the common intention in 1760. It is fair that it be given this interpretation today.

60 The distinction between a commercial right and a right to trade for necessaries or sustenance was discussed in *Gladstone*, supra, where Lamer C.J., speaking for the majority, held that the Heiltsuk of British Columbia have "an aboriginal right to sell herring spawn on kelp to an extent best described as commercial" (para. 28). This finding was based on the evidence that "tons" of the herring spawn on kelp was traded and that such trade was a central and defining feature of Heiltsuk society. McLachlin J., however, took a different view of the evidence, which she concluded supported a finding that the Heiltsuk derived only sustenance from the trade of the herring spawn on kelp. "Sustenance" provided a manageable limitation on what would otherwise be a free-standing commercial right. She wrote at para. 165:

> Despite the large quantities of herring spawn on kelp traditionally traded, the evidence does not indicate that the trade of herring spawn on kelp provided for the Heiltsuk anything more than basic sustenance. There is no evidence in this case that the Heiltsuk accumulated wealth which would exceed a sustenance lifestyle from the herring spawn on kelp fishery. [Emphasis added.]

In this case, equally, it is not suggested that Mi'kmaq trade historically generated "wealth which would exceed a sustenance lifestyle". Nor would anything more have been contemplated by the parties in 1760.

61 Catch limits that could reasonably be expected to produce a moderate livelihood for individual Mi'kmaq families at present-

day standards can be established by regulation and enforced without violating the treaty right. In that case, the regulations would accommodate the treaty right. Such regulations would not constitute an infringement that would have to be justified under the *Badger* standard.

APPLICATION TO THE FACTS OF THIS CASE

62 The appellant is charged with three offences: the selling of eels without a licence, fishing without a licence and fishing during the close season with illegal nets. These acts took place at Pomquet Harbour, Antigonish County. For Marshall to have satisfied the regulations, he was required to secure a licence under either the *Fishery (General) Regulations*, SOR/93–53, the *Maritime Provinces Fishery Regulations*, SOR/93–55, or the *Aboriginal Communal Fishing Licences Regulations*, SOR/93–332.

63 All of these regulations place the issuance of licences within the absolute discretion of the Minister. Section 7(1) of the *Fisheries Act*, R.S.C., 1985, c. F–14, so provides:

> 7. (1) Subject to subsection (2), the Minister may, <u>in his absolute discretion</u>, wherever the exclusive right of fishing does not already exist by law, issue or authorize to be issued leases and licences for fisheries or fishing, wherever situated or carried on. [Emphasis added.]

The *Maritime Provinces Fishery Regulations* provides that the Minister "may issue" a commercial fishing licence (s. 5). The *Aboriginal Communal Fishing Licences Regulations* state as well that the Minister "may issue" a communal licence to an aboriginal organization to carry on food fishing and related activities (s. 4). The licences described in the *Fishery (General) Regulations* are all discretionary as well, although none of those licences would have assisted the appellant in this situation.

64 Furthermore, there is nothing in these regulations which gives direction to the Minister to explain how she or he should

exercise this discretionary authority in a manner which would respect the appellant's treaty rights. This Court has had the opportunity to review the effect of discretionary licensing schemes on aboriginal and treaty rights: *Badger*, supra, *R. v. Nikal*, [1996] 1 S.C.R. 1013 , *R. v. Adams*, [1996] 3 S.C.R. 101, and *R. v. Côté*, [1996] 3 S.C.R. 139 . The test for infringement under s. 35(1) of the *Constitution Act*, 1982 was set out in *Sparrow*, supra, at p. 1112:

> To determine whether the fishing rights have been interfered with such as to constitute a prima facie infringement of s. 35(1), certain questions must be asked. First, is the limitation unreasonable? Second, does the regulation impose undue hardship? Third, does the regulation deny to the holders of the right their preferred means of exercising that right? The onus of proving a prima facie infringement lies on the individual or group challenging the legislation.

Lamer C.J. in *Adams*, supra, applied this test to licensing schemes and stated as follows at para. 54:

> In light of the Crown's unique fiduciary obligations towards aboriginal peoples, <u>Parliament may not simply adopt an unstructured discretionary administrative regime which risks infringing aboriginal rights in a substantial number of applications in the absence of some explicit guidance.</u> If a statute confers an administrative discretion which may carry significant consequences for the exercise of an aboriginal right, the statute or its delegate regulations must outline specific criteria for the granting or refusal of that discretion which seek to accommodate the existence of aboriginal rights. In the absence of such specific guidance, the statute will fail to provide representatives of the Crown with sufficient directives to fulfil their fiduciary duties, and the statute will be found to represent an infringement of aboriginal rights under the Sparrow test. [Emphasis added.]

Cory J. in *Badger*, supra, at para. 79, found that the test for infringement under s. 35(1) of the *Constitution Act*, 1982 was the same for both aboriginal and treaty rights, and thus the words of Lamer C.J. in *Adams*, although in relation to the infringement of aboriginal rights, are equally applicable here. There was nothing at that time which provided the Crown officials with the "sufficient directives" necessary to ensure that the appellant's treaty rights would be respected. To paraphrase *Adams*, at para. 51, under the applicable regulatory regime, the appellant's exercise of his treaty right to fish and trade for sustenance was exercisable only at the absolute discretion of the Minister. Mi'kmaq treaty rights were not accommodated in the Regulations because, presumably, the Crown's position was, and continues to be, that no such treaty rights existed. In the circumstances, the purported regulatory prohibitions against fishing without a licence (*Maritime Provinces Fishery Regulations*, s. 4(1)(a)) and of selling eels without a licence (Fishery (General) Regulations, s. 35(2)) do prima facie infringe the appellant's treaty rights under the Treaties of 1760–61 and are inoperative against the appellant unless justified under the *Badger* test.

65 Further, the appellant was charged with fishing during the close season with improper nets, contrary to s. 20 of the *Maritime Provinces Fishery Regulations*. Such a regulation is also a prima facie infringement, as noted by Cory J. in *Badger*, supra, at para. 90: "This Court has held on numerous occasions that there can be no limitation on the method, timing and extent of Indian hunting under a Treaty", apart, I would add, from a treaty limitation to that effect.

66 The appellant caught and sold the eels to support himself and his wife. Accordingly, the close season and the imposition of a discretionary licensing system would, if enforced, interfere with the appellant's treaty right to fish for trading purposes, and the ban on sales would, if enforced, infringe his right to trade for sustenance. In the absence of any justification of the regulatory prohibitions, the appellant is entitled to an acquittal.

DISPOSITION

67 The constitutional question stated by the Chief Justice on February 9, 1998, as follows:
Are the prohibitions on catching and retaining fish without a licence, on fishing during the close time, and on the unlicensed sale of fish, contained in ss. 4(1)(a) and 20 of the Maritime Provinces Fishery Regulations and s. 35(2) of the Fishery (General) Regulations, inconsistent with the treaty rights of the appellant contained in the Mi'kmaq Treaties of 1760–61 and therefore of no force or effect or application to him, by virtue of ss. 35(1) and 52 of the Constitution Act, 1982? should be answered in the affirmative. I would therefore allow the appeal and order an acquittal on all charges.

The reasons of Gonthier and McLachlin JJ. were delivered by
MCLACHLIN J. (dissenting) —

I. INTRODUCTION

68 The issue in this case is whether the appellant Marshall, a Mi'kmaq Indian, possesses a treaty right that exempts him from the federal fisheries legislation under which he was charged with fishing without a licence, fishing with a prohibited net during the closed period, and selling fish caught without a licence.
69 At trial, Marshall admitted that he caught and sold 463 pounds of eels without a licence and with a prohibited net within closed times. The only issue at trial was whether he possessed a treaty right to catch and sell fish that exempted him from compliance with the federal fisheries legislation and mandated his acquittal. The trial judge held that he did not. The Nova Scotia Court of Appeal dismissed his appeal. Marshall now appeals to this Court.
70 I conclude that the Treaties of 1760–61 created an exclusive trade and truckhouse regime which implicitly gave rise to a limited Mi'kmaq right to bring goods to British trade outlets so long as this regime was extant. The Treaties of 1760–61 granted

neither a freestanding right to truckhouses nor a general underlying right to trade outside of the exclusive trade and truckhouse regime. The system of trade exclusivity and correlative
British trading outlets died out in the 1780s and with it, the incidental right to bring goods to trade. There is therefore no existing right to trade in the Treaties of 1760–61 that exempts the
appellant from the federal fisheries legislation. The charges
against him stand.

II. RELEVANT TREATY AND CONSTITUTIONAL PROVISIONS

71 *Trade Clause in Treaties of 1760–61*
And I do further engage that we will not traffick, barter or
Exchange any Commodities in any manner but with such persons or the managers of such Truck houses as shall be appointed
or Established by His Majesty's Governor at [insert location of
closest truck house] or Elsewhere in Nova Scotia or Accadia.
Constitution Act, 1982
35. (1) The existing aboriginal and treaty rights of the aboriginal peoples of Canada are hereby recognized and affirmed.

III. JUDGMENTS

72 The trial judge, Embree Prov. Ct. J., concluded ([1996]
N.S.J. No. 246 (QL)) that the trade clause in the Treaties of
1760–61 imposed an obligation on the Mi'kmaq to trade only
at English truckhouses or with licensed traders. The clause gave
the Mi'kmaq a limited "right to bring" their trade goods (the
products of their hunting, fishing and gathering lifestyle) to such
outlets or traders to trade. The trial judge found that when the
exclusive trade obligation and the system of truckhouses and
licensed traders fell into disuse, the "right to bring" disappeared. He concluded, at para. 125:

It was a pre-requisite to the Mi'kmaq being able to trade
under the terms of the trade clause that the British provide

truckhouses or appoint persons to trade with. When the British stopped doing that, the requirement (or if I had taken the Defence view, the option) to trade with truckhouses or licensed traders disappeared. The trade clause says nothing about that eventuality and it is my view that no further trade right arises from the trade clause.

73 The trial judge was unequivocal on the limited nature of this Treaty "right to bring" goods to truckhouses and licensed traders to trade. He concluded that the British did not intend to convey, and would not have conveyed, a trading right beyond the limited right to trade at truckhouses and with licensed traders within the exclusive trade regime, and that the Mi'kmaq appreciated and understood the position and objectives of the British. In light of these conclusions, he rejected the appellant's claim that the Treaties granted him a treaty right to catch and sell fish. He found, at para. 129, that such an interpretation was not even among the "various possible interpretations of the common intention" of the Mi'kmaq and the British.

74 The Court of Appeal ((1997), 159 N.S.R. (2d) 186), per Roscoe and Bateman JJ.A., affirmed the trial judge's decision that the Treaties of 1760–61 did not grant a treaty right to catch and sell fish. The court found, at p. 200, that "the mercantile nature of the British economy; the fact that the Governor had been instructed not to place any subject in a preferential trading position; and the fact that, pursuant to this Treaty, the Mi'kmaq were submitting to British law" all lent support to the trial judge's conclusion. Unlike the trial judge, however, the Court of Appeal concluded that the Treaties did not grant any right to trade, not even a limited "right to bring" goods to truckhouses. The court held that the mere reference to trading at truckhouses in the trade clause of the Treaties of 1760–61 could not, without more, constitute the grant of a right to trade. The Treaties of 1760–61 were peace treaties, not land cession treaties, and hence no grant of rights could be presumed. Moreover, the negative language of the clause was unlike that traditionally found in rights-granting treaties. The Court of Appeal concluded, at p.

200, that the Treaties of 1760–61 were negotiated following a long period of British-Mi'kmaq hostilities and that "[t]rade was not central to the Treaties but a vehicle by which the British could encourage the maintenance of a friendly relationship with the Mi'kmaq". The requirement imposed upon the Mi'kmaq to trade solely at truckhouses was characterized as a mechanism to help ensure the maintenance of peace. Thus, while the Treaties made trade at truckhouses "permissible", they did not confer a legal right on the Mi'kmaq to do so. The Court of Appeal upheld the trial judge's decision and dismissed the appeal.

IV. THE ISSUES

75 The ultimate issue before the Court on this appeal is whether the appellant possesses a treaty right which exempts him from the federal fisheries legislation under which he is charged. The arguments urged in support of this position, however, are more difficult to articulate. The appellant's oral and written submissions, taken together, suggest that he contends that the Treaties of 1760–61 granted either or both of two separate rights, one unlimited, one more restricted. The appellant's arguments may be summarized as follows:

A. *The Rights Claimed*
1 The treaties conferred on the Mi'kmaq a general right to trade.
2 Alternatively, or in addition, the treaties conferred on the Mi'kmaq a right to truckhouses or licensed traders.

B. *Justification Arguments*
1 In the event a general right to trade is established, the federal fisheries legislation governing fishing and trade in fish fails to accommodate this treaty right to trade.
2 The government has not shown that this failure is justified as required by s. 35 of the Constitution Act, 1982.
3 Therefore the federal fisheries legislation does not apply to the appellant and he is entitled to be acquitted.

Alternatively, or in addition:

1 In the event a right to truckhouses or licensed traders is established, the government has been in breach of its treaty obligations since the 1780s.
2 The government has not shown that this infringement is justified as required by s. 35 of the Constitution Act, 1982.
3 Therefore the federal fisheries legislation does not apply to the appellant and he is entitled to be acquitted.

76 I will first consider the principles of interpretation relevant to this appeal. I will then consider in turn the appellant's "general trade right" and "right to trading outlets" arguments.

77 It should be noted that the appellant does not argue for an aboriginal (as distinct from treaty) right to trade on this appeal.

V. DISCUSSION

A. *What Principles of Interpretation Apply to the Interpretation of the Treaty Trade Clause?*

78 This Court has set out the principles governing treaty interpretation on many occasions. They include the following.

1 Aboriginal treaties constitute a unique type of agreement and attract special principles of interpretation: *R. v. Sundown*, [1999] 1 S.C.R 393, at para. 24; *R. v. Badger*, [1996] 1 S.C.R. 771 , at para. 78; *R. v. Sioui*, [1990] 1 S.C.R. 1025, at p. 1043; *Simon v. The Queen*, [1985]
2 S.C.R. 387 , at p. 404. See also: J. [Sákéj] Youngblood Henderson, "Interpreting *Sui Generis* Treaties" (1997), 36 *Alta. L. Rev.* 46; L. I. Rotman, "Defining Parameters: Aboriginal Rights, Treaty Rights, and the *Sparrow* Justificatory Test" (1997), 36 *Alta. L. Rev.* 149.2 Treaties should be liberally construed and ambiguities or doubtful expressions should be resolved in favour of the aboriginal signatories: *Simon*, supra, at p. 402; *Sioui*, supra, at p. 1035; *Badger*, supra, at para. 52.

3 The goal of treaty interpretation is to choose from among the various possible interpretations of common intention the one which best reconciles the interests of both parties at the time the treaty was signed: Sioui, supra, at pp. 1068–69.

4 In searching for the common intention of the parties, the integrity and honour of the Crown is presumed: *Badger*, supra, at para. 41.

5 In determining the signatories' respective understanding and intentions, the court must be sensitive to the unique cultural and linguistic differences between the parties: *Badger*, supra, at paras. 52–54; *R. v. Horseman*, [1990] 1 S.C.R. 901 , at p. 907.

6 The words of the treaty must be given the sense which they would naturally have held for the parties at the time: *Badger*, supra, at paras. 53 et seq.; *Nowegijick v. The Queen*, [1983] 1 S.C.R. 29, at p. 36.

7 A technical or contractual interpretation of treaty wording should be avoided: *Badger*, supra; *Horseman*, supra; *Nowegijick*, supra.

8 While construing the language generously, courts cannot alter the terms of the treaty by exceeding what "is possible on the language" or realistic: *Badger*, supra, at para. 76; Sioui, supra, at p. 1069; Horseman, supra, at p. 908.

9 Treaty rights of aboriginal peoples must not be interpreted in a static or rigid way. They are not frozen at the date of signature. The interpreting court must update treaty rights to provide for their modern exercise. This involves determining what modern practices are reasonably incidental to the core treaty right in its modern context: *Sundown*, supra, at para. 32; *Simon*, supra, at p. 402.

79 Two specific issues of interpretation arise on this appeal. The answer to each is found in the foregoing summary of principles.
80 The first issue of interpretation arises from the Court of Appeal's apparent suggestion that peace treaties fall in a different category from land cession treaties for purposes of interpretation, with the result that, when interpreting peace treaties,

there is no "presumption" that rights were granted to the aboriginal signatories in exchange for entering into the treaty. This raises the issue of whether it is useful to slot treaties into different categories, each with its own rules of interpretation. The principle that each treaty must be considered in its unique historical and cultural context suggests that this practice should be avoided.

81 The second issue of interpretation raised on this appeal is whether extrinsic evidence can be used in interpreting aboriginal treaties, absent ambiguity. Again, the principle that every treaty must be understood in its historical and cultural context suggests the answer must be yes. It is true that *in R. v. Horse*, [1988] 1 S.C.R. 187 , at p. 201, this Court alluded with approval to the strict contract rule that extrinsic evidence is not admissible to construe a contract in the absence of ambiguity. However, subsequent decisions have made it clear that extrinsic evidence of the historic and cultural context of a treaty may be received absent ambiguity: *Sundown,* supra, at para. 25; *Badger,* supra, at para. 52. As Cory J. wrote in *Badger,* supra, at para. 52, courts interpreting treaties "must take into account the context in which the treaties were negotiated, concluded and committed to writing".

82 The fact that both the words of the treaty and its historic and cultural context must be considered suggests that it may be useful to approach the interpretation of a treaty in two steps. First, the words of the treaty clause at issue should be examined to determine their facial meaning, in so far as this can be ascertained, noting any patent ambiguities and misunderstandings that may have arisen from linguistic and cultural differences. This exercise will lead to one or more possible interpretations of the clause. As noted in *Badger,* supra, at para. 76, "the scope of treaty rights will be determined by their wording". The objective at this stage is to develop a preliminary, but not necessarily determinative, framework for the historical context inquiry, taking into account the need to avoid an unduly restrictive interpretation and the need to give effect to the principles of interpretation.

83 At the second step, the meaning or different meanings which have arisen from the wording of the treaty right must be considered against the treaty's historical and cultural back-drop. A consideration of the historical background may suggest latent ambiguities or alternative interpretations not detected at first reading. Faced with a possible range of inter-pretations, courts must rely on the historical context to deter-mine which comes closest to reflecting the parties' common intention. This determination requires choosing "from among the various possible interpretations of the common intention the one which best reconciles" the parties' interests: Sioui, supra, at p. 1069. Finally, if the court identifies a particular right which was intended to pass from generation to genera-tion, the historical context may assist the court in determining the modern counterpart of that right: Simon, supra, at pp. 402–3; *Sundown*, supra, at paras. 30 and 33.

84 In the case on appeal, the trial judge heard 40 days of trial, the testimony of three expert witnesses, and was presented with over 400 documents. After a meticulous review of this evidence, the trial judge stated, at para. 92:

> With the full benefit of the cultural and historical context, I now need to address the following questions. What did the Mi'kmaq and the British agree to and intend to agree to in the Treaties of 1760 and 1761? Directly related to that are the questions of Mi'kmaq understanding of these treaties' contents. Did they understand and agree to all of the written portions of the treaties before me? Were there other state-ments or promises made orally which the Mi'kmaq consid-ered were part of these treaties and which have an impact on their meaning? Did the Mi'kmaq consider that previous trea-ties were renewed by and combined with the 1760–61 Trea-ties? Are there any other aspects of the historical record, whether referred to me by Counsel for the defendant or oth-erwise, which reflect on the contents or the proper under-standing of the contents of these treaties?

The trial judge's review of the historical context, the cultural differences between the parties, their different methods of communication, and the pre-treaty negotiations, led him to conclude that there was no misunderstanding or lack of agreement between the British and the Mi'kmaq that trade under the treaties was to be carried out in accordance with the terms of the trade clause. Having come to this conclusion, the trial judge turned again to the historical context to interpret the content of such terms, in accordance with the parties' common intention. In my opinion, the trial judge's approach to the interpretation of the Treaties of 1760–61 is in keeping with the principles governing treaty interpretation. With the greatest respect for the contrary view of my colleague, Justice Binnie, I find no basis for error in the trial judge's approach.

B. Do the Treaties of 1760–61 Grant a General Right to Trade?

85 At trial, the appellant argued that the treaty trade clause conferred on the Mi'kmaq a general trading right. The trial judge rejected this submission, finding that the treaties conferred only a limited "right to bring" goods to truckhouses and licensed traders to trade. The Court of Appeal went even further, finding that the treaties conferred no trade right at all. Before this Court, the appellant once again advances the argument that the Treaties of 1760–61 conferred a general trade right on the Mi'kmaq.

86 Before addressing whether the words of the treaties, taken in their historic and cultural context support a general treaty right to trade, it is necessary to distinguish between a right to trade under the law applicable to all citizens, and a treaty right to trade. All inhabitants of the province of Nova Scotia or Acadia enjoyed a general right to trade. No treaty was required to confer such a right as it vested in all British subjects. The Mi'kmaq, upon signing the Treaties of 1760–61 and thereby acknowledging the jurisdiction of the British king over Nova Scotia, automatically inherited this general right. This public right must be distinguished from the asserted treaty right to trade. Treaty

rights are by definition special rights conferred by treaty. They are given protection over and above rights enjoyed by the general populace. Only rights conferred by treaty are protected by s. 35 of the Constitution Act, 1982. I note that while rights enjoyed by the general populace can be included in treaties, where this occurs, they become separate and distinct treaty rights subject to a higher level of protection. The appellant in this case must establish a distinct treaty right if he is to succeed.

(1) The Wording of the Trade Clause

87 This brings me to the words of the treaty trade clause. It states:

> And I do further engage that we will not traffick, barter or Exchange any Commodities in any manner but with such persons or the managers of such Truck houses as shall be appointed or Established by His Majesty's Governor at [insert location of closest truck house] or Elsewhere in Nova Scotia or Accadia.

The clause is short, the words simple. The Mi'kmaq covenant that they will "not traffick, barter or Exchange any Commodities in any manner but with [British agents]" (emphasis added). The core of this clause is the obligation on the Mi'kmaq to trade only with the British. Ancillary to this is the implied promise that the British will establish truckhouses where the Mi'kmaq can trade. These words do not, on their face, confer a general right to trade.

88 The next question is whether the historic and cultural context in which the treaties were made establishes a general right to trade, having due regard for the need to interpret treaty rights generously. I will deal first with the linguistic and cultural differences between the parties, then with the historical record generally.

(2) Cultural and Linguistic Considerations

89 The trial judge found that there was no misunderstanding or lack of agreement between the British and the Mi'kmaq that trade under the treaties was to be carried out in accordance with

the terms of the trade clause, and that the Mi'kmaq understood those terms. He addressed and discounted the possibility that the French-speaking Mi'kmaq might not have understood the English treaty terms. The record amply supports this conclusion. French missionaries, long allied with the Mi'kmaq, were employed by the British as interpreters in the treaty negotiations. In the course of the negotiations, the Mi'kmaq were referred to an earlier treaty entered into by the Maliseet and Passamaquody, containing a similar trade clause in French. Some of the Mi'kmaq appeared to have acquired English; the records speak of Paul Laurent of LaHave, a Mi'kmaq Sakamow and one of the first signatories, as speaking English. More generally, by the time the Treaties of 1760–61 were entered into, the record suggests that the Mi'kmaq had developed an understanding of the importance of the written word to the British in treaty-making and had a sufficiently sophisticated knowledge of the treaty-making process to compare and discern the differences between treaties. The trial judge was amply justified in concluding that the Mi'kmaq understood the treaty process as well as the particular terms of the treaties they were signing. There is nothing in the linguistic or cultural differences between the parties to suggest that the words of the trade clause were not fully understood or appreciated by the Mi'kmaq.

(3) The Historical Context and the Scope of the Trade Clause

90 After a meticulous review of the historical evidence, the trial judge concluded that: (1) the Treaties of 1760–61 were primarily peace treaties, cast against the background of both a long struggle between the British and the French in which the Mi'kmaq were allied with the French, and over a decade of intermittent hostilities between the British and the Mi'kmaq; (2) the French defeat and withdrawal from Nova Scotia left the Mi'kmaq to co-exist with the British without the presence of their former ally and supplier; (3) the Mi'kmaq were accustomed to and in some cases dependent on trade for firearms, gunpowder, food and European trade goods; and (4) the British wanted peace and a safe environment for settlers and, despite recent victories, did not feel completely secure in Nova Scotia.

91 Considering the wording of the trade clause in this historical context, the trial judge concluded that it was not within the common intention of the parties that the treaties granted a general right to trade. He found that at the time of entering the treaties, the Mi'kmaq wanted to secure peace and continuing access to European trade goods. He described the Mi'kmaq concerns at the time as very focussed and immediate. The British, for their part, wanted peace in the region to ensure the safety of their settlers. While the British were willing to support the costly truckhouse system to secure peace, they did not want the Mi'kmaq to become a long-term burden on the public treasury. To this end, the trial judge found that the British wanted the Mi'kmaq to continue their traditional way of life. The trial judge found that the interpretation of the treaty trade clause which best reconciled the intentions of both parties was that the trade clause imposed an obligation on the Mi'kmaq to trade only at British truckhouses or with licensed traders, as well as a correlative obligation on the British to provide the Mi'kmaq with such trading outlets so long as this restriction on Mi'kmaq trade existed. This correlative obligation on the British gave rise to a limited Mi'kmaq "right to bring" goods to trade at these outlets. When the British ceased to provide trading outlets to the Mi'kmaq, the restriction on their trade fell as did the limited "right to bring" which arose out of the system of mutual obligations.

92 Although trade was central to the Treaties of 1760–61, it cannot be doubted that achieving and securing peace was the preeminent objective of both parties in entering into the treaties. See: "As Long as the Sun and Moon Shall Endure": A Brief History of the Maritime First Nations Treaties, 1675 to 1783 (1986), at pp. 101–2; The MAWIW District Council and Indian and Northern Affairs Canada, "We Should Walk in the Tract Mr. Dummer Made": A Written Joint Assessment of Historical Materials ... Relative to Dummer's Treaty of 1725 and All Other Related or Relevant Maritime Treaties and Treaty Negotiations (1992), at pp. 23–24, 31–34 and 90; and L. F. S. Upton, Micmacs and Colonists: Indian-White Relations in the Maritimes, 1713–1867 (1979), at p. 63.

93 The desire to establish a secure and successful peace led each party to make significant concessions. The Mi'kmaq accepted that forging a peaceful relationship with the British was essential to ensuring continued access to European trade goods and to their continued security in the region. To this end, the Mi'kmaq agreed to limit their autonomy by trading only with the British and ceasing all trading relations with the French. Agreeing to restricted trade at truckhouses made the limit on Mi'kmaq autonomy more palatable as truckhouses were recognized as vehicles for stable trade at guaranteed and favourable terms. See: O. P. Dickason, "Amerindians Between French and English in Nova Scotia, 1713–1763", *American Indian Culture and Research Journal*, X (1986), 31, at p. 46; and MAWIW District Council and Indian and Northern Affairs Canada, supra, at pp. 23, 31 and 32.

94 The British, for their part, saw continued relations between the Mi'kmaq and the French as a threat to British dominance in the region and to British-Mi'kmaq relations. Although the fall of the French in 1760 established British power in the region, the trial judge concluded, at para. 90, that the British "did not feel completely secure in Nova Scotia". Evidence submitted at trial indicated that the British feared the possibility of a renewed military alliance between the Mi'kmaq and the French as late as 1793. These concerns of the British are reflected in the Treaties of 1760–61, which, in addition to restricting Mi'kmaq trade, prevent the Mi'kmaq from attacking British settlers and from assisting any of the Crown's enemies. The British were also acutely aware that trading between unregulated private traders and the Mi'kmaq was often unfair and the cause of many disruptions of the peace. Preventing such disruptive practices was a central concern of the Nova Scotia governors and the British Board of Trade who hoped to cement the fragile peace in the region.

95 To secure the peace, the British therefore required the Mi'kmaq to trade only at truckhouses, even though truckhouses ran counter to the British policy not to place the Crown in a monopolistic trading position and imposed a significant financial burden on the public purse. The Nova Scotia government in

"Remarks on the Indian Commerce Carried on by the Government of Nova Scotia 1760, 1761 and part of 1762", expressed the view that the benefits of "Settling [of] the Province and securing the Peace of the New Settlers" were "much more than an Equivalent for any exceedings" in cost, (see: R. O. MacFarlane, "Indian Trade in Nova Scotia to 1764", *Report of the Annual Meeting of the Canadian Historical Association with Historical Papers* (1935), 57, at pp. 59–60; Upton, supra, at p. 63; J. Stagg, *Anglo-Indian Relations in North America to 1763 and an Analysis of the Royal Proclamation of 7 October 1763* (1981), at p. 278; W. E. Daugherty, *Maritime Indian Treaties in Historical Perspectiv*e (1983); and *"We Should Walk in the Tract Mr. Dummer Made ..."*, supra, at p. 90. On British policy see: Letter from the British Board of Trade to Lieutenant Governor Belcher, March 3, 1761, and June 23, 1761; Board of Trade and Privy Council Minutes, June 23 and July 2, 1761).

96 To achieve the mutually desired objective of peace, both parties agreed to make certain concessions. The Mi'kmaq agreed to forgo their trading autonomy and the general trading rights they possessed as British subjects, and to abide by the treaty trade regime. The British, in exchange, undertook to provide the Mi'kmaq with stable trading outlets where European goods were provided at favourable terms while the exclusive trade regime existed. This is the core of what the parties intended. The wording of the trade clause, taken in its linguistic, cultural and historical context, permits no other conclusion. Both the Mi'kmaq and the British understood that the "right to bring" goods to trade was a limited right contingent on the existence of a system of exclusive trade and truckhouses. On the historical record, neither the Mi'kmaq nor the British intended or understood the treaty trade clause as creating a general right to trade.

97 The parties' pre-treaty negotiations and post-treaty conduct point to the same conclusion. I turn first to the pre-treaty negotiations. British negotiations with the Mi'kmaq took place against the background of earlier negotiations with the Maliseet and Passamaquody on February 11, 1760. These negotiations led to the treaty of February 23, 1760, the first of the 1760–61

Treaties. When Mi'kmaq representatives came to negotiate peace with the British 18 days later on February 29, 1760, they were informed of the treaty entered into by the Maliseet and Passamaquody and agreed to make peace on the same conditions. The minutes record that at the very outset of the February 11, 1760, meeting, the Maliseet and Passamaquody representatives were informed:

> ... that it was now expected that they should engage, in behalf of their Tribes, that they will not aid or assist any of His Majesty's Enemies, nor hold any Correspondence or Commerce with them.

The Maliseet and Passamaquody consented to this term of trade exclusivity. After some discussion about "hostages" the following exchange took place:

> His Excellency then demanded of them, Whether they were directed by their Tribes, to propose any other particulars to be Treated upon at this Time. To which they replied that their Tribes had not directed them to propose any thing further than that there might be a Truckhouse established, for the furnishing them with necessaries, in Exchange for their Peltry, and that it might, at present, be at Fort Frederick.
>
> Upon which His Excellency acquainted them that in case of their now executing a Treaty in the manner proposed, and its being ratified at the next General Meeting of their Tribes the next Spring, a Truckhouse should be established at Fort Frederick, agreable to their desire, and likewise at other Places if it should be found necessary, for furnishing them with such Commodities as shall be necessary for them, in Exchange for their Peltry & and that great care should be taken, that the Commerce at the said Truckhouses should be managed by Persons on whose Justice and good Treatment, they might always depend; and that it would be expected that the said Tribes should not Trafic or Barter and Exchange any Commodities at any other Place, nor with any

other Persons. Of all which the Chiefs expressed their entire Approbation. [Nova Scotia Executive Council Minutes, February 11, 1760.]

98 The pre-treaty negotiations between the British and the Maliseet and the Passamaquody, indicate that the aboriginal leaders requested truckhouses in response to their accommodation of the British desire for restricted trade. The negotiations also indicate that the British agreed to furnish truckhouses where necessary to ensure that the Maliseet and the Passamaquody could continue to acquire commodities and necessities through trade. The negotiations highlight the concessions that both the aboriginal and the British signatories made in order to secure the mutually desired objective of peace. The negotiations also indicate that both parties understood that the treaties granted a specific, and limited, right to bring goods to truckhouses to trade.

99 This finding is confirmed by the post-treaty conduct of the Mi'kmaq and the British. Neither party's conduct is consistent with an expectation that the treaty granted the Mi'kmaq any trade right except the implied "right to bring" incidental to their obligation to trade exclusively with the British. Soon after the treaties were entered into, the British stopped insisting that the Mi'kmaq trade only with them. The British replaced the expensive truckhouses with licensed traders in 1762. The system of licensed traders, in turn, died out by the 1780s. Mi'kmaq adherence to the exclusive trade and truckhouse regime was also ambiguous. Records exist of Mi'kmaq trade with the French on the islands of St. Pierre and Miquelon in 1763 and again in 1767: Upton, supra, at pp. 64–65.

100 The fall of the licensed trading system marked the fall of the trading regime established under the Treaties. This left the Mi'kmaq free to trade with whomever they wished, like all other inhabitants of the colonies. The British expressly confirmed that the obligation on the aboriginal signatories to trade exclusively with the British fell with the demise of the truckhouse and licensed trader system at a meeting between two

Maliseet Sakamows and the Lieutenant Governor of Nova Scotia on July 18, 1768:

> Chiefs 9.
> We shall be glad that the Prices of Goods were regulated, as formerly, for Beaver skins were Sold at a better price than some people will now give for them.
> Answer
> here is no Restriction on your Trade you may Traffick with those who sell Cheapest, which will be more for your Interest than limitting the Price of Beaver.
> (Nova Scotia Executive Council Minutes, July 18, 1768.)

101 The record thus shows that within a few years of the signing of the Treaty, the Mi'kmaq treaty obligation to trade only with the British fell into disuse and with it the correlative British obligation to supply the Mi'kmaq with trading outlets. Both parties contributed to the demise of the system of mutual obligations and, apart from a lament that prices were better regulated under the truckhouse system, neither seems to have mourned it. The exclusive trade and truckhouse system was a temporary mechanism to achieve peace in a troubled region between parties with a long history of hostilities. To achieve this elusive peace, the parties agreed that the trading autonomy possessed by all British subjects would be taken away from the Mi'kmaq, and that compensation for the removal of this right would be provided through the provision of preferential and stable trade at truckhouses. When the restriction on the Mi'kmaq trade fell, the need for compensation for the removal of their trading autonomy fell as well. At this point, the Mi'kmaq were vested with the general non-treaty right to hunt, to fish and to trade possessed by all other British subjects in the region. The conditions supporting the right to bring goods to trade at truckhouses, as agreed to by both parties, ceased to exist.

102 The historical context, as the trial judge points out, supports the view that the British wanted the Mi'kmaq to maintain their traditional way of life and that trade was important to the Mi'kmaq. From this, Binnie J. suggests that the purpose of the

treaty trading regime was to promote the self-sufficiency of the Mi'kmaq, and finds a treaty right to hunt, to fish, and to trade for sustenance. Yet, with respect, the historical record does not support this inference. The dominant purpose of the treaties was to prevent the Mi'kmaq from maintaining alliances with the French. To this end, the British insisted on a treaty term that the Mi'kmaq trade exclusively with British agents at British trading outlets — the truckhouses. Implicit in this is the expectation that the Mi'kmaq would continue to trade. But it does not support the inference that the treaty clause conveyed a general right to trade and to sustenance. The treaty reference to the right to bring goods to truckhouses was required by and incidental to the obligation of the Mi'kmaq to trade with the British, and cannot be stretched to embrace a general treaty right to trade surviving the exclusive trade and truckhouse regime. To do so is to transform a specific right agreed to by both parties into an unintended right of broad and undefined scope.

103 The importance of trade to the Mi'kmaq was recognized in two ways. First, as discussed above, so long as the Mi'kmaq were bound to an exclusive covenant of trade with the British, the British promised to provide the Mi'kmaq with truckhouses at which they could trade on favourable terms and obtain the European products they desired. Second, as noted, upon entering into a treaty with the British and acknowledging the sovereignty of the British king, the Mi'kmaq automatically acquired all rights enjoyed by other British subjects in the region. Although these rights were supplanted by the exclusive trade and truckhouse regime while it was extant, when this regime came to an end, the Mi'kmaq trading interest continued to be protected by the general laws of the province under which the Mi'kmaq were free to trade with whomever they wished.

104 I conclude that the trial judge did not err — indeed was manifestly correct — in his interpretation of the historical record and the limited nature of the treaty right that this suggests.

(4) The Argument on the Treaty of 1752

105 The appellant suggests that when the Treaties of 1760–61 are considered together with the earlier Treaty of 1752, the inference arises that the parties understood the trade clause of

the later treaties to confer a general trade right on the Mi'kmaq. The Treaty of 1752 stated that "the said Indians shall have free liberty to bring for Sale to Halifax or any other Settlement within this Province, Skins, feathers, fowl, fish or any other thing they shall have to sell, where they shall have liberty to dispose thereof to the best Advantage" (emphasis added). These words, unlike the words of the Treaties of 1760–61, arguably confer a positive right to trade. The appellant admits that this broad right, if that is what it was, was supplanted by the quite different negative wording of the Treaties of 1760–61. However, he suggests that when the exclusive trade-truckhouse regime of the Treaties of 1760–61 fell into disuse, the more general trade right of the Treaty of 1752 was revived. The difficulty with this argument is that the Treaty of 1752 was completely displaced by the new Treaties of 1760–61, which pointedly made no reference to a general right to trade. Moreover, the different wording of the two treaties cannot be supposed to have gone unperceived by the parties. To conclude that the parties would have understood that a general right to trade would be revived in the event that the exclusive trade and truckhouse regime fell into disuse is not supportable on the historical record and is to "exceed what is possible on the language", to paraphrase from *Sioui*, supra.

106 In summary, a review of the wording, the historical record, the pre-treaty negotiations between the British and the Maliseet and Passamaquody, as well as the post-treaty conduct of the British and the Mi'kmaq, support the trial judge's conclusion that the treaty trade clause granted only a limited "right to bring" trade goods to truckhouses, a right that ended with the obligation to trade only with the British on which it was premised. The trial judge's conclusion that the treaties granted no general trade right must be confirmed.

C.   Do the Treaties of 1760–61 Grant a Right to Government Trading Outlets?

107 The appellant suggests both in the alternative and in addition, that the trial judge's decision makes it clear that the

Treaties of 1760–61 granted a right to truckhouses or licensed traders which was breached by the government's failure to provide such outlets after the 1780s. In the absence of government outlets and any justification for the failure to provide them, the appellant suggests that the federal fisheries regulations are inconsistent with his right to a Mi'kmaq trade vehicle and therefore are null and void in their application to him and other treaty beneficiaries. This argument rests on one aspect of the trial judge's finding, while ignoring the other. Specifically, it asserts the right to truckhouses as an independent freestanding treaty right, while ignoring the finding that this was a dependent right to bring goods to truckhouses collateral to the obligation to trade exclusively with the British. It follows from the trial judge's finding that the "right to bring" goods to trade at truckhouses died with the exclusive trade obligation upon which it was premised, that the treaties did not grant an independent right to truckhouses which survived the demise of the exclusive trade system. This right therefore cannot be relied on in support of an argument of a trade right in the modern context which would exempt the appellant from the application of the fisheries regulations.

108 Even if the appellant surmounted the trial judge's finding that the "right to bring" died with the exclusive trade obligation upon which it was premised, he has failed to establish how a breach of the obligation to provide trading outlets would exempt him from the federal fisheries regulations and, specifically, acquit him of illegally catching fish and illegally selling them to a private party. In my opinion, it is difficult to see how a government obligation to provide trading outlets could be stretched to include a treaty right to fish and a treaty right to trade the product of such fishing with private individuals. Even a broad conception of a right to government trading outlets does not take us to the quite different proposition of a general treaty right to take goods from the land and the sea and sell them to whomever one wishes.

109 This brings me to a variation on the appellant's argument of a right to trading outlets. When pressed on the exact nature

and scope of the trade right asserted, the appellant at times seemed to suggest that this did not matter. A finding that the treaties granted a right to truckhouses or licensed traders, undefined as it might be in scope and modern counterpart, would shift the onus to the government to justify its failure to provide such trading outlets, he suggested. The absence of any justification would put the government in breach and preclude it from applying its regulations against the appellant.

110 The appeal of this argument cannot be denied. It engages, at a superficial glance, many of the concerns that underlie the principles of interpretation addressed at the outset of these reasons. The treaty rights of aboriginal peoples should be interpreted in a generous manner. The honour of the Crown is presumed and must be upheld. Ambiguities must be resolved in favour of the aboriginal signatories. Yet the argument, in my opinion, cannot succeed.

111 A claimant seeking to rely on a treaty right to defeat a charge of violating Canadian law must first establish *a treaty right that protects, expressly or by inference, the activities in question*, see: *Sioui*, supra, at pp. 1066–67. Only then does the onus shift to the government to show that it has accommodated the right or that its limitations of the right are justified.

112 To proceed from a right undefined in scope or modern counterpart to the question of justification would be to render treaty rights inchoate and the justification of limitations impossible. How can one meaningfully discuss accommodation or justification of a right unless one has some idea of the core of that right and its modern scope? How is the government, in the absence of such definition, to know how far it may justifiably trench on the right in the collective interest of Canadians? How are courts to judge whether the government that attempts to do so has drawn the line at the right point? Referring to the "right" in the generalized abstraction risks both circumventing the parties' common intention at the time the treaty was signed, and functioning illegitimately to create, in effect, an unintended right of broad and undefined scope.

113 Instead of positing an undefined right and then requiring justification, a claim for breach of a treaty right should begin by defining the core of that right and seeking its modern counterpart. Then the question of whether the law at issue derogates from that right can be explored, and any justification for such derogation examined, in a meaningful way.

114 Based on the wording of the treaties and an extensive review of the historical evidence, the trial judge concluded that the only trade right conferred by the treaties was a "right to bring" goods to truckhouses that terminated with the demise of the exclusive trading and truckhouse regime. This led to the conclusion that no Crown breach was established and therefore no accommodation or justification required. The record amply supports this conclusion, and the trial judge made no error of legal principle. I see no basis upon which this Court can interfere.

VI. JUSTIFICATION

115 Having concluded that the Treaties of 1760–61 confer no general trade right, I need not consider the arguments specifically relating to justification.

VII. CONCLUSION

116 There is no existing right to trade in the Treaties of 1760–61 that exempts the appellant from the federal fisheries regulations. It follows that I would dismiss the appeal.

Appeal allowed, GONTHIER and MCLACHLIN JJ. dissenting.

Notes

1 All of the thousands of judicial decisions in Canada are catalogued so that they can be easily referenced and retrieved. The decisions of the Supreme Court of Canada are no different; the designation "[1999] 3 S.C.R. 456" is simply the catalogue number of the first Marshall decision by year, volume, and page number. For ease of reference, I will refer to this decision throughout this book as *Marshall (No. 1)*.

2 *Miller v. Jackson*, [1977] Q.B. 966.

3 S.N.S. 1760.

4 There is nothing to suggest that he had a government licence to trade with natives.

5 Dr William Wicken, professor of History, who testified as an expert witness for the accused in both *Marshall (No. 1)* and *Stephen Marshall*, says "tensions were fuelled by the free flow of alcohol" between natives and fishermen-traders, and "the chances of misunderstanding and hostility were acute." (*Encounters with Tall Sails and Tall Tales*, PhD thesis, McGill University, 267–9). A letter to the governor of Massachusetts in 1727 described the problem: "some of our men goe out & carry them strong liquor and make the Indians Drunk and get their furrs for a small Matter so that when they get out of their Drink & see that their Furrs are gone They are mad & care not what Mischief They doe, a Ready way to bring on Outrages & Murders if not the Warr again. I Humbly am of Opinion That it is Needful either to prohibit trading with them or to Regulate their trading ...," R.O.

MacFarlane, *Indian Relations in New England, 1620–1760: A Study of a Regulated Frontier* (Cambridge, Mass.: Harvard University Press, 1933), 364.

6 *Marshall (No. 1)* Crown Documents, #113.
   It should be noted that in July 1761 the King in London repealed the 1760 Nova Scotia statute. But it was a fundamental rule of colonial law that statutes repealed by the King were valid law in the colony where they originated *until notice* of their repeal was received by the Governor of the colony (Joseph Chitty, *A Treatise on the Law of the Prerogatives of the Crown* London: Joseph Butterworths & Sons, (1820), 34; and Labaree, *Royal Government in America*, New Haven: Yale University Press, (1930), 218). Notice of the repeal of the 1760 statute did not reach Nova Scotia's Governor until early 1762 (letter of Jonathan Belcher, 18 January 1762, *Marshall (No. 1)*, Crown Document #136). So the 1760 statute very clearly caught Reverend Seycombe. Strangely, Justice Binnie appears to have thought that Reverend Seycombe's diary entry was 1758 – "235 years previously" to Mr Marshall's fishing expedition in August 1993. But the diary entry is clearly dated August 1761, and the testimony confirmed that date of the diary: evidence of Dr W. Wicken, 1 June 1995, 2,803.

7 Trial transcript, evidence of Dr S. Patterson, 19 April 1995, 189–90.

8 This point is confirmed in William C. Wicken, *Mi'Kmaq Treaties on Trial*, (Toronto: University of Toronto Press, 2002), 21; only one document showed the Mi'Kmaq selling eels.

9 Rory Leishman, *Against Judicial Activism* (Montreal: McGill-Queen's University Press, 2006), 247.

10 Debates of the Nova Scotia House of Assembly, 22 and 26 October 1998, 2,497–8, 2,659.

11 The native accused in *R. v. Stephen Marshall* challenged my appointment to prosecute the appeal of this case, suggesting that lawyers employed by the Department of Justice could not lawfully be appointed to the Prosecution Service. But this challenge was rejected by the Nova Scotia Court of Appeal: [2002] N.S.J. No. 154.

12 An exhaustive examination of these media reports is found in Ken Coates, *The Marshall Decision and Native Rights*, (Montreal: McGill-Queen's University Press, 2000).

CHAPTER ONE

1 John Adamson, *The Noble Revolt – The Overthrow of Charles* I (London: Weidenfeld and Son, 2007), 116–18.

2 Ibid., 505.

3 Cited in Winston S. Churchill, *A History of the English Speaking Peoples, The New World*, vol. 2 (New York: Dodd, Mead, 1974 reprint), 175.

4 An Act of the Commons of England Assembled in Parliament for Erecting of an High Court of Justice for the Trying and Judging of Charles Stuart, King of England, 6 January 1649 in David Iagomarsino and Charles Wood, *The Trial of Charles I* (Hanover, New Hampshire: Dartmouth College / University Press of New England, 1989), 25.

5 Ibid., 75; The Kings Trial, Monday, 22 January 1649.

6 Ibid., 65, 75.

7 Antonia Fraser, *Cromwell Our Chief of Men* (London: Granada, 1981), 420.

8 Hugh Trevor-Roper, 'Epilogue: The Glorious Revolution' in *The Anglo-Dutch Moment*, J. Israel, ed. (Cambridge: Cambridge University Press, 1991), 485.

9 "The Declaration of Rights," 13 February 1689, in Maurice Ashley, *The Glorious Revolution of 1688*, (New York: Scribner, 1966), 206.

10 Israel, *The Anglo-Dutch Moment*, 10.

11 Joseph Chitty, *Prerogatives of the Crown* (London: Joseph Butterworth and Son, 1820), 30.

12 *R. v. Stephen Marshall et al.*, trial evidence of Dr S. Patterson, vol. 36 (26 April 2000), 5320–1. I would be remiss not to highlight this testimony of Dr Patterson. He was testifying six months after the decision of the Supreme Court of Canada in *Marshall (No. 1)*, and he was at that time the only one, of all the many lawyers and academics who had examined the decision, to recognize the massive constitutional error made by the Court in *Marshall (No. 1)*. His courage in testifying in contradiction of the pronouncement of our country's highest court should not be minimized.

13 Section 35 is not one of the 34 sections that constitute the Charter.

CHAPTER TWO

1 Michael Klarman, "The Judges Versus the Union: The Development of British Labour Law 1867–1913," *Virginia Law Review* 75, (1989): 1,487.

2 *Priestly v. Fowler*, (1837) 3 M+W 1.

3 R.L. Howells "Priestly v. Fowler and the Factory Acts" 1963, *Modern Law Review* 26, no. 4, (1963): 367 at 375, n50, citing 1854 Mines Report, 24.

4 James M. Cameron, *The Pictonian Colliers* (Halifax, NS: NS Museum, 1974).

5 Per Pollock CB, *Vose v. Lancs + Yorks Ry* (1858) 27 LJ Ex 249.

6 *AG Can v. AG Ontario (Labour Conventions)*, [1937] AC 326; *AG Can v. AG Ontario (Unemployment Insurance)*, [1937] AC 355.

7 1937 15 Can. Bar Rev. 478, 485.

8 *Constitution Act*, 1940, 3–4 Geo. VI, c. 36.

9 Legislation governing Residential Tenancies, Condominiums, Labour Standards and Sale of Goods are a few of the many examples.

10 *R. v. Drybones*, [1970] S.C.R. 282.

11 *Curr v. The Queen*, [1972] S.C.R. 889 at 899 per Laskin J.

12 *Scott v. Sandford*, (1857) 60 US 393.

13 Peter Hogg, *Constitutional Law in Canada* (5th, Carswell Looseleaf), vol. 2, (Scarborough, Ontario: Thompson Carswell, 2008), 36–8.

14 Ibid., 36–6.

15 *Hunter et al. v. Southam Inc.* (1984) 11 D.L.R. (4th) 641 at 650 (S.C.C.) per Dickson J; *Law Society of British Columbia v. Andrews*, [1989] 1 S.C.R. 143, at para. 38.

16 *Egan v. Canada*, [1995] 2 S.C.R. 513; *Vriend v. Alberta*, [1998] 1 S.C.R. 493; *Egale v. Canada (AG)* (2003) 225 D.L.R. (4th) 472 (BCCA); *Halpern v. Canada (AG)* (2003) 65 OR (3rd) 161 (On. C.A.).

17 *Chaoulli v. Quebec*, [2005] 254 D.L.R. 4th 577.

18 *R. v. Big M Drug Mart*, [1985] 1 S.C.R. 295.

19 *Doucet-Boudreau v. AGNS*, [2003] 3 S.C.R. 3.

20 *Health Studies and Support-Facilities Subsector Bargaining Association v. British Columbia*, [2007] 2 S.C.R. 391.

21 F.L. Martin and Rainer Knopff, *The Charter Revolution and the Court Party* (Peterborough, Ontario: Broadview Press, 2000) 22, 34.

22 Ibid., 149.

23 See, for example, Rory Leishman, *Against Judicial Activism, the Decline of Freedom and Democracy in Canada*, (Montreal: McGill-Queen's University Press, 2006), 37, 78.

24 MacKay, "The Legislature, The Executive and The Courts: The Delicate Balance of Power or who is Running this Country Anyway" *Dalhousie Law Journal* 24, no. 2 (2001): 37–74. Discussions of the Charter "Dialogue" are found in 45 *Osgoode Hall Law Journal*, no. 1 (Spring 2007).

25 Keynote address delivered at Osgoode Hall Law School, York University, Toronto, *Globe and Mail*, 13 April 2000: A17. Justice Abella was then a judge of the Ontario Court of Appeal.

26 (1990) 70 D.L.R. (4th) 385.

27 (1986) 36 D.L.R. (4th) 246 at 255.

28 36 D.L.R. (4th) 246 at 255, 257.

29 36 D.L.R. (4th) 246 at 260. In a DFO sting operation in 1982 Musqueam band members sold an undercover officer seventeen tons of "food fish." The lower court noted that "the conclusion of commercial sales of food fish is all but inescapable": 36 D.L.R. (4th) 246 at 257.

30 36 D.L.R. (4th) 246 at 257.

31 36 D.L.R. (4th) 246 at 258.

32 Hogg, *Constitutional Law in Canada* (5th ed, Carswell Looseleaf), vol. 1, 6–10, 33–2; Kent Roach, *Constitutional Remedies in Canada* (Canada Law Book) 2006, 2–32; *Canadian Bar Association v. British Columbia*, [2006] B.C.J. No. 1342 at para. 118; *Cape Breton Regional Municipality v. AGNS*, [2008] N.S.J. No. 154.

33 "That the right is controlled in great detail by the regulations does not mean that the right is thereby extinguished.": 70 D.L.R. (4th) 385 at 400.

34 "an existing aboriginal right cannot be read so as to incorporate the specific manner in which it was regulated.": 70 D.L.R. (4th) 385 at 396.

35 70 D.L.R. (4th) 385 at 396.

36 Ibid., 409.

37 Ibid., 407, 409.

38 Ibid., 409.

39 Ibid., 411.

40 Cited in R.S. Sharpe and Kent Roach, *Brian Dickson: A Judge's Journey* (Toronto: University of Toronto Press, 2003), 449. The authors

review the personal papers of former Chief Justice Brian Dickson, which uniquely include memoranda recording the views of judges involved in the case, together with draft decisions and other material that is not usually accessible to the public.

41 70 D.L.R. (4th) 385 at 413–14.

42 *R. v. Van der Peet* (1996) 137 D.L.R. (4th) 289 at paras 42, 43.

43 70 D.L.R. (4th) 385 at 411.

44 The British Columbia Court of Appeal took a more cautious approach than that of the Supreme Court of Canada. It said that only the right to fish for food purposes was a constitutionally protected native right. The method of fishing was a different thing. It did not receive constitutional protection. Government could regulate the time, place, and method of fishing without running into the constitution. 36 D.L.R. 4th 246 at 277.

45 [1996] 2 S.C.R. 507, para. 30.

46 Ibid., paras 31, 44.

47 Ibid., paras 44–6.

48 Ibid., para. 59.

49 Ibid., para. 68.

50 Ibid., para. 64.

51 [2006] S.C.J. No. 54.

52 *R. v. Stephen Marshall*, [2005] 2 S.C.R. 220, per McLachlin C.J., at para. 34.

53 Native people on the east coast made "limited use of forest products"(*R. v. Stephen Marshall*, per Curran Prov. Ct. J., para. 95). Their technology did not permit them to "exploit mature timber resources" (*R. v. Stephen Marshall*, para. 44 per Scanlan J.).

54 [1996] 138 D.L.R. (4th) 657.

55 *Re s. 193 and 195.1 of Criminal Code* [1990] 1 S.C.R. 1,123, 1,163.

56 [1997] 153 D.L.R. (4th) 193.

57 Ibid., para. 119.

58 [1973] S.C.R. 313.

59 Ibid., per Judson J., 328.

60 *Delgamuukw*, [1997] 153 D.L.R. (4th) 153, at para. 115.

61 Evidence of Dr W. Wicken, *R. v. Stephen Marshall*, Transcript Vol. 13, 2,047–55 citing the work of Frank Speck. See evidence of Dr Alex Von Guernet, Transcript Vol. 51, 7,588–89, 7633–36.

62 *Delgamuukw*, [1997] 153 D.L.R. (4th) 193, para. 112.

63 Ibid., paras 111, 128.

64 Ibid., paras 128–31.

65 Ibid., para. 127.

66 As explained by Dr Alex Von Guernet at trial in *R. v. Stephen Marshall*. Nova Scotia natives participating in the market economy for furs in the seventeenth and eighteenth centuries exploited local wildlife populations to the point of extinction. Trial Transcript, Vol. 50, 7,508–12, Vol. 55, 8266–70. See also Shepard Kreck, *The Ecological Indian: Myth and history*, (New York: W.W. Norton, 1999).

67 *Delgamuukw*, [1997] 153 D.L.R. (4th) 193 at paras 113, 129.

68 See *Marshall v. Peguis Band* (1990) 71 D.L.R. (4th) 193 at 225; *Guerin et al. v. The Queen*, (1984) 13 D.L.R. (4th) 321 at 340.

69 *R. v. Marshall/R. v. Bernard*, [2005] S.C.C. 43 at paras 85–96.

70 A Bill entitled an Act for the Regulation of the Indian Trade, 7 July 1762.

71 The suggestion that non-native settlers had to take title from a Crown grant (*Delgamuukw*, para. 129) is met by the response that subjects of the Crown, such as natives in Nova Scotia, were free to sell their lands to other subjects. As Kent McNeil says in *Common Law Aboriginal Title*, Oxford: Clarendon Press (1989) "prohibition of private purchases from indigenous landholders appears to have been a matter of policy backed by legislation when adopted, rather than a consequence of the application of English law" (227).

72 *Delgamuukw*, [1997] 153 D.L.R. (4th) 193, para. 195.

73 Ibid., para. 165.

74 [2005] S.C.R. 220, joint reasons.

75 Ibid., paras 56, 58, and 66.

76 [2004] 3 S.C.R. 511.

77 Ibid., para. 16, 17.

78 *R. v. Badger*, [1996] 1 S.C.R. 771 at para. 41; *R. v. Taylor* (1981), 34 OR (2nd) 360 (Ont. C.A.) at 367. *Marshall (No. 1)* at paras 48–51, per Binnie J.

79 *Haida*, [2004] 3 S.C.R. 511, para. 20, and para. 38, "consultation and accommodation ... is an essential corollary to the honourable process of reconciliation that s. 35 demands."

80 "Charter Myths," *UBC Law Review* 33, No. 1 (1999): 23 at 31.

81 "Judicial Independence and Judicial Activism." Address to the Canadian Bar Association Council Awards Luncheon, 21 August 1999, in F.L. Morton, *Law, Politics and the Judicial Process in Canada* (Calgary, Alberta: University of Calgary Press, 2002) 602 at 613. Interestingly, Justice L'Heureux-Dubé made these comments only one month before the release of the decision in *Marshall (No. 1)*.

82 "Charter Myths," 33.

CHAPTER THREE

1 *R. v. Syliboy* [1929] D.L.R. 307.

2 The Treaty of 1752 was not "kept." It was terminated by hostilities, a point that will be dealt with later.

3 *R. v. Isaac* [1975] 13 N.S.R. (2nd) 460.

4 Mr Isaac was represented by Bruce Wildsmith, then a young law professor at Dalhousie Law School. The case marks the beginning of Mr Wildsmith's able advocacy on behalf of Mi'kmaq in the Maritime Provinces. Most of the significant cases subsequently decided by the courts were argued by Mr Wildsmith, and much of the change in native rights law in the Maritime Province is attributable to his very capable work.

5 *R. v. Paul and George* [1977] 24 N.S.R. (2nd) 313.

6 *R. v. Simon* [1985] 71 N.S.R. (2nd) 15.

7 *R. v. Denny* [1990], 94 N.S.R. (2nd) 253.

8 *R. v. Sparrow*, [1990] 1 S.C.R. 1075, discussed in chapter 2.

9 See *R. v. Simon*, [2002] N.B.J. No. 248, para. 8; *R. v. Francis*, [1996] N.B.J. No. 220.

10 See, for example, *R. v. Lavigne*, [2005] N.B.J. No. 92. *R. v. McCoy*, [1992] 127 N.B.R. (2nd) 328 at para. 2.

11 See, for example, *R. v. McCoy*, [1991] N.B.J. No. 1146, reversed, but not on this point, [1993] N.B.J. No. 597 (NBCA); *R. v. Hamilton*, [1993] N.B.J. No. 486.

12 *R. v. Drew*, [2003] NLSCTD 105 at para. 1,027, aff'd [2006] NLCA 53.

13 *R. v. Peter Paul*, [1996], 182 N.B.R. (2nd) 270 (Arsenault ProvCtJ); (1997), 193 N.B.R. (2nd) 321 (Turnbull J).

14 *R. v. Peter Paul*, [1998] N.B.J. No. 126.

15 *Fredericton Daily Gleaner*, editorial, 24 April 1998, cited in Ken Coates, *Re Marshall Decision and Native Rights* (Montreal: McGill-Queen's University Press, 2000).

16 Ibid.

CHAPTER FOUR

1 As an undergraduate student at Mount Allison University, I was privileged to study under Dr Reid. He is, in his field of expertise, a leading scholar of Maritime history.

2 (1985), 71 N.S.R. (2nd) 15, para. 30.

3 Opening remarks of counsel for the accused, Bruce Wildsmith, 21 November 1994, 28.

4 Opening remarks of Crown counsel, 21 November 1994, 14.

5 It needs mention that at the conclusion of the defendant's evidence at trial, the trial judge permitted the Crown to recall Dr Patterson on the basis that the focus of the trial had changed from the Treaty of 1752 after Dr Patterson had completed his original testimony. The trial judge's objective in taking this step was to allow the Crown to adduce additional evidence to ensure it was not prejudiced by the defendant's change of position. A close review of the transcript reveals more argument than evidence. Counsel for Mr Marshall objected to question after question that Crown counsel attempted to ask, arguing they were beyond the proper scope of rebuttal testimony. Little was accomplished.

6 Dr S. Patterson, *The Marshall Case: Treaty Rights and the Task of Blending History and Law*, paper prepared for Aboriginal Law Programme, Winnipeg, 29 April 2000, 12.

7 It is not suggested that there was anything improper in this, or in any other aspect of Mr Wildsmith's presentation of the case. The point is that at the trial, where matters of fact are meant to be closely examined, the document that would be seen as centrally important by the Supreme Court of Canada was not considered significant.

8 *Marshall (No. 1)* per Embree, Prov. Ct. J., para. 127.

9 Had normal procedure been followed, the defence would have been forced to choose its position at the outset. If the defence had chosen

the Treaty of 1752, the Crown's evidence in reply would have very likely been fatal. If the defence had chosen to rely on the Halifax Treaties, the Crown's evidence in response would not have been restricted to "rebuttal" evidence.

10 These treaties are sometimes referred to as the "Treaties of 1760–61." They will be referred to here as the "Halifax Treaties" of that period to distinguish them from treaties made with native peoples outside Halifax in roughly the same period.

11 Para. 5. The Court referred to this treaty for the very practical reason that not all the Halifax Treaties have been preserved, and the treaty with the LaHave band exemplified the terms of the other Halifax Treaties. Judge Embree, in the trial Court, referred to the same treaty for the same reason (para. 70). Both Courts are to be faulted in this. The LaHave Treaty, dated 10 March 1760, was entirely irrelevant to the case. Mr Marshall was from Cape Breton and at a Treaty Ceremony in June of 1761, the Cape Breton chief, among others, signed a Halifax Treaty. The Cape Breton Treaty has not been preserved, but others from the same ceremony have. Those are the treaties that should have been referenced. But by referring to the LaHave Treaty, Justice Binnie was repeatedly distracted by the date of that treaty (see paras 7, 16, 19, 20) and distracted from the record of the June 1761 Treaty discussions which, as will be discussed at length in the text, are inconsistent with the majority finding of a treaty right to hunt, fish, and gather for trade.

12 Brief of Argument of Federal Crown, Nova Scotia Provincial Court, para. 165.

13 *Marshall (No. 1)* per Embree, Prov. Ct. J., para. 125.

14 Ibid., paras 74–5.

15 Ibid., para. 116.

16 Ibid., paras 125–6.

17 Referencing the thorough and detailed post-trial brief filed by the federal Crown, dated 23 February 1996, especially 26–9.

18 Evidence of Dr W. Wicken, 20 September 1995, 3422. The disease arrived in Nova Scotia with an ill-fated French naval fleet that sought refuge in Halifax Harbour in 1746, having been sent to recover Fortress Louisbourg, which had been captured by New Englanders in 1745. The fleet was smashed by a hurricane and decimated by

disease. It sheltered in the harbour, then returned to France without ever attacking Louisbourg.

19 "Ceremonials at Concluding a Peace with the Several Districts of the General MickMack Nation of Indians in His Majesty's Province of Nova Scotia." The document was discussed in the federal Crown's post-trial brief, 33–4. *Marshall (No. 1)* Crown Documents, #127.

20 Evidence of Dr W. Wicken, 21 September 1995, 3706.

21 Evidence of Dr John Reid, 17 May 1995, 1172.

22 *Marshall (No. 1)*, Ruling of Embree, Prov.Ct.J., 9 May 1995, 531.

23 Fred Anderson, *The Crucible of War: The Seven Years War and the Fate of Empire in British North America 1754–1766* (New York: Alfred Knopf, 2000), 383; William Fowler, *Empires at War: The Seven Years War and the Struggle for North America 1754–1763* (Vancouver: Douglas & McIntyre, 2005), 220–1; Geoffrey Jules Marcus, *Quiberon Bay, The Campaign in Home Waters, 1759* (London: Hollis and Carter, 1960).

24 Arthur Herman, *To Rule the Waves* (New York: Harper Collins, 2004), 290.

25 Anderson, *Crucible of War*, 395.

26 *Marshall (No. 1)* per Embree, Prov. Ct. J., para. 127.

27 Evidence of Dr W. Wicken, 31 May 1995, 2624–31.

28 Evidence of Dr W. Wicken, 31 May 1995, 2631.

29 Evidence of Dr W. Wicken, 21 September 1995, 3720.

30 Evidence of Dr W. Wicken, 30 May 1995, 2580–4; 22 September 1995, 2788–9.

31 Evidence of Dr W. Wicken, 30 May 1995, 2574; 31 May 1995, 2746, 2762; 22 September 1995, 3,797.

32 Evidence of Dr W. Wicken, 1 June 1995, 2788.

33 Evidence of Dr W. Wicken, 21 September 1995, 3750–1.

34 Evidence of Dr W. Wicken, 1 June 1995, 2786–801.

35 Evidence of Dr W. Wicken, 30 May 1995, 2495–7.

36 *Marshall (No. 1)*, Embree, Prov.Ct.J., paras 96, 122, 127.

37 Ibid., para. 97.

38 In 2002 Dr Wicken published *Mi'kmaq Treaties on Trial*, (Toronto: University of Toronto Press). While the book gives an interesting account of his experiences as an expert witness, it is largely a reiteration of his evidence respecting the Mi'kmaq treaties, which was

rejected by the trial judge. It focuses primarily on the Treaty of 1726, which the trial judge determined (paras 103–5) was not incorporated into the Halifax Treaties. The 1726 Treaty was consequently irrelevant to the decision of the trial court or the appeal courts.

39 There is a simple explanation for this, as described by Dr Stephen Patterson. An original, handwritten copy of the 1752 Treaty survives to this day, as recorded by the clerk to the Nova Scotia Executive Council in 1752. The treaty recites that it was between the British governor and "Major Jean Baptiste Cope Chief Sachem of the xxx Tribe of Mick Mack Indians, Inhabiting the Eastern Coast of the said Province." That is exactly what it says. The "xxx" probably means that the clerk did not know or could not spell the name of Chief Cope's band, the Shubenacadie-Musquodoboit band. When this treaty was first published in 1869, the editors dropped the "xxx," so it looks as though Cope was "Chief Sachem of the Tribe of Mick MacK Indians Inhabiting the Eastern Coast ... " As a consequence of this editorial change in 1869 it became widely held among Mi'kmaq peoples in the Maritime Provinces that the 1752 Treaty was made by their "Chief Sachem" and embraced all Mi'kmaq. Even today the myth survives to the point that in the 1980s native leaders convinced politicians in Nova Scotia to celebrate "Treaty Day" in October (October 1) when the 1752 Treaty was negotiated. Each year in Nova Scotia, politicians and native leaders gather to commemorate a treaty that applied to only one Mi'kmaq band, was tossed in a fire by natives to symbolize its termination, was followed by a bitter war, and was replaced by a 1760–61 Halifax Treaty; accordingly it has no enduring modern-day relevance. Evidence of Dr Patterson in *R. v. Stephen Marshall*, 26 April 2000, vol. 36, 5476–93; 1 May 2000, vol. 37, 5496–598.

40 Testimony of Gilbert Sewell, *R. v. Gray*, [2004] N.B.J. No. 291.

41 *Marshall (No. 1)*, Embree, Prov. Ct. J., paras 97, 132.

42 *Marshall (No. 1)*, Binnie, J., para. 5.

43 *R. v. Stephen Marshall*, Scanlan J., para. 8

44 *R. v. Stephen Marshall*, para. 7; notwithstanding this, the federal government has executed agreements with nearly every Mi'kmaq band in respect of "Marshall fishing rights" and committed hundreds

of millions of taxpayer's dollars, on the questionable basis that *all* Mi'kmaq have "Marshall" treaty rights.

45 *Marshall (No. 1)*, Defence Document #159.

46 These treaties of 1760–61 were of two sorts: the Halifax Treaties, executed by the governor or lieutenant-governor at Halifax; and treaties with British officers in the field. *R. v. Stephen Marshall*, per Scanlan J., para. 13; Evidence of Dr W. Wicken in *Marshall (No. 1)*, 31 May 1995, 2,741.

47 In *Newfoundland v. Drew*, [2003] NLSCTD 105, a judge in Newfoundland said that the 1726 Treaties were terminated by hostilities (para. 1,027). An earlier decision in New Brunswick held that the same treaties had not been terminated by hostilities: *R. v. Paul: R. v. Polchies*, [1988] 4 CNLR 107 (NBQB).

48 The part of the 1726 Treaty, cited above, that natives, "shall not be molested in their persons, Hunting, fishing and Planting grounds ... " is not part of what the 1760 Halifax Treaty incorporates, but the native side still argued that it was implicitly incorporated.

49 *Marshall (No. 1)*, Embree, Prov. Ct. J., para. 105; similarly, the trial judge in *R. v. Bernard*, [2000] N.B.J. No. 138, reviewed the same evidence and concluded that the Mi'kmaq treaties were "stand alone treaties which did not renew previous treaties" (para. 75).

50 Opening remarks of Crown Counsel, 21 November 1994, 18.

51 Cited in J.B. Brebner, *New England's Outpost: Acadia Before the Conquest of Canada*, (New York: Burt Franklin, 1973 reprint), 257, where Governor Lawrence's rule is described as a "dictatorship" (234).

52 An interesting wrinkle is that the instructions to Governor Cornwallis at the time of the founding of Halifax in 1749 provided for the election of an Assembly. In the early years after the founding of Halifax, this instruction was not obligatory, and the Assembly was not summoned for nearly a decade. In the mid–1750s, the Board of Trade became more insistent, and eventually forced a reluctant Charles Lawrence to hold elections: see Brebner, ch. IX. Years later Lord Mansfield decided, in *Campbell v. Hall* (1774) Lofft 655, that the Crown's prerogative was limited after the grant of the Assembly. But whatever the constitutional position before 1758, it is undoubted

that in 1758, at the establishment of the Assembly, the prerogative became limited.

53 *Marshall (No. 1)*, Embree, Prov. Ct. J., para. 67.

54 *Marshall (No. 1)*, Embree, Prov. Ct. J., paras 115, 116.

55 *An Act Giving further Encouragement for the Importation of Naval Stores*, 8 Geo I, c.12; *An Act for the better preservation of his Majesty's Woods in America*, 2 Geo II, c.35.

56 "A great part of white pine timber in this Province, from 29 Inches Upward, are found defective upon opening them. I believe these defects often proceed from fires which the Indians formerly set on the meadows, which slightly running over, consumed the dead herbage and produced better seed for the Moose Deer – These fires often spread lightly into the woods and scorched the trees in different degrees." Letter of J. Wentworth, 20 March 1790, Defence Documents, *R. v. Bernard*, Tab 317.

57 *Marshall (No. 1)*, Embree, Prov. Ct. J., para. 115.

58 Alewives are herring.

59 Evidence of Dr W. Wicken, 23 May 1995, 1703. He also said that cod was harvested, but pointed to no evidence in the period between contact (approximately 1500) and the period of the Halifax Treaties of 1760/61 for this assertion. Later on he added that the Mi'kmaq harvested shellfish, and he referred vaguely to "other types of anadromous and catadronus fish."

60 Evidence of Dr W. Wicken, 29 May 1995, 2322; 26 May 1995, 2272; 1 June 1995, 2,806.

61 Evidence of Dr John Reid, 17 May 1995, 1286–7, 1189, 11192.

62 *Marshall (No. 1)*, Embree, Prov. Ct. J., para. 115.

63 Dr Patterson said merely that trading fish at truckhouses was not prohibited so, "it's fair to assume that it was permissible": Evidence, 19 April 1995, 156. Dr Reid said merely that because the treaty referred to trade, and because the Mi'kmaq traded fish and furs "this implies that there should be a right to fish and a right to trade the product of fishing": Evidence, 12 May 1995, 975. This was a legal analysis, not a historical one. Dr Wicken said he "assumed" that natives could trade fish at truckhouses: Evidence, 31 May 1995, 2636. The only evidence he could summon was by reference to Hudson Bay Company Records from James Bay where, he said, natives brought fresh fish to

trade at company trading posts for the consumption of the individual who ran the post. The example is obviously irrelevant to Nova Scotia, and could not, in any event, be fairly characterized as a substantial commercial trade. Dr Wicken has since confirmed that "there is no direct evidence of a trade in food from the truckhouse accounts." Wicken, *Mi'Kmaq Treaties on Trial*, 200.

CHAPTER FIVE

1 John Sopinka and Mark Gelowitz, *The Conduct of an Appeal* (2nd ed), Toronto: Butterworths Canada Ltd (2000), 282. Justice Binnie would note at para. 18 in *Marshall (No. 1)* that an appeal court must defer to a trial judge's findings of fact, which "should not be overturned unless made on the basis of a 'palpable and overriding error.'"
2 *R. v. Marshall* [1997], 146 D.L.R. (4th) 257 at 269 (NSCA).
3 Ibid., 273.
4 Already in the eighteenth century, "liberty" or freedom was "deeply implanted" in the British Constitution. William Blackstone, *Commentaries on the Laws of England*, Book the First, Oxford: Clarendon Press (1765), 123.
5 Not until much later in the nineteenth century did legislatures begin regulating the fishery in and around the Maritime Provinces.
6 *Marshall (No. 1)*, NSCA, 272.
7 Ibid., 273.
8 Ibid., 277.

CHAPTER SIX

1 Justice McLachlin was appointed Chief Justice of Canada in January 2000, a few months after the decision in *Marshall (No. 1)* was issued by the court.
2 *Marshall (No. 1)*, per Binnie J., para. 19.
3 Ibid., para. 7 and see para. 4.
4 Ibid., para. 7.
5 Ibid., para. 14.
6 Ibid., para. 26.
7 Ibid., para. 29, citing Defence Document #107.

8 Ibid., para. 54.

9 Ibid., para. 19. Note that in this sentence he references the "Mi'kmaq," while the document relates not to the Mi'kmaq, but to the *Maliseet*, a point that will be elaborated later.

10 Ibid., paras 35, 44, 52.

11 Ibid., para. 4.

12 Ibid., paras 58, 59. The obvious practical problem with this distinction is that it is practically impossible to differentiate the two. As one judge later wrote, "even a large harvesting operation may operate at a loss" (Scanlan J., *R. v. Stephen Marshall*, para. 27). In that scenario, would such a "commercial" operation be within the scope of the treaty? After all, its earnings would be less than the "moderate livelihood" described by Justice Binnie.

13 *Marshall (No. 1)*, per McLachlin J., para. 70.

14 Ibid., paras 97, 98.

15 Ibid., para. 102.

16 Ibid., para. 93.

17 Ibid., paras 86, 102–3.

18 Ibid., para. 83.

19 Ibid., para. 78.

20 Ibid., para. 80.

21 Ibid., para. 80. Justice Binnie's reasons equally reject the distinction made by the Court of Appeal, paras 9–14. It should be noted that it is debated whether Nova Scotia's native treaties did not also have significant implications respecting lands.

22 And perhaps in Quebec: see *R. v. Sioui*, [1990] 1 S.C.R. 1025.

23 It may be that the principles summarized by Justice McLachlin are appropriate to encompass treaty obligations, but the court has never confronted the issue and, at the very least, it needs to acknowledge the significant and binding character of native treaty obligations.

CHAPTER SEVEN

1 A detailed description of that reaction is found in Ken Coates, *The Marshall Decision and Native Rights* (Montreal: McGill-Queen's University Press, 2000).

2 *Chronicle Herald,* "Ottawa Pleads for Goodwill," 25 September 1999.

3 *Daily Gleaner,* 30 September 1999, cited in Coates, *The Marshall Decision,* 136. And, more chilling: "I'm used to blood. Fish blood. Indian blood – it's all the same to me." "Justice Takes a Fall in NB," *National Post,* 5 October 1999.

4 Coates, *The Marshall Decision,* 13.

5 "We've Never Surrendered Our Land," *Telegraph Journal.* 25 October 1999.

6 "Indian Affairs Minister Calls for Talks," *Chronicle Herald,* 15 October 1999.

7 *Marshall (No. 1),* para. 67.

8 Justice Cory was absent in *Marshall (No. 2)* as he had retired from the court. The decision in *Marshall (No. 2)* is the decision of the Court; no specific judge is identified as the author.

9 *Marshall (No. 2),* para. 2.

10 Ibid., para. 6.

11 Ibid., para. 19.

12 Ibid., para. 38.

13 *R. v. Badger,* [1996] 1 S.C.R. 771 at para. 97.

14 *Marshall (No. 2),* para. 38.

15 Ibid., para. 17.

16 Philip Saunders, "Getting Their Feet Wet: The Supreme Court and Practical Implementation of Treaty Rights in the Marshall Case," *Dalhousie Law Journal* (spring 2000): 23, 48, 74.

17 Mr Wildsmith has expressed his "shock" and "sense of betrayal" at *Marshall (No. 2),* pointing out that it is inconsistent with *Marshall (No. 1)* and that the aboriginal community was not provided with an opportunity to be heard on the issues discussed in *Marshall (No. 2).* The Court, he said, "bowed to the intense controversy that resulted from its decision" and "yield[ed] to political considerations ... commenting on issues that came to the court through the media and not through the parties": *Vindicating Mi'Kmaq Rights: The Struggle Before, During and After Marshall* (2001) 19 Windsor Year Book Access to Justice, 203.

18 McLachlin CJ, in *British Columbia v. Haida,* [2004] 3 S.C.R. 511, para. 11.

CHAPTER EIGHT

1 *Marshall (No. 1)*, per Embree, Prov. Ct. J., para. 112.
2 Ibid., paras 113–16.
3 Ibid., para 116.
4 *Marshall (No. 1)*, per Binnie J., paras 19, 30, 52, 54.
5 Ibid., para. 19.
6 Ibid., para. 52.
7 *Marshall (No. 1)*, per Embree, Prov.Ct.J., para. 99.
8 *Marshall (No. 1)*, per Binnie J., para. 20.
9 He referred to the document only in passing at para. 99.
10 There is a passing reference to the document in Mr Marshall's written submission to the trial judge (12 January 1996, para 117), but it is not suggested there that the document reflected a native demand.
11 Evidence of Dr W. Wicken, 2 June 1995, 3141.
12 Appellant's Factum at the Supreme Court of Canada, 12 March 1998 at para 23, "A *crucial interchange* over the treaties of 1760–61 occurred on February 11, 1760" [emphasis in the original]. While the language in that document that "Their Tribes had not directed them to propose any thing further than that there might be Truckhouses established" was emphasized in the factum, it is not entirely clear even from the factum that this language would be characterized as a native demand. However, in the oral argument at the Supreme Court of Canada on 5 November 1998, counsel for Mr Marshall clearly characterized the passage in that way. Reference to the language of the 11 February 1760 document and its "crucial importance" was the very first point made by counsel for Mr Marshall in oral argument. He said that the document was "of such overriding importance and received so little consideration by the lower courts and, indeed, by my learned friend, that I would like to get to it right away."
13 I am not suggesting here or elsewhere that there was anything improper on the part of Mr Marshall's counsel in changing their position or advancing this argument. To the contrary, it was a brilliantly effective tactic. The problem is in how it was handled by the Supreme Court of Canada.
14 *Marshall (No. 1)*, per Binnie J., para. 3.
15 Ibid., para. 17.

16 Justice Binnie's summary of the "balance of power" reflects very closely the evidence given by Dr W. Wicken at Trial Transcript, 31 May 1995, 2622 and following. The trial judge rejects this evidence at para 127, and his findings at paras 90 and 91 have a different emphasis. Whereas Justice Binnie said the Mi'kmaq were a "considerable fighting force" (para. 17), the trial judge said their ability to fight was "substantially reduced." Whereas Justice Binnie described the period as one of "great military and political turmoil" (para. 3), the trial judge referred to British military victories and said they "had cause to be more confident than ever before" in their strength in Nova Scotia.

17 *Marshall (No. 1)*, per Embree, Prov. Ct. J., para. 127.

18 Evidence of Dr W. Wicken, 30 May 1995, 2590.

19 To his credit, counsel for Mr Marshall did refer to the document in his factum at the Supreme Court of Canada, at para. 21.

20 *Marshall (No. 1)*, per Binnie, J., para. 20.

21 Evidence of Dr Patterson, 29 November 1994, 1016–1017.

22 Evidence of Dr John Reid, 16 May 1995, 1015; Evidence of Dr W. Wicken, 30 May, 1995, 2602.

23 *Marshall (No. 1)*, per Binnie, J., para. v25. While the earlier correspondence General Whitmore refers to was not in evidence in *Marshall (No. 1)*, it was in evidence in *R. v. Stephen Marshall*, and it describes natives surrendering: "Thirty-four French people have surrendered & also seven Indians, among them Jeanot Pequide Onalouet Chief of the Indians of This Island; they have taken The Oaths of Allegiance to His Britannick Majesty and promised to be faithful good subjects in all times to come." [Letter of General Whitmore, 1 December 1759, Ex.17 #156].

24 *Marshall (No. 1)*, per Binnie J., para. 47.

25 Evidence of Dr S. Patterson, 29 November 1994, 1067 and following.

26 Evidence of Dr S. Patterson, 29 November 1994, 1049–50.

27 One document that Justice Binnie did reference (at para. 24) was a letter dated later in 1758, after the fall of Louisbourg, from the British to a French priest. Father Maillard had retreated to Merigomish with a group of Acadians and Mi'kmaq. The British wrote recommending surrender, confirming that "you will enjoy all your possessions, your liberty, property with the free exercise of your religion."

To the extent that this letter could be characterized as a British promise of peace "terms," it says nothing about treaty rights to have access
to the region's resources or to trade.

28 *R. v. Stephen Marshall*, Scanlan J. paras 12, 13.

29 *Marshall (No. 1)*, per Binnie J., paras 36, 37.

30 The complete list is as follows: Paul Lawrence, "Chief of a Tribe that
before the war lived at La Have"; Louis Francis, "Chief of Merimichi";
Denis Winmouet, "Chief of Tabugimkik"; Etienne Alchaba, "Chief of
Pohomoosh"; Claud Atonash, "Chief of Gediack"; Michel
Alexcotimpk, "Chief of Keshpugowitk"; Joseph A [ ]"Chief of
Chignectou"; John N[ ], "Chief of Pictou"; Baptist L[ ], "Chief of Isle of
St. John's"; Reni, "Chief of Nalkitgonish"; Jeanot Pigaluet, "Chief of
Cape Breton"; Claud, "Chief of Chigabennakadik"; Michael
Algamatimpk, "Chief of Keshpugowitk"; [Otelary Argualett], "Chief
of Minas"; Augustine Michael, "Chief of Richibouctou."

CHAPTER NINE

1 *Marshall (No. 1)*, Embree, Prov. Ct. J., para. 92.

2 Ibid., para. 105.

3 *Marshall (No. 1)*, per Binnie, J., para. 26.

4 *Marshall (No. 1)*, Embree, Prov. Ct. J., para. 99. There is a glancing
reference to the document at para. 96.

5 It is not referenced in Mr Marshall's Factum in the Court of Appeal.
It is referenced twice in his reply Factum (paras 12, 20) in that Court,
but not to suggest a "demand." I have not had access to the tran-
scripts of oral submissions in the Court of Appeal as they have not
been preserved.

6 *Marshall (No. 1)*, per Binnie, J., para. 27.

7 *Marshall (No. 1)*, Embree, Prov. Ct. J., para. 107.

8 Evidence of Dr S. Patterson, 29 November 1994, 1,079. *Marshall
(No. 1)*, Crown documents #127 and #128.

9 While the Cape Breton Treaty does not survive, those treaties signed
that day by the "Merimichi" chief and the "Jediack" chief do survive.
They are the standard form Halifax Treaties. *Marshall (No. 1)*,
Crown documents #127 and #128.

10 *Marshall (No. 1)*, per Binnie, J., para. 52; see also paras 7, 19, 35.

11 *R. v. Van der Peet*, [1996] 2 S.C.R. 507 at para. 69.

CHAPTER TEN

1 There are some exceptions whereby the law of the Prerogative gives the King powers that can be effected in a treaty, but they are not relevant here.
2 George Chalmers, *Opinions of Eminent Lawyers* (Burlington: C. Goodrich, 1858) 625–28, 627; see also 623.
3 Evidence of Dr John Reid, 11 May 1995, 824.
4 Evidence of Dr John Reid, 11 May 1995, 832.
5 Evidence of Dr John Reid, 11 May 1995, 835, 836, 842, 848.
6 Evidence of Dr S. Patterson, 29 November 1994, 999.
7 Evidence of Dr S. Patterson, 29 November 1994, 1000.
8 The treaty is reproduced at appendix V of the decision of Embree, Prov. Ct. J. in *Marshall (No. 1)*.
9 *Marshall (No. 1)*, per Binnie J., paras 14, 40, 43.
10 Ibid., para. 45.
11 Ibid., paras 58, 59.
12 *Marshall (No. 1)*, per Binnie J., para. 32.
13 Dr Wicken was unaware of the constitutional point. On cross-examination, there was this exchange:
"Q ... treaties were not binding on the English populace unless they were enacted in the statute. Do you know that?
A. No, I don't know that."
Evidence of Dr W. Wicken, 18 September 1995, 3228.
Dr Patterson did not discuss the point, because his evidence was preoccupied with the Treaty of 1752 and the question of whether it survived the hostilities of the 1750s. Not until Dr Patterson had left the witness stand did it become clear that the defence would rely on the Treaties of 1760–61 for their defence.
14 Factum of the Federal Crown, Supreme Court of Canada, dated June 1998, paras 60, 76.

CHAPTER ELEVEN

1 *Marshall (No. 1)*, per McLachlin, J., paras 86, 103.

2 Ibid., para. 91.

3 *Marshall (No. 1)*, per Binnie, J., para. 45. He also said that a "general right enjoyed by all citizens" can be made, "the subject of an *enforceable* treaty promise."

4 Ibid., para. 47.

5 Ibid., para. 47.

6 Ibid., para 37.

7 Ibid., para. 38.

8 "High Court Accused of Distorting History," *National Post*, 28 October 1999, A1.

9 Evidence of Dr S. Patterson, 29 November 1994, 1078.

10 Evidence of Dr S. Patterson, 12 October 1995, 4115–16.

11 Ibid., 4154.

12 Ibid., 4189.

13 Evidence of Dr S. Patterson, 13 October 1995, 4216.

14 This point was first suggested by Philip Saunders, Dean of the Dalhousie Law School.

15 Theodore F.T. Plucknett, *A Concise History of the Common Law*, 5th ed. (London: Butterworths, 1956), 23.

16 The discussion here is a much condensed summary of the comments in William Sharp McKechnie, *Magna Carta*, 2nd ed. (New York: Burt Franklin, 1914).

17 Respecting the application of the Magna Carta, and in particular its provisions respecting fishing, to British North America, see *R. v. Nikal*, [1996] 1 S.C.R. 1013 at paras 30, 32 ; *A.G.B.C. v. A.G. Canada*, [1914] A.C. 153; *In Re Provincial Fisheries* (1895) 26 S.C.R. 444, per Strong CJ, Gwynne J. *Uniacke v. Dickson* (1848) 2 N.S.R. 287 is often cited as the leading decision that English law was received in Nova Scotia in 1758, but even before that time judges in Nova Scotia had adopted the view that the statute laws of England applied in the colony: George Chalmers, *Opinions of Eminent Lawyers*, vol. 1 (London: Reed and Hunter, 1814), 198. In *R. v. Calder*, [1973] S.C.R. 313, Judson J. said that the Magna Carta was always the law throughout the British Empire (395).

18 *A.G. Canada v. A.G. Quebec*, [1921] 1 A.C. 413 (P.C.).

19 The fishery was "not a regal franchise"; Joseph Chitty, *Prerogatives of the Crown* (London: Joseph Butterworth, 1820), 142.

CHAPTER TWELVE

1 "High Court Accused of Distorting History," *National Post*, 28 October 1999.
2 B. Wildsmith, "Vindicating Mi'kmaq Rights" (2001) 19 Windsor Year Book Access Just. 203.
3 Ian Stewart, "Good Cop and Bad Cop: The Canadian State and the East Coast Fishery," Centre for Research and Information on Canada, June 2004.
4 "Indian Brook rejects 20m Fisheries Offer," *The Chronicle Herald*, 25 March 2004, B1.
5 *R. v. Simon*, [2002] N.B.J. No. 248, para. 20.
6 Stewart, 3.
7 "N.B. crab fishermen threaten to shut down season"; "Fiery protest engulfs fishery," *The Globe and Mail*, 5 May 2003.
8 "Governments, Mi'kmaq agree to talks," *The Chronicle Herald*, 24 February 2007, B3.
9 Frances Widdowson and Albert Howard remark in *Disrobing the Aboriginal Industry*, (Montreal: McGill-Queen's University Press, 2008), 83–7, that in the past thirty years there has been "surprisingly little progress" in treaty negotiations across Canada, despite expenditures of "untold millions" to support the process. These "negotiations that never end," the authors argue, are a "public make-work project for lawyers" in which those involved "benefit financially from prolonging the process." In this province the "Made in Nova Scotia" approach to negotiations may yet avoid the same interminable fate.

CHAPTER THIRTEEN

1 Technically, the "Summary Conviction Appeal Court."
2 *R. v. Stephen Marshall*, Scanlan J., para. 8.
3 Ibid., paras 12, 13.
4 See *Arsenault v. Canada*, [2008] F.C.J. No. 604 at paras 1–5.
5 In *Marshall (No. 2)* the Court was careful to note that in future cases it would be up to a claimant to establish membership in a community with which one of the local treaties was made (para. 17).

6 *An Act Giving further Encouragement for the importation of Naval Stores*, 8 Geo I, c.12 (1721); *An Act for the better preservation of his Majesty's Woods in America*, 2 Geo II, c.35 (1729).

7 It should be noted that the proposed concession predated, and was therefore not informed by, the Supreme Court of Canada decision in *Haida* (discussed in chapter 2) endorsing a "duty to consult" with native peoples. New Brunswick's proposed concession was entirely different in nature, involving a supposed treaty right to consult and accommodate that would have been more burdensome than even a *Haida* obligation.

8 These points were mentioned in argument in the Nova Scotia Court of Appeal, but as an aside only, because that Court was bound by the decision in *Marshall (No. 1)*. Only the Supreme Court of Canada can overrule itself.

9 Factum of the Attorney General of Nova Scotia in *R. v. Stephen Marshall et al* dated 15 September 2004 at para. 87.

10 Factum, paras 87–122, and Intervenor Factum of the Attorney General of Nova Scotia in *R. v. Bernard* dated 12 November 2004, paras 1–5, 16–49.

11 *R. v. Stephen Marshall; R. v. Bernard*, per McLachlin, C.J., para. 16. It is odd that these sentences are written in the singular, "the appellant Crown." There were joint reasons for decision in two cases, and there were *two* appellant Crowns: Nova Scotia and New Brunswick. Unlike Nova Scotia, New Brunswick did not challenge the decision in *Marshall (No. 1)*. As we have seen, New Brunswick had been prepared to concede that it extended broadly to encompass Native exploitation of all natural resources.

12 *Brant Dairy v. Milk Comm. of Ont.* [1973] S.C.R. 131, 152–153; *Paquette v. The Queen* [1977] 2 S.C.R. 189, 197; *McNamara Construction v. The Queen* [1977] 2 S.C.R. 655, 661; *Keizer v. Hanna* [1978] 2 S.C.R. 342, 347; *Vetrovec v. The Queen* [1982] 1 S.C.R. 811, 830; *Min. of Indian Affairs v. Ranville* [1982] 2 S.C.R. 518, 527; *Argentina v. Mellino* [1987] 1 S.C.R. 356, 547; *Re Bill 30 (Ont. Separate School Funding)* [1987] 1 S.C.R. 1148, 1195; *Clark v. CNR* [1988] 2 S.C.R. 680, 704; *Brooks v. Canada Safeway* [1989] 1 S.C.R. 1219, 1243–50; *Central Alta. Dairy Pool v. Alta.* [1990] 2 S.C.R. 48, para. 51; *R. v. B. (K. G.)* [1993] 1 S.C.R. 740, paras 62–72; *R. v. Robinson* [1996] 1 S.C.R. 683, para. 16; *United States v. Burns* [2001]

1 S.C.R. 283, paras 131, 144; *R. v. Henry* [2005] 3 S.C.R. 609, paras 43–7; *Health Services and Support – Facilities Subsector Bargaining Assn. v. B.C.* [2007] 2 S.C.R. 391, para. 36; These cases are cited in Hogg, *Constitutional Law of Canada*, 5th ed., vol. 1 (Looseleaf), Scarborough, Ontario: Thompson Carswell (2008), 8–22.

13 *Green v. US* [1958] 356 US 165, 195.

14 *Delgamuukw*, para. 186; *Sparrow*, 406.

15 *R. v. Stephen Marshall*; *R. v. Bernard*, per McLachlin, C.J., para. 21.

16 Ibid., para. 34.

17 Ibid., para. 26.

18 Ibid., paras 19, 21, 26.

19 Ibid., para. 20.

20 The majority went on to confirm that treaty rights are not "frozen in time" but can "evolve." But they said that such evolution means "the same sort of activity carried on ... by modern means" ... "the activity must be essentially the same" (Ibid., para. 25).

21 Ibid., para. 16.

22 Ibid., paras 18, 19.

23 *Marshall (No. 1)*, per Binnie J., para. 7.

24 Ibid., para. 7.

25 *R. v. Stephen Marshall*; *R. v. Bernard*, per McLachlin, C.J., para. 20.

26 Ibid., paras 21–4.

27 In shaping the law, judges properly have regard to the "policy" of the law that they fashion. That is a legitimate judicial endeavour and is quite different from the sort of considerations of policy discussed here.

CHAPTER FOURTEEN

1 Michel Bastarache, a judge of the Supreme Court of Canada (now retired), who was not involved in the *Marshall (No. 1)* decision, suggested in a 2001 interview that the Court was perceived, in light of the case, as "very result oriented and inventing rights that weren't even in the treaties," and was "seen as being unduly favourable to the native position in all cases, and that it sort of has an agenda for extending [aboriginal] rights." He said that he did not agree with the majority decision. "S.C.C. Wrong Forum for Native Land Claims," *Lawyers's Weekly* 20, no. 34 (19 January 2001).

Index

Abenaki, 113, 114
aboriginal title, 7, 38, 84, 129, 130, 132, 133
academic debate, 102
Acadians, 54, 94, 112
Alchaba, Etienne, 103
Arbuthnot, Colonel, 96–8

balance of power, 95
Big Cove First Nation, 103
Bill of Rights, 18
BNA Act, 14, 20
Burnt Church, 6, 82, 83, 104, 127, 128

Calder v. Attorney General (British Columbia), 38
Canadian Bill of Rights, 25, 26
Canso, 54, 124
Cape Breton, 44, 56, 60, 61, 100; reserves, 104
chain of treaties, 62–3, 72, 90, 104, 105, 107
Chapel Island, 44
Charles I, 15, 16, 17; trial, 16
Charles II, 17
colonies, 19

commercial logging, 6, 37, 47, 129, 130, 132, 133, 135
commercial rights, 46, 49
common employment, 24
Constitution, Canada, 9, 10–22
Constitution Act, 1867, 20
Constitution Act, 1982, 21, 22, 31
consult, duty to, 40
Court of Appeal: court of error, 71, 89, 93, 94; decision in *Marshall (No. 1)*, 71–4, 120; fact finding, 71; of New Brunswick, 47, 129, 130
Cromwell, Oliver, 16, 17

Daigle, Joe, 129, 130
Declaration of Rights, 18
Delgamuukw v. British Columbia, 37, 47
Denning L.J., 4
disease, 55
division of powers, 20, 21
Douglas Treaties, 81
Dudley, Governor, 113, 114, 116

eels, sale of, 3, 4, 5, 69

Embree, John, Provincial Court Judge, 48
equitable access, 86
errors of fact, 71, 92–3
errors of law, 71
Eskasoni, 45–6

Fifth Amendment, 25, 26
fish, species harvested, 69
fishing: agreements, 127, 128, 133, 149; licences, 127, 128, 139, 148, 149
Fort Beausejour, 54, 94, 101
Fort Cumberland, 100
Fort Frederick, 96, 97, 101, 115
Fortress Louisbourg, 54, 94, 101
Framework Agreement, 130
Francis, Louis, 103
Frye, Colonel, 100, 103

Glorious Revolution, 14–21, 65
Governor, constitutional position, 65–6, 112–17
Governor's Farm Ceremony, 55–7, 58, 59, 100, 104, 108, 118, 123, 124

Haida v. British Columbia, 40, 147
Honour of the Crown, 41
hostages, 97
House of Assembly, 19, 20, 65, 112–16

Indian Brook, 45
Instructions. See Royal Instructions

intervenors, 7, 75

James II, 17, 18
judicial activism, 9, 12, 13, 23–43, 87–8; traditional role of judges, 21

LaHave Treaty, 53
legal academics, 10
lobster fishery, 82, 84
logging, 129, 132–5

MacKenzie, James, 127
MacRae, Ian, 48
Magna Carta, 134
Maillard, 55
Maliseet & Passamaquoddy, 51, 63, 77, 90, 91, 92, 96, 97, 99, 106, 108, 109, 110, 114, 115
Marshall, Donald Jr, 12
Marshall Response Initiative, 133–4
Massachusetts House of Representatives, 113, 114, 116
McLachlin J.: dissent, 78; principles of treaty interpretation, 79
media, 10, 83–4
Michael, Augustine, 103
Minister of Fisheries, Nova Scotia, 7
Mirimachi, 103, 104, 132
moderate livelihood, 5, 83
Montcalm, General, 94

necessaries, 116, 125
numbered treaties, 81

obiter dictum, 61
Office of Aboriginal Affairs,
 Nova Scotia, 130

Paré, Michael, 48
parliamentary sovereignty
 (supremacy), 14, 18, 21, 22,
 117
Passamaquoddy. See Maliseet &
 Passamaquoddy
Patterson, Dr Stephen, 19, 48,
 50, 51, 98, 99, 120–2, 127
Pigaluet, Jeanot, 103
pine trees, laws preserving, 68,
 134, 135
pipelines, 128
planters, 55, 112
Pokemouche, 104
Pomquet Harbour, 3, 87
Protestants, foreign, 54
Public Prosecution Service, Nova
 Scotia Independence, 8

Quebec, 54, 94
Quiberon Bay, 57

R. v. Adams, 37
R. v. Bernard, 129, 132, 134,
 139–41
R. v. Denny, 45
R. v. Isaac, 44
R. v. Sappier & Polchies, 37
R. v. Simon, 45, 49, 52
R. v. Sparrow, 30–5, 147
R. v. Stephen Marshall, 6, 7, 11,
 21, 40, 62, 86, 101, 129, 132,
 134, 137, 139–41

R. v. Syliboy, 44, 45
R. v. Van der Peet, 35–7, 147
reconciliation, 12
Red Bank, 104
Reid, Dr John, 48
Richibouctou, 103
rights of subjects, 73, 79,
 118–23, 125
Robinson Treaties, 81
Royal Instructions, 73, 120, 135
royal prerogative, 15, 17, 18, 19,
 20, 65, 112, 113, 125
Royal Proclamation, 1763, 39

Seven Years' War, 54, 57, 94
Seycombe, Reverend John, 3, 4,
 69, 115
Shippegan, 104, 128
Shubenacadie Band, 44, 52, 127
stay, 84, 85
St Mary's Bay, 6, 83
Supreme Court of Canada: decision in Marshall (No. 1),
 75–81; decision in Marshall
 (No 2), 84–8; 11 February
 1760 document, 77–8, 79,
 91–9, 104, 106, 107; equitable
 access, 86; finding of fact,
 93–4, 103; majority decision,
 75–8; minority decision,
 78–81; moderate livelihood,
 78; principles of treaty interpretation, 80–1; regulated
 treaty rights, 85; right to
 'bring,' 78; rights of subjects,
 79, 118–19; traditional territory, 87; treaty negotiations,

77; treaty right, 78; trial judge errors, 76, 90–1; way of life, 120–3

Supreme Court, United States, 25, 26

surrenders, 55–7, 94–8, 100–1; demands, 57, 91–101, 110

trade regulation, 4, 19, 113–14

trade union movement, 24

Treaty of 1725–26, 47, 54, 62, 63, 97, 104

Treaty of 1749, 54, 97, 104

Treaty of 1752, 44–52, 60–5, 73, 98, 99, 104

Trial Court, 48–70; chain of treaties, 62–3, 90; change in position, 20, 49, 50; competing historical approaches, 58–9; evidence not elaborated, 20, 51; evidence of fishing, 68–71; evidence of trade in fish, 69; key negotiations, 106; newly discovered treaties,

60–1; procedure, 20, 50, 51; treaties on same conditions, 107–8; treaty at issue, 61; way of life, 66–68; written treaties, 64–5

truckhouse: clause in Halifax Treaties, 52–3, 58, 72, 76, 115; clause in Treaty of 1752, 49, 63; demise of system, 53, 62, 67, 74, 78, 119, 123; required legislation, 114–17

Trudeau, Pierre, 9, 149

West Nova Fisherman's Coalition, 84, 85, 87

Whitmore, General, 100

Wicken, Dr William, 48

Wildsmith, Bruce, 48

William & Mary, 18

Wolfe, General, 54, 94

workers' compensation, 24

Zscheile, Eric, 48